POSTCARD HISTORY SERIES

Roanoke
IN VINTAGE POSTCARDS

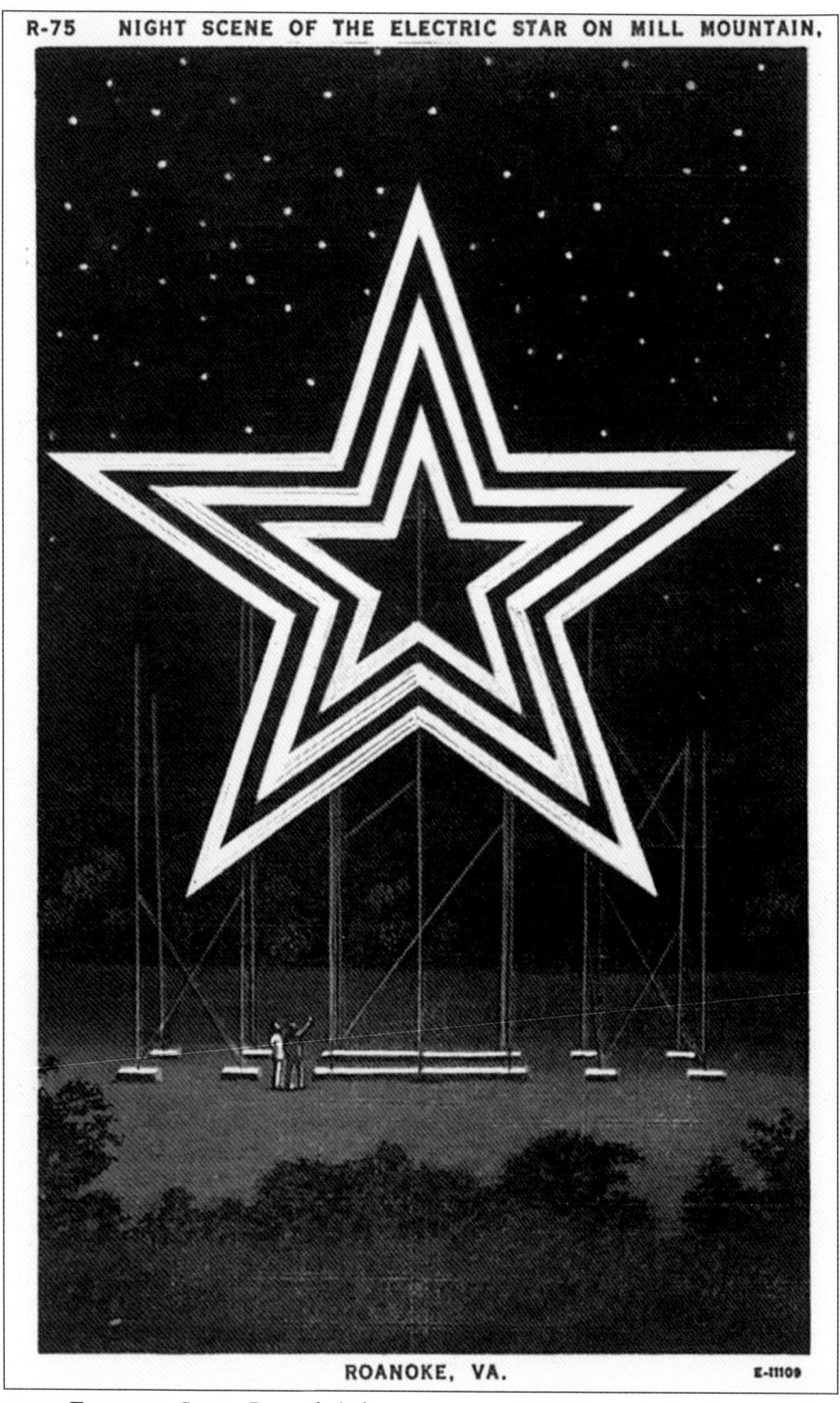

ROANOKE ELECTRIC STAR. Roanoke's large star atop Mill Mountain has become the city's signature symbol, giving Roanoke the label of "Star City of the South."

POSTCARD HISTORY SERIES

Roanoke
IN VINTAGE POSTCARDS

Nelson Harris

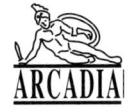

Copyright © 2002 by Nelson Harris.
ISBN 0-7385-1439-X

First published 2002.
Reprinted 2003, 2004.

Published by Arcadia Publishing
an imprint of Tempus Publishing Inc.
Charleston SC, Chicago, Portsmouth NH, San Francisco

Printed in Great Britain.

Library of Congress Catalog Card Number: 2002103790

For all general information contact Arcadia Publishing at:
Telephone 843-853-2070
Fax 843-853-0044
E-Mail sales@arcadiapublishing.com

For customer service and orders:
Toll-Free 1-888-313-2665

Visit us on the internet at http://www.arcadiapublishing.com

This book is dedicated in memory of my mother, Gaynelle Simpson Harris.

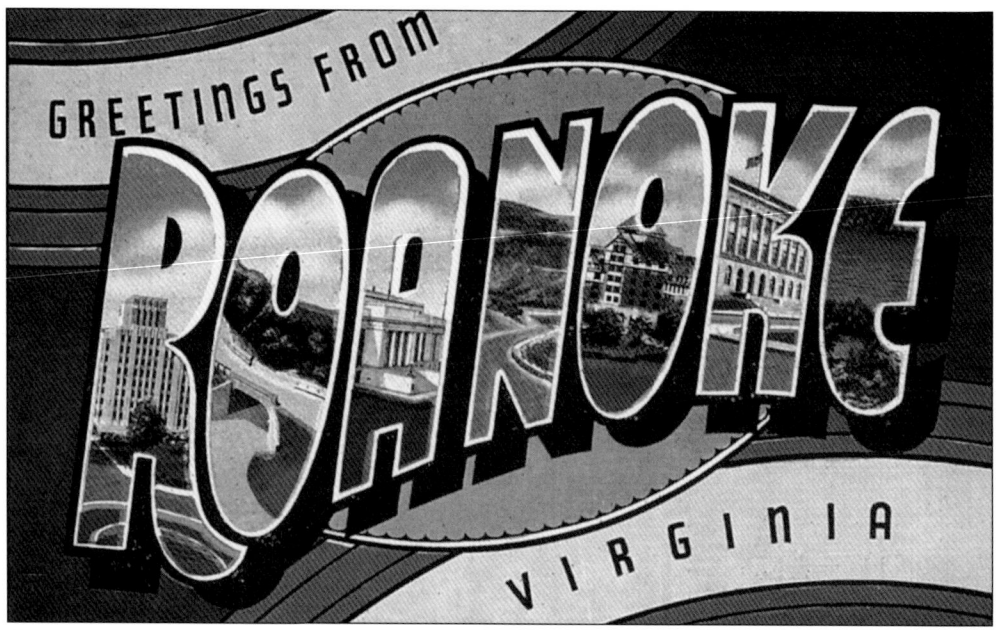

GREETINGS FROM ROANOKE, VIRGINIA. This cover card was part of a packet of postcards promoting Roanoke to visitors as a center of commerce and place of natural beauty.

Contents

Acknowledgments 6

Introduction 7

1. Norfolk and Western Railroad 9

2. Religion and Education 25

3. Government and Commerce 39

4. Streets and Bridges 53

5. Recreation and Leisure 73

6. Scenery and Travel 95

7. Healthcare 121

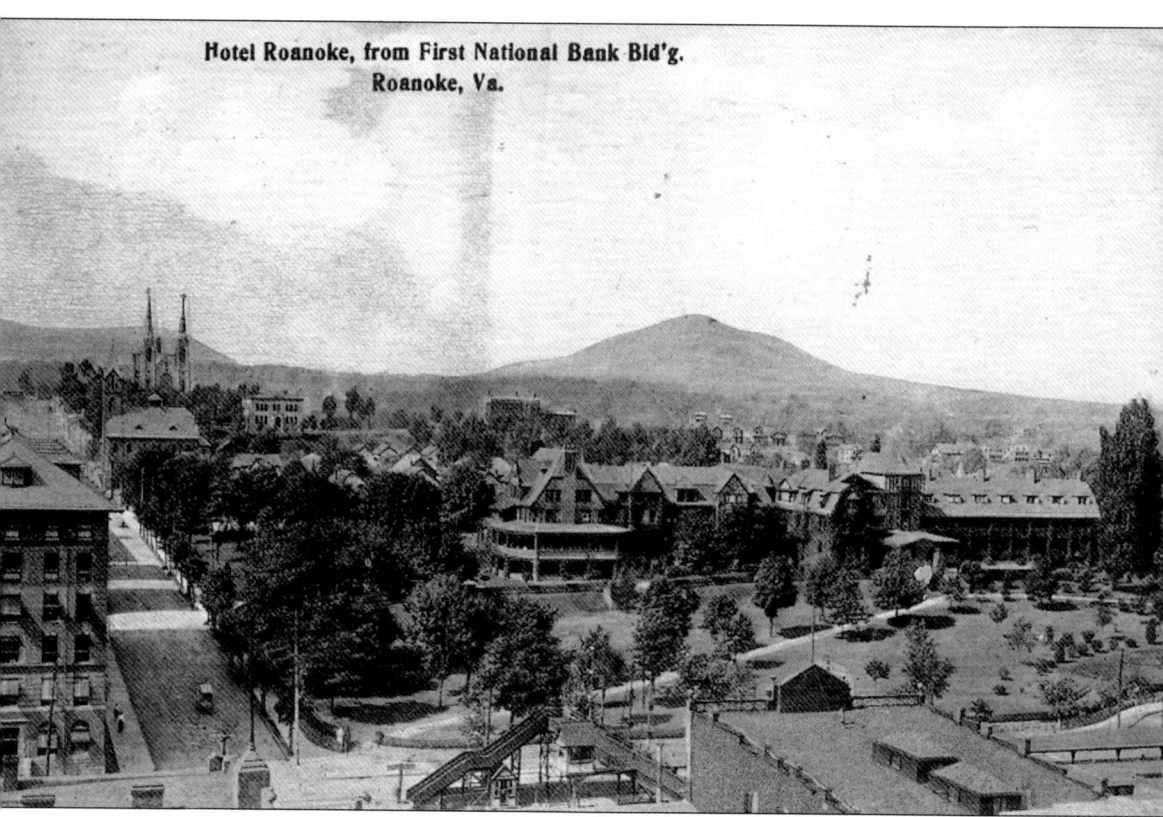

HOTEL ROANOKE FROM FIRST NATIONAL BANK BUILDING, 1912. This postcard shows a number of Roanoke's more notable buildings—the Hotel Roanoke, the Norfolk and Western Office Building, and St. Andrews Catholic Church.

INTRODUCTION

Settled in 1740, but not officially chartered until 1882, the City of Roanoke has long held a position of prominence in Southwestern Virginia. Being the largest urban center west of Virginia's capitol, Richmond, Roanoke emerged initially as a booming railroad town in the late 1800s. In fact, rumor has it that it was the railroad that actually named the city after the Roanoke River. Originally called "Big Lick" after large salt deposits prevalent in the area, railroad officials thought that name too backward for a main depot along their rail line. Consequently, town fathers were advised, "Call it Roanoke." And so it was.

With the coming of the railroad and the decision by the Norfolk & Western Railroad (N&W) to locate their headquarters in Roanoke, the city experienced tremendous population and economic growth in the late 19th and early 20th centuries. The community rapidly attracted new industries and commercial ventures mostly linked with the rail economy. While Roanoke is no longer a rail center, its economic interests have become diverse, creating a vibrant downtown and varied cultural amenities.

Roanoke is also known for its surrounding environment. Nestled among the Blue Ridge Mountains, the city is just minutes off the Blue Ridge Parkway and Appalachian Trail, and is dissected by the Roanoke River. In fact, it was Roanoke's natural surroundings that prompted the first European explorers to traverse the valley in 1671, writing that the area had "blue mountains and a snug flat valley beside the upper Roanoke River." Ever since, people have been drawn to the beauty and ecology of the Roanoke region.

Known affectionately as the "Star City of the South," Roanoke's signature symbol is the large lighted star perched atop Mill Mountain. Erected over a half-century ago by local merchants as a way to attract holiday shoppers, the Mill Mountain Star stands watch over her changing city. Roanoke's star is the largest of its kind in the United States and can be seen for miles. Roanokers arriving by plane know their hometown is close when the star can be seen from the airliner window. Usually white, the star was lit red, white, and blue for the nation's bicentennial in 1976 and in support of our troops' fight against terrorism during the aftermath of September 11, 2001. The Mill Mountain Star is today recognized as a registered historic landmark.

Roanoke in Vintage Postcards captures a portion of the city's history through the visual imagery of the picture postcard. The cards depict Roanoke at the turn of the last century with its dirt streets, trolley tracks, and horse-drawn carriages and its subsequent development into the early 1960s. What emerges is an interesting collage of sights, events, and structures that have marked Roanoke's past and influenced its present. Many have disappeared from Roanoke's cityscape, while others have remained over the decades albeit altered either in form or function.

Being interested in my city's history and having been a postcard collector of some years, this book allows me the opportunity to merge those interests in what I hope will be an enjoyable and informative look at Roanoke's past. The towered facade of the Terry Building, the ornate architecture of the Academy of Music, and the pavilion-graced lawn of Mountain Park are but a few of the vintage images within these pages. Beyond being merely elements of a bygone Roanoke, these cards recollect the vision and ambitions of Roanokers that have given rise to today's "Star City of the South."

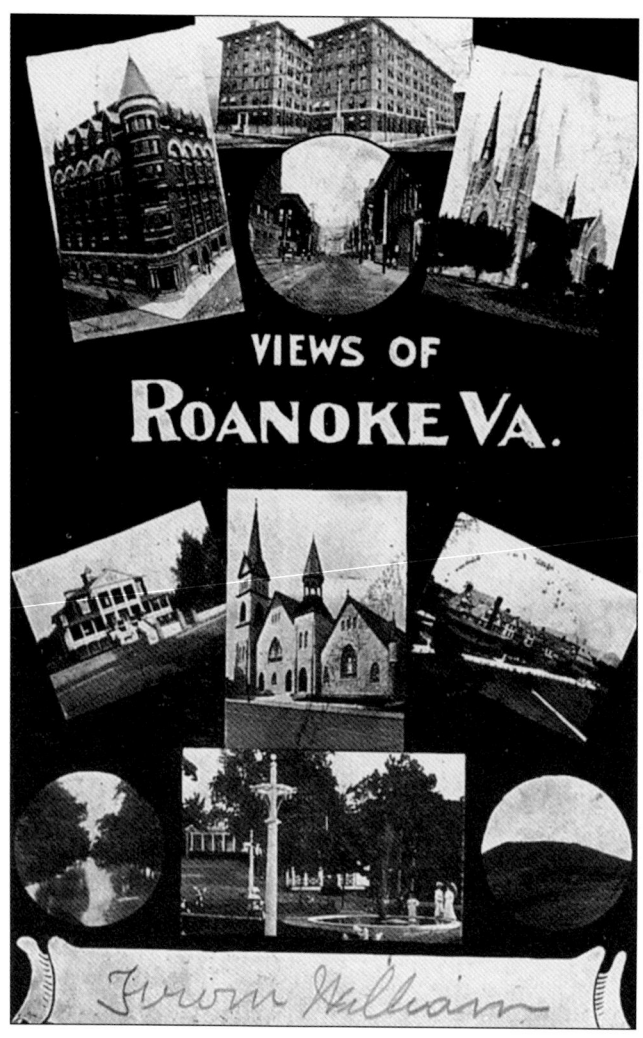

VIEWS OF ROANOKE, VIRGINIA. One of the earliest ways to effectively promote a city was the picture postcard. Here is an early cover of a postcard booklet.

One
Norfolk & Western Railroad

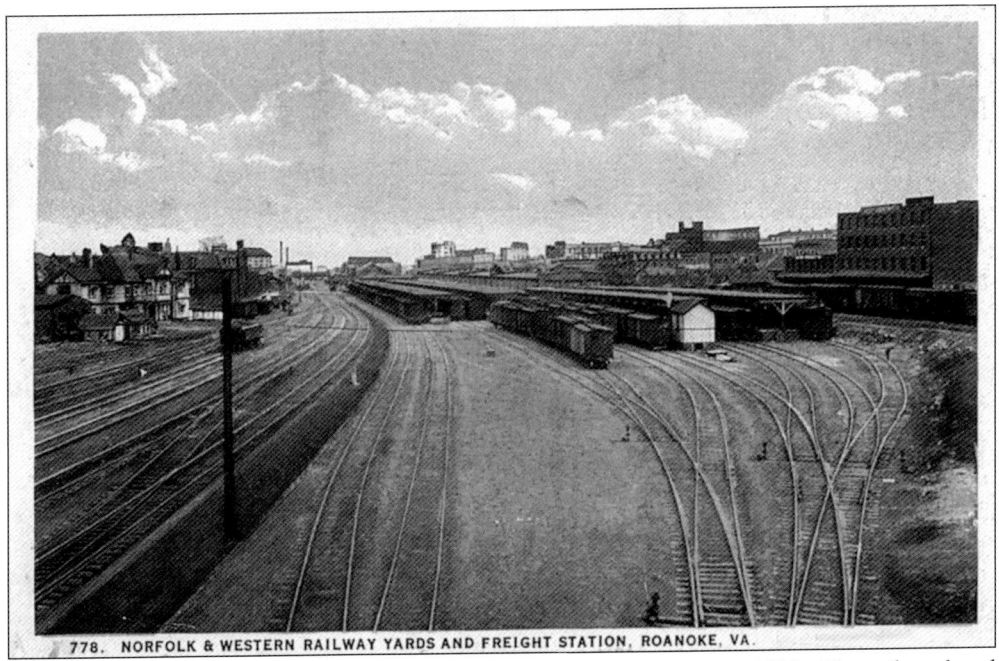

778. NORFOLK & WESTERN RAILWAY YARDS AND FREIGHT STATION, ROANOKE, VA.

Norfolk & Western Railway Yards and Freight Station, 1920. The rail yard and freight station cut through the heart of Roanoke and still do today, giving the city a rich rail history and flavor.

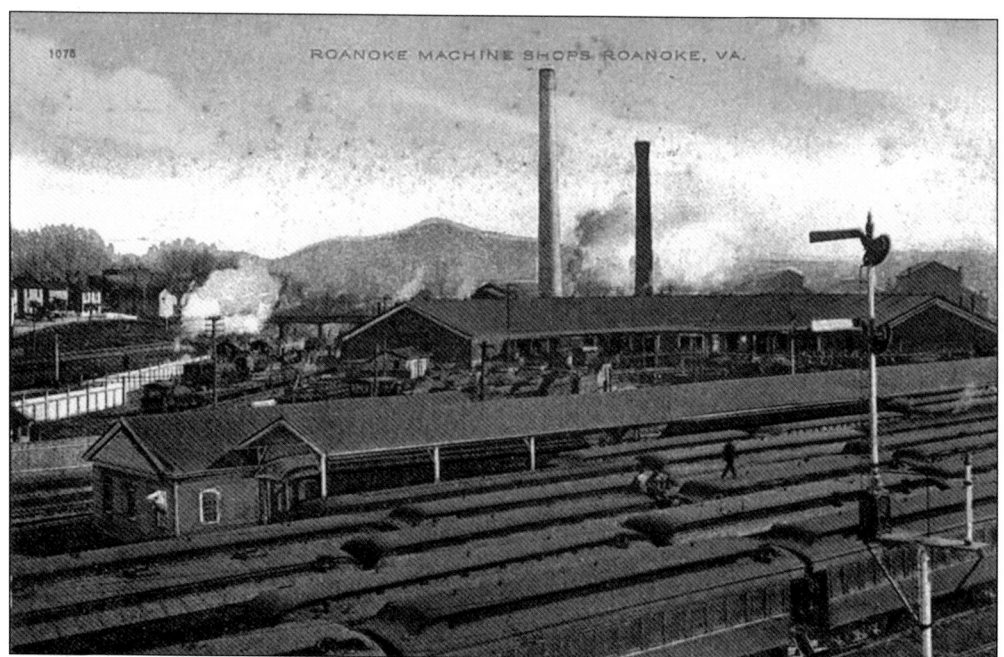

ROANOKE MACHINE SHOPS, 1910. The Roanoke Machine Shops produced some of the finest engines for the Norfolk & Western Railroad and employed hundreds of Roanoke citizens.

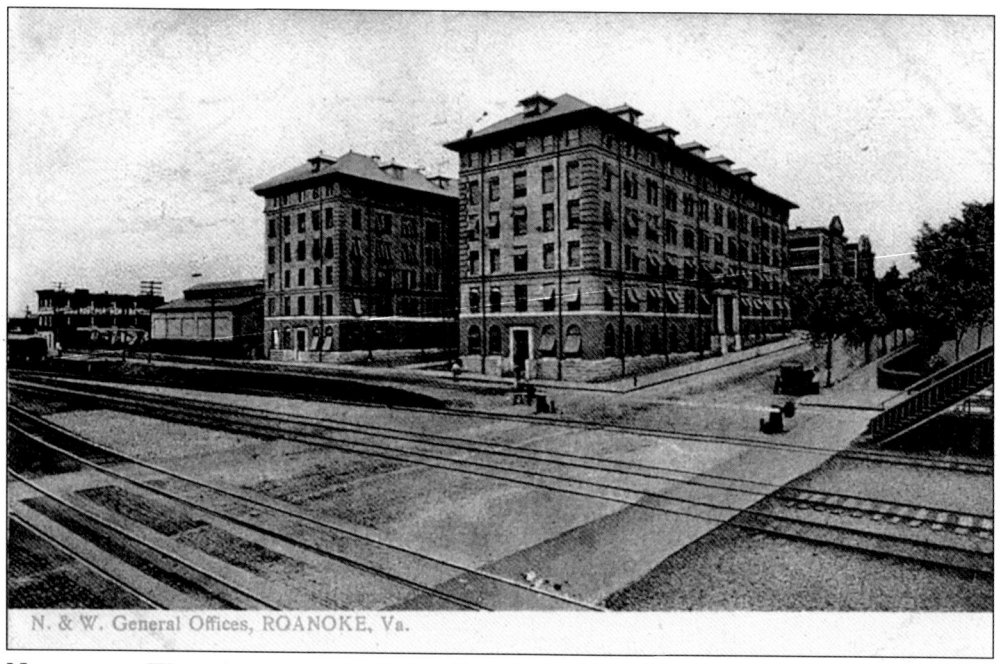

NORFOLK & WESTERN GENERAL OFFICE BUILDING, 1912. The N&W general office building was erected around the turn of the century. The two buildings still remain and have been converted into upscale apartments. Known as "8 Jefferson Place," the buildings represent Roanoke's finest address in downtown living.

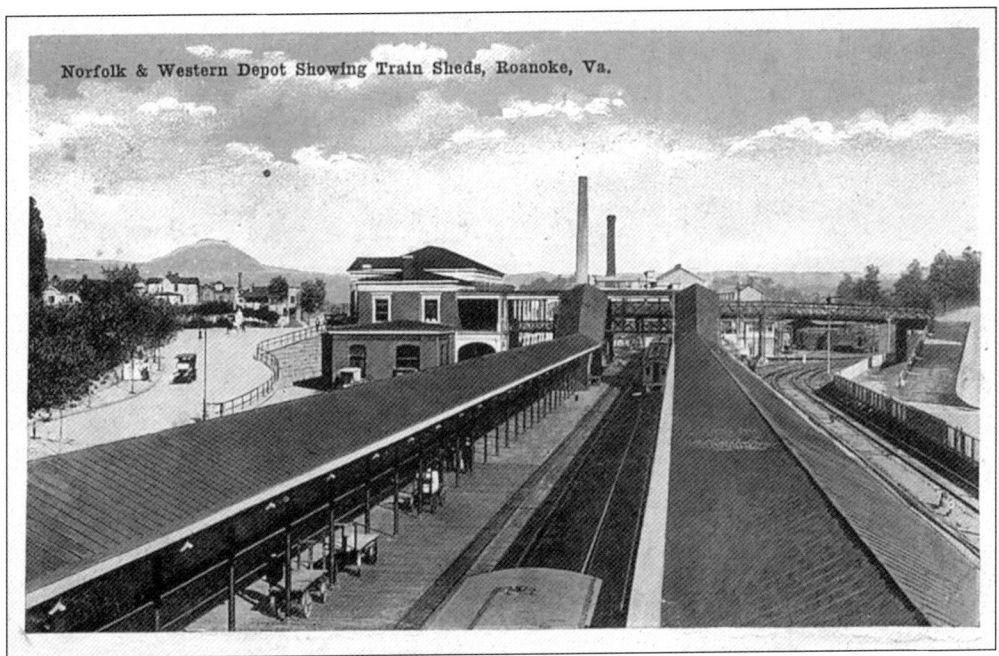

NORFOLK & WESTERN DEPOT SHOWING TRAIN SHEDS, 1919. The depot was once one of the busiest venues in Roanoke. Passenger trains could transport Roanokers to all major eastern cities. The sheds no longer remain, but the depot does although passenger rail service was discontinued in the early 1970s.

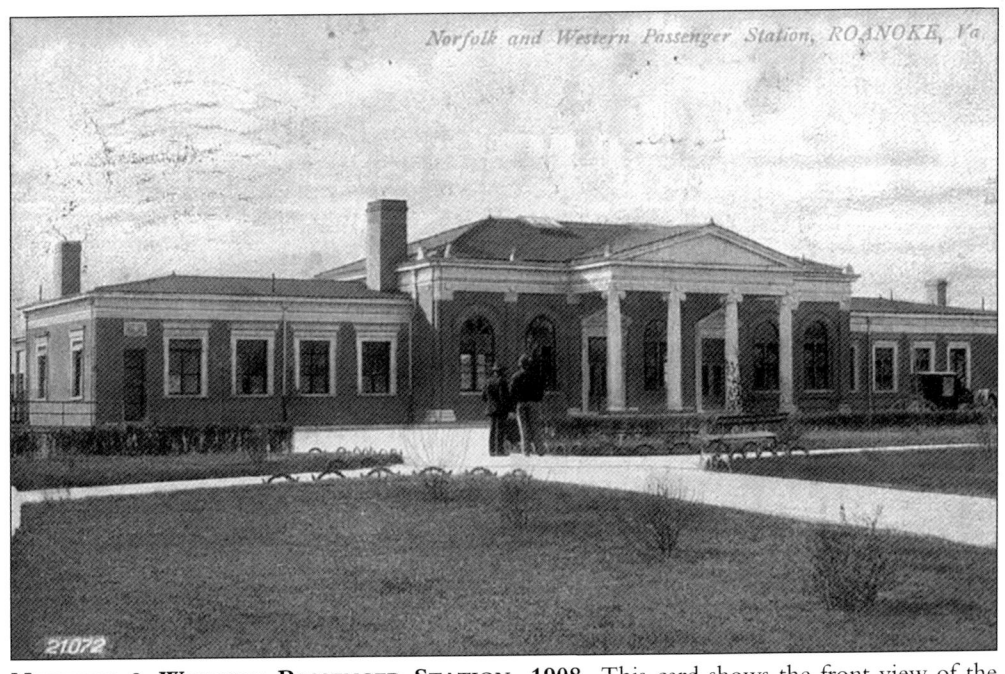

NORFOLK & WESTERN PASSENGER STATION, 1908. This card shows the front view of the passenger station with its original columns that graced the facade before the railroad modernized the station's appearance.

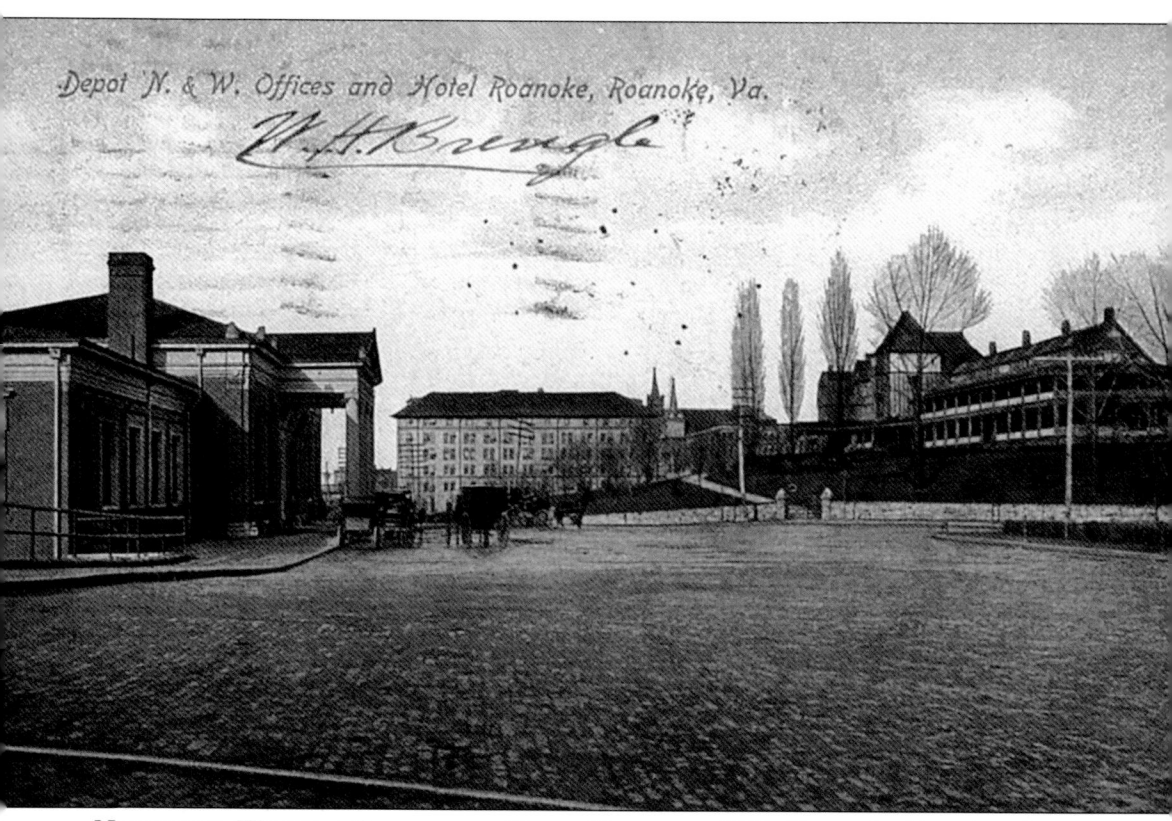

NORFOLK & WESTERN OFFICES AND HOTEL ROANOKE, 1907. Shown in this unique image is the rail depot on the left, the general office building in the background, and the Hotel Roanoke to the right. The hotel was built by the railroad to accommodate its passengers and company officials. Notice the large brick plaza spanning the hotel and depot entrances.

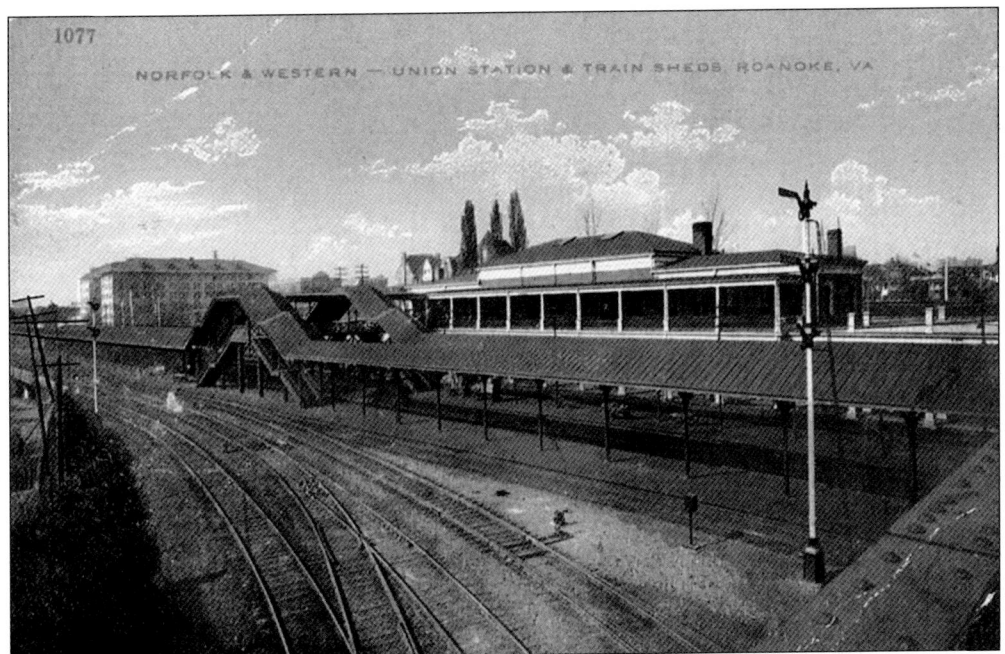

NORFOLK & WESTERN—UNION DEPOT AND TRAIN SHEDS, 1910. This postcard shows the depot and massive train sheds from a different perspective, the backside. Note the raised pedestrian bridge in the center allowing access over the rail lines.

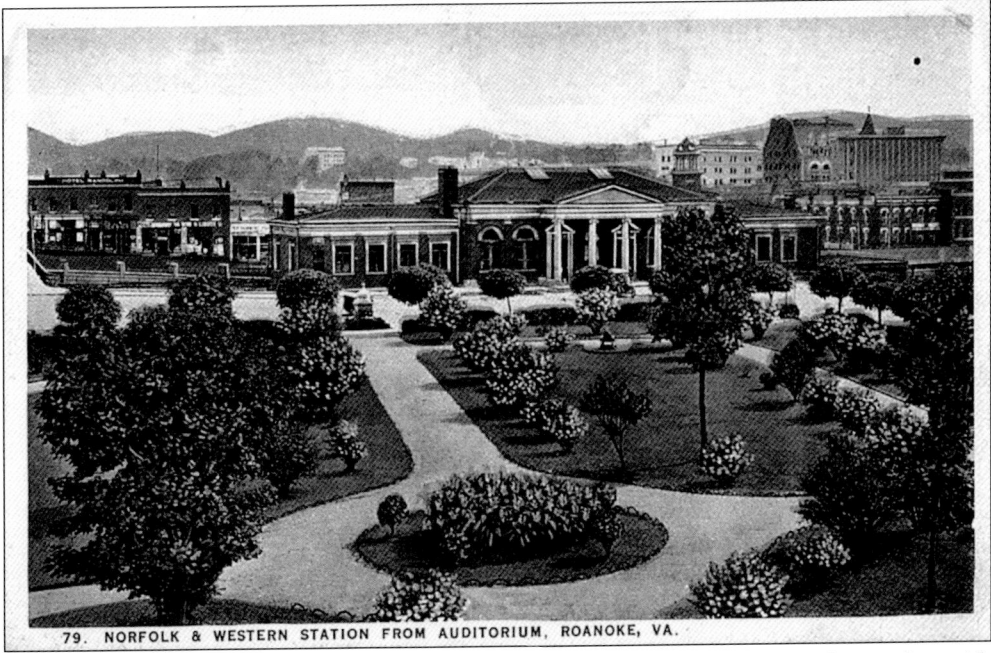

NORFOLK & WESTERN STATION FROM AUDITORIUM, 1925. A landscaped park complete with fountain once lay in front of the depot. No longer in existence, the park was considered to be one of the most beautiful in its day.

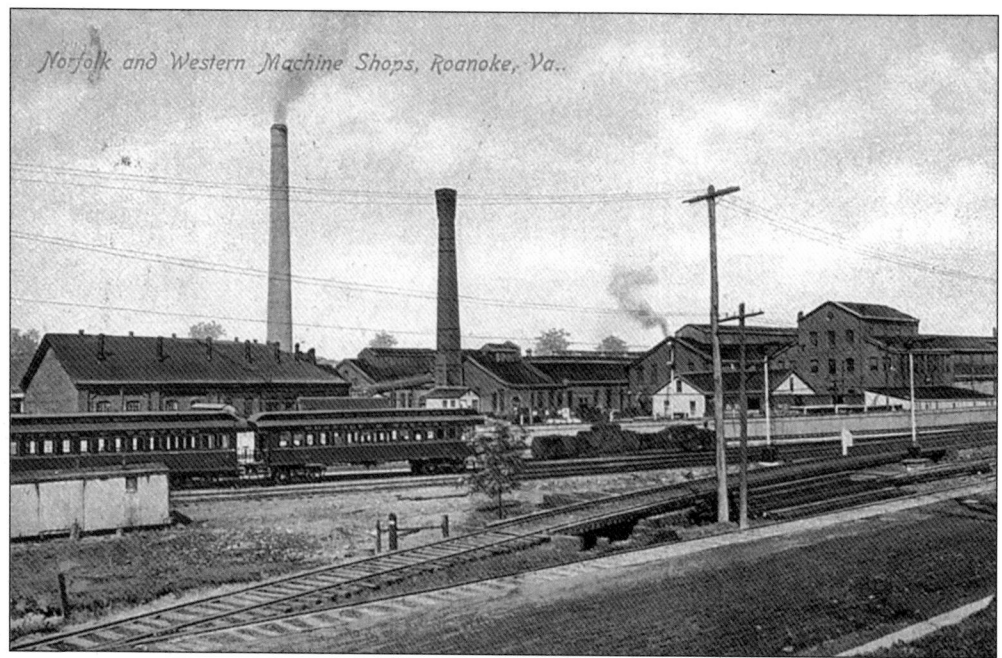

NORFOLK & WESTERN MACHINE SHOPS, 1908. Another view of the Roanoke Machine Shops displays the various buildings that housed the numerous trades necessary for the railroad's operation. Notice the passenger trains idled in the foreground.

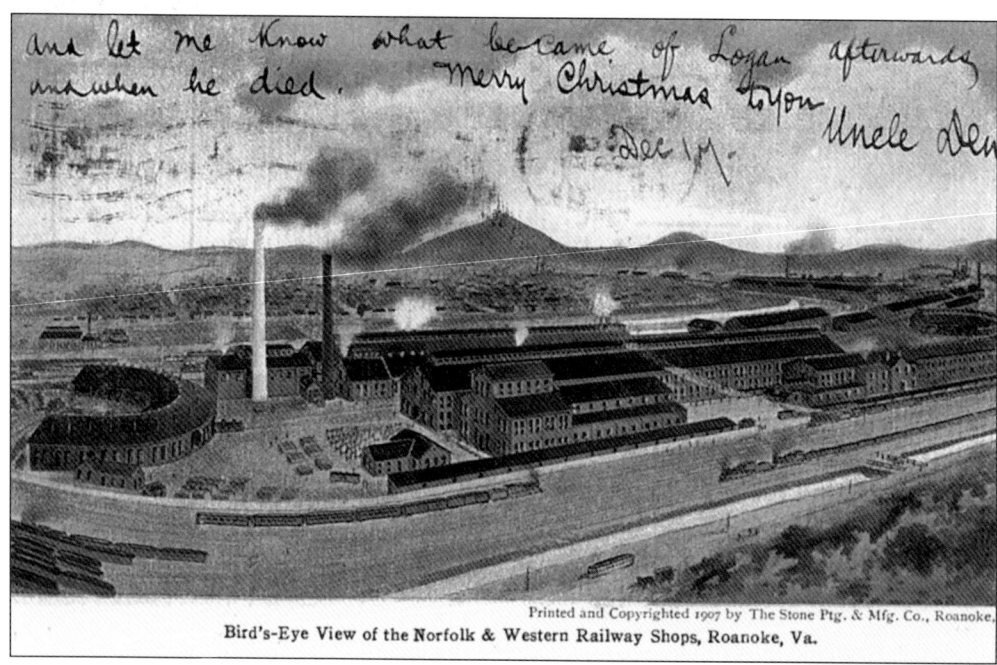

BIRD'S EYE VIEW OF NORFOLK & WESTERN RAILWAY SHOPS, 1907. This aerial view shows 22 distinctive structures as part of the rail shop complex.

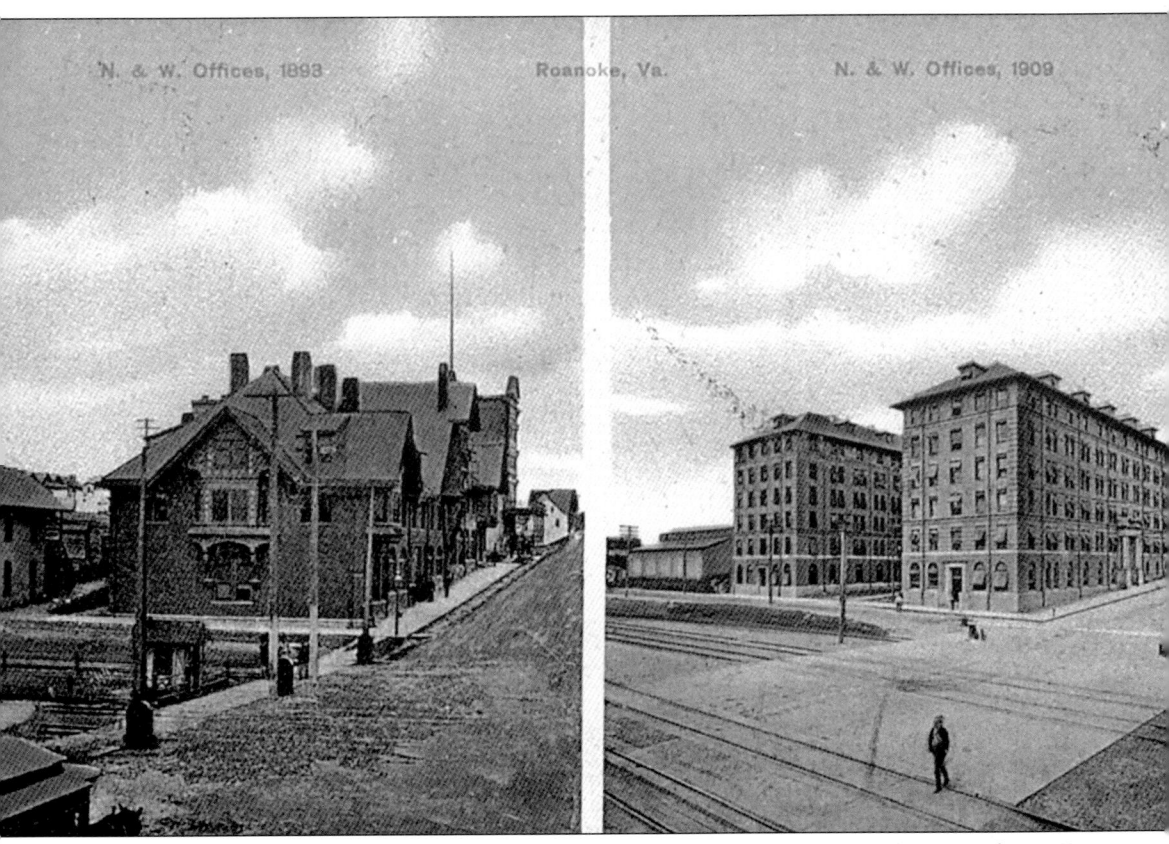

NORFOLK & WESTERN OFFICE BUILDINGS, 1909. This divided card shows the original N&W office building as it looked in 1893 and the "new" building of 1909.

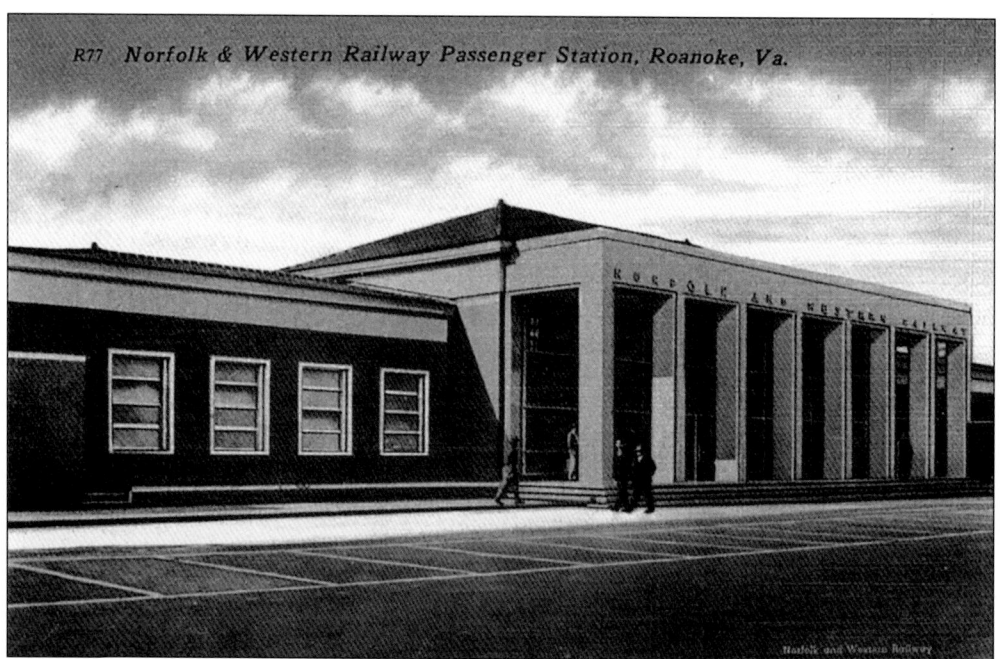

NORFOLK & WESTERN RAILWAY PASSENGER STATION, 1950. The modernized appearance of the railroad passenger station was achieved by replacing the ornate columns to create a more contemporary architectural style. The passenger station serves today as a museum and visitors center.

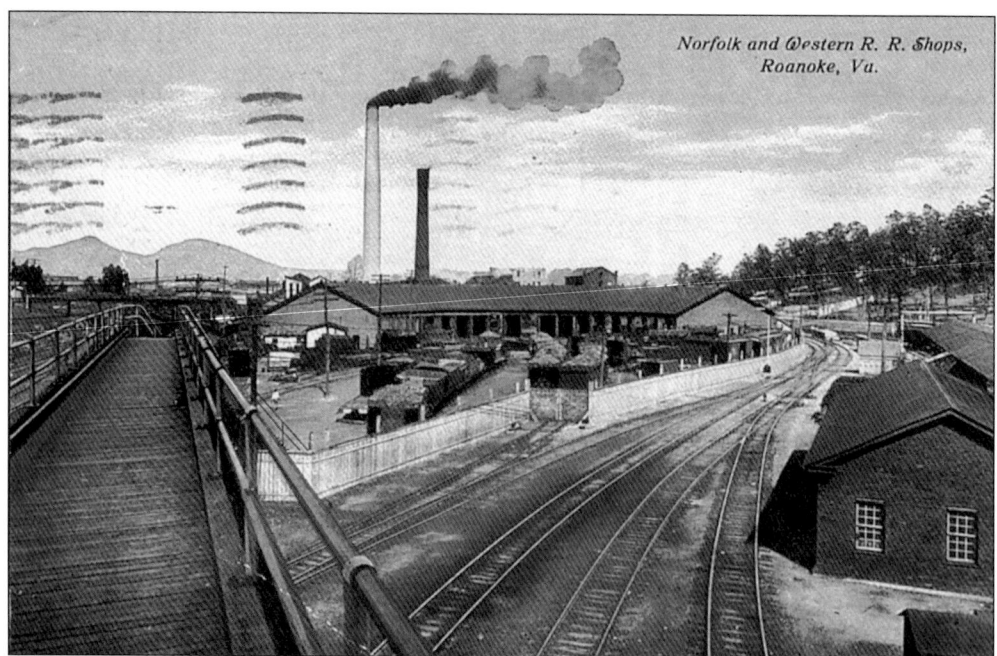

NORFOLK & WESTERN RAILROAD SHOPS, 1911. Railroad machine shops were connected by several bridges that kept the buildings accessible and allowed workers safe access over the tracks.

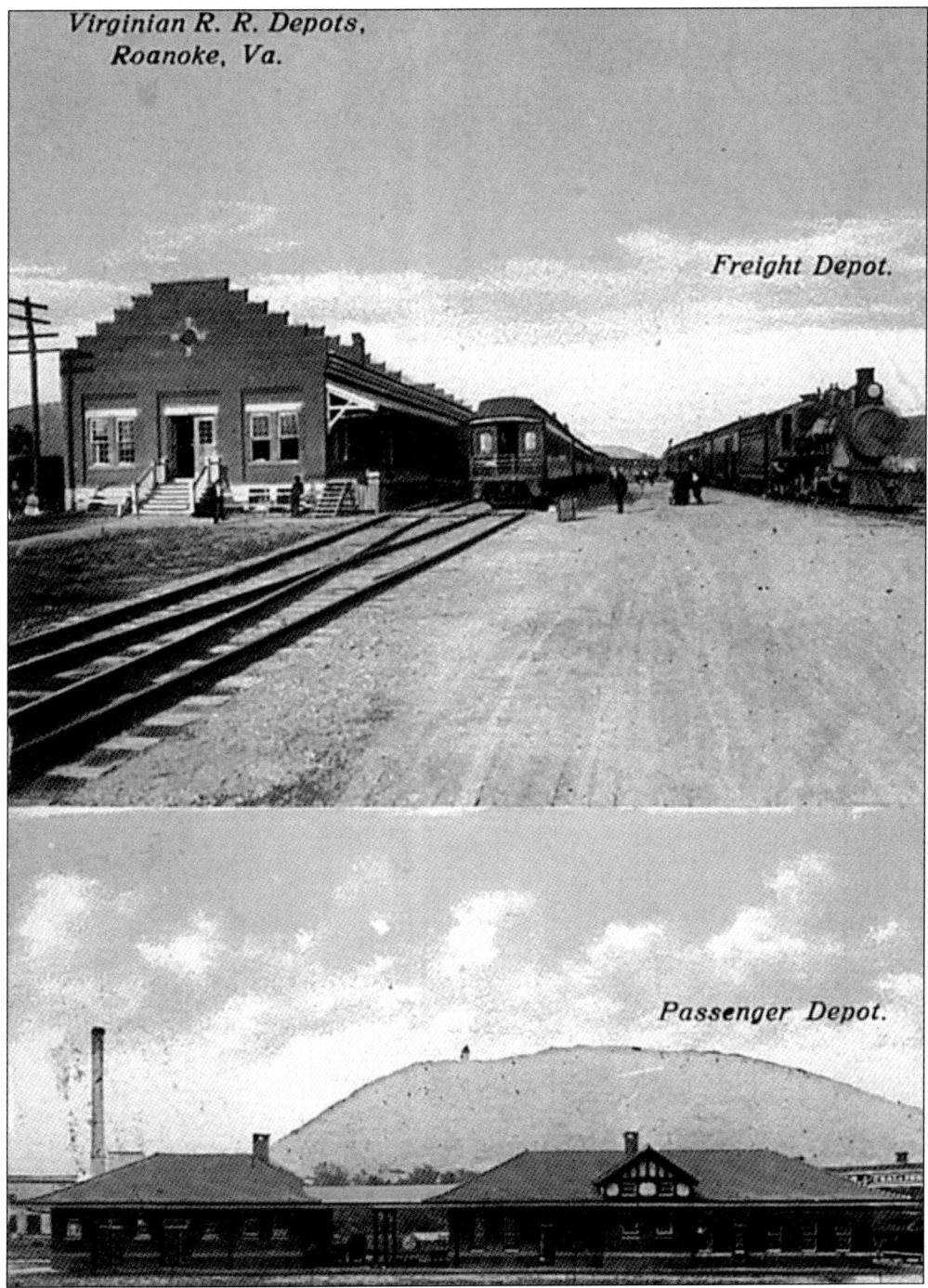

VIRGINIAN RAILROAD DEPOTS, 1911. Eventually, the Virginian Railroad would merge with the N&W, but until then, the Virginian had a passenger depot, which closed in 1959, and a freight depot. Aunt Mannie and Uncle Artie used this card to write their nephew in Delaware the following about their rail trip: "We were in Roanoke yesterday, today at Natural Bridge, and tomorrow expect to go to Luray Caverns. Enjoying our trip very much."

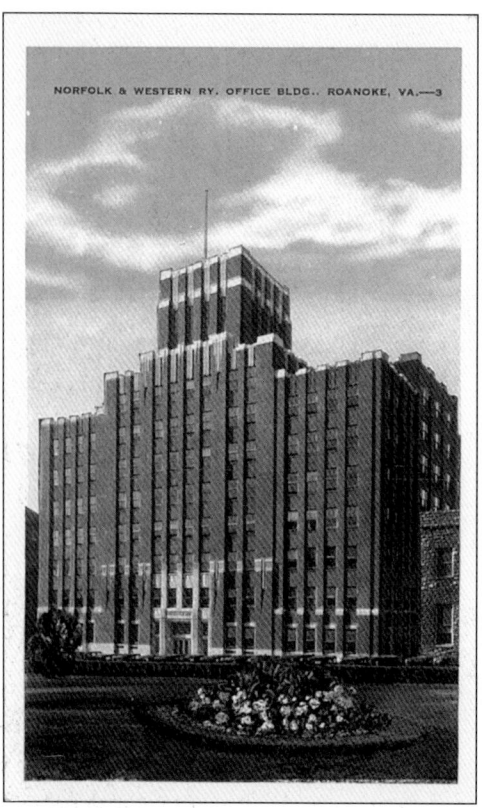

NORFOLK & WESTERN OFFICE BUILDING, 1950. As the N&W Railway grew, so did the need for a new office building. Roanoke no longer serves as headquarters for the railroad, but the office building today is known as the Roanoke Higher Education Center, a facility housing programs of 16 educational institutions.

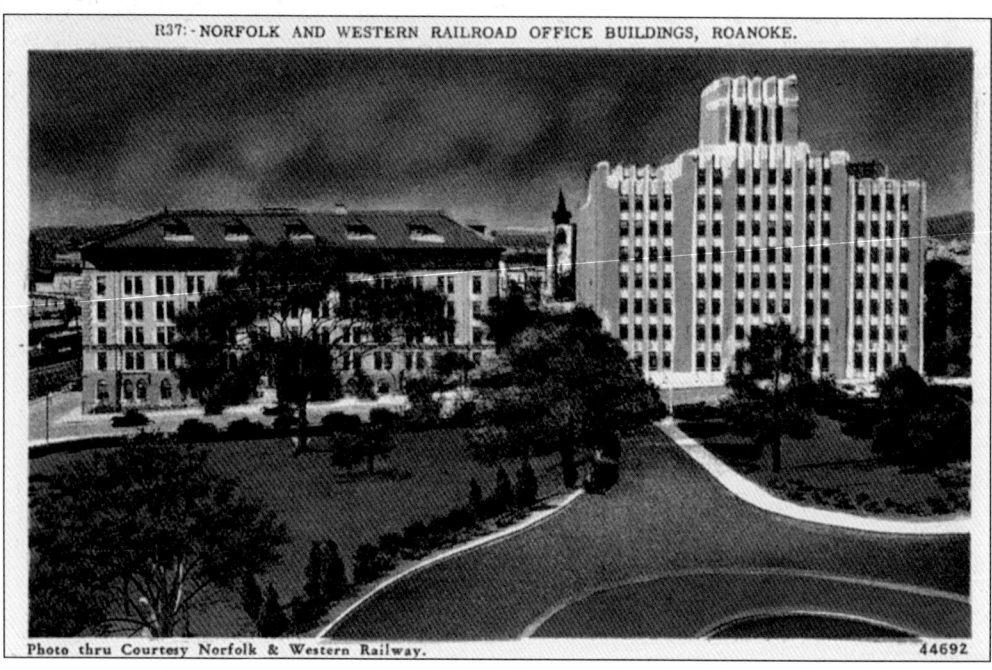

NORFOLK & WESTERN OFFICE BUILDINGS, 1950. This card shows the close proximity of the two former N&W office buildings.

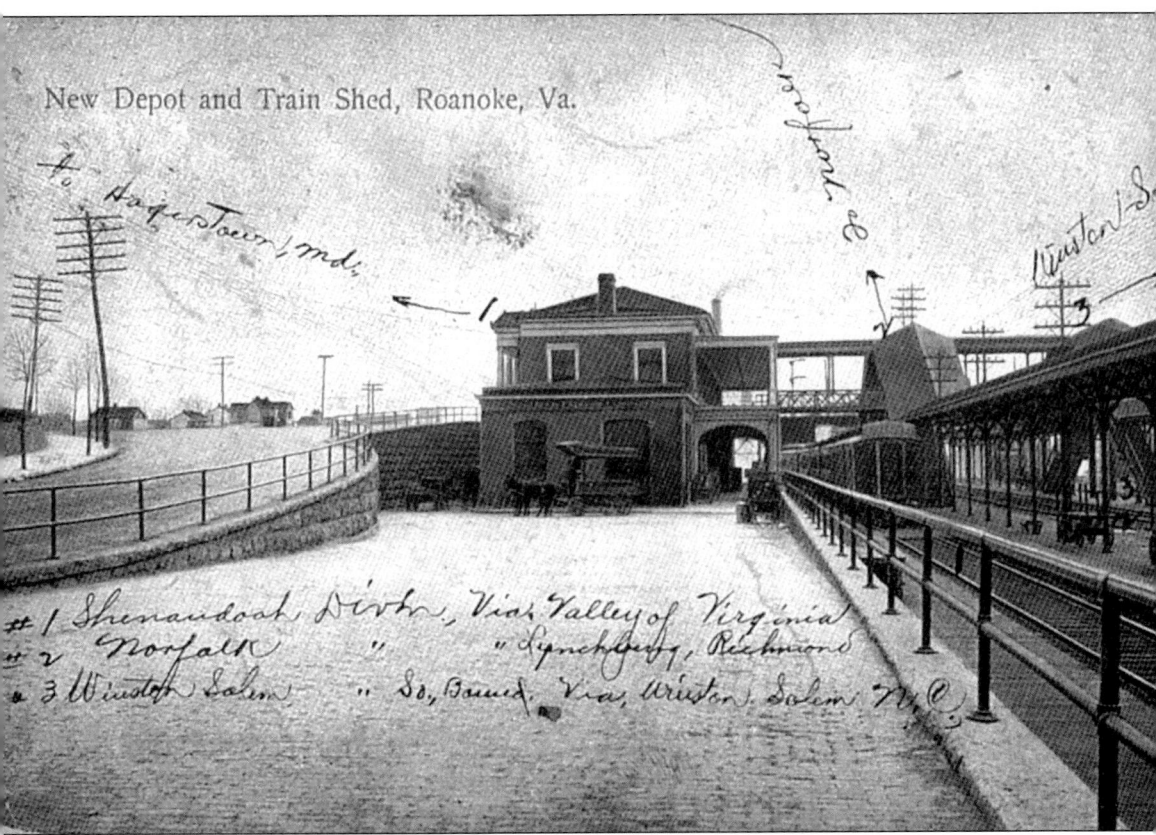

NORFOLK & WESTERN DEPOT AND TRAIN SHED, 1911. This card depicts another view of the N&W passenger station. The sender has scribbled on the front arrows to the three main tracks—one to Lynchburg, another for the Shenandoah Valley and Hagerstown, Maryland, and the third to Winston-Salem, North Carolina.

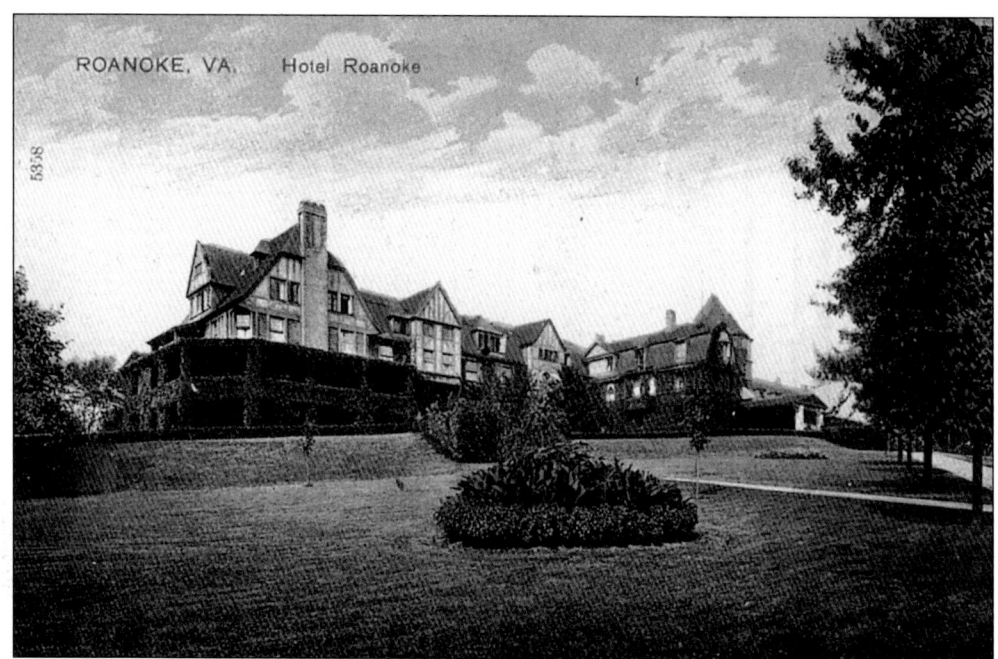

HOTEL ROANOKE, 1907. As a service to its passengers and company officials, the Norfolk & Western Railway built and operated the Hotel Roanoke. This early card shows the hotel with its ivy-adorned balconies and massive lawn.

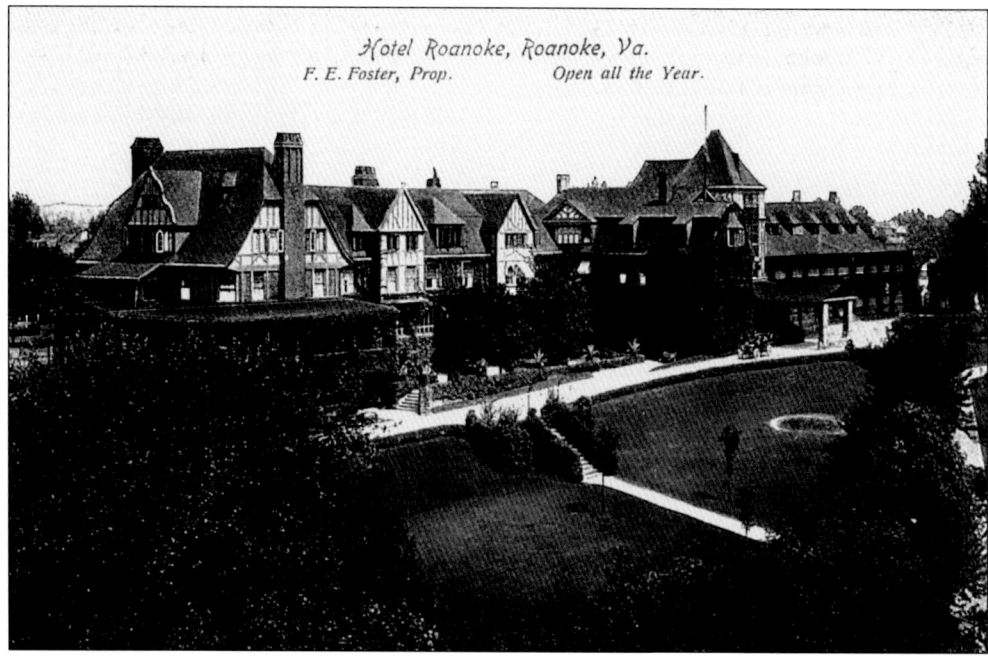

HOTEL ROANOKE, 1915. This card shows in more detail the 10-acre park-like surroundings of the hotel and the broad balconies. At the time this card was printed, F.E. Foster was proprietor and the card boasted "open all the year."

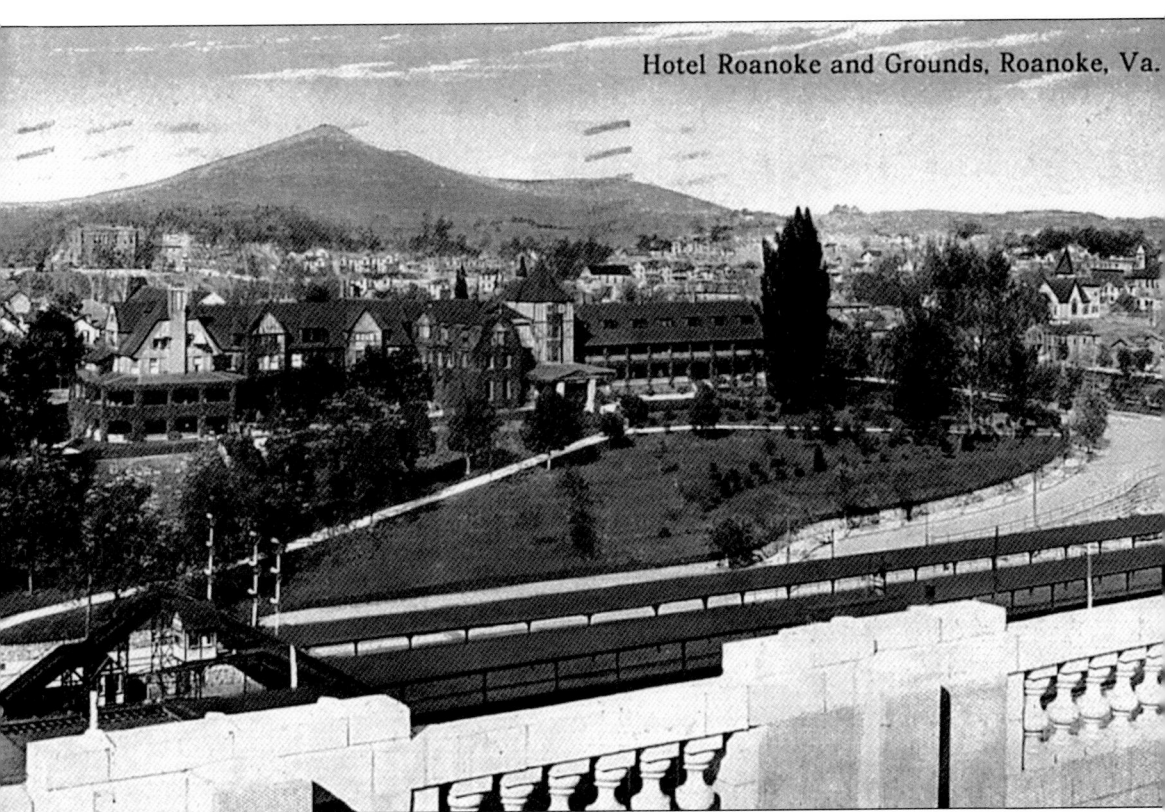

Hotel Roanoke and Grounds, 1915. This view of the hotel from atop a building in downtown Roanoke shows the closeness of the hotel to residential areas and the passenger depot (note the train sheds in the foreground).

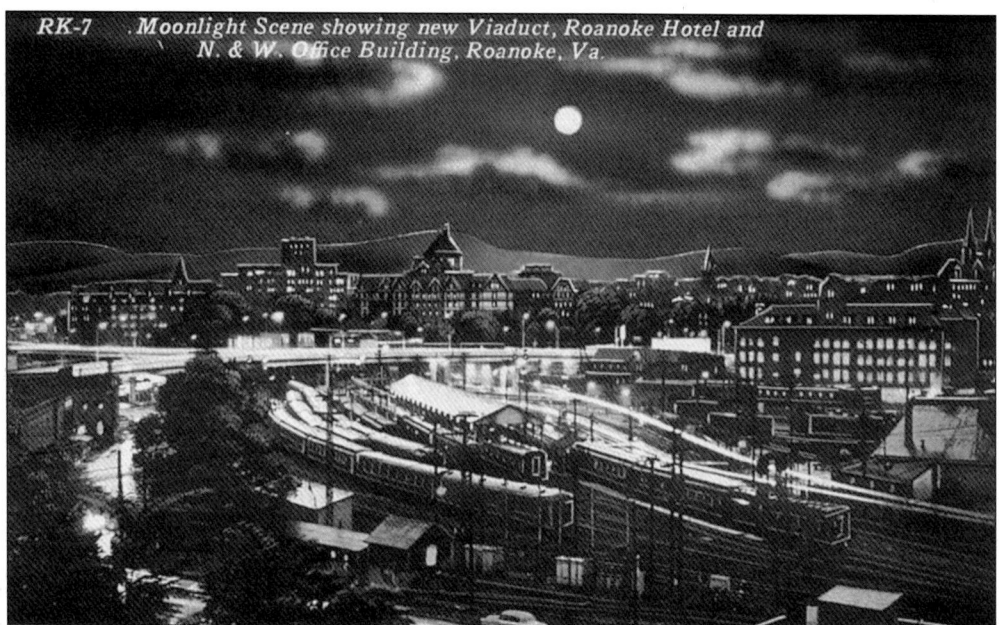

Moonlight Scene Showing New Viaduct, Roanoke Hotel, and N&W Office Buildings, 1960. The Hotel Roanoke was centered in the heart of Roanoke's bustling rail and commercial activities. This card shows the emerging skyline of what would become Roanoke by mid-century.

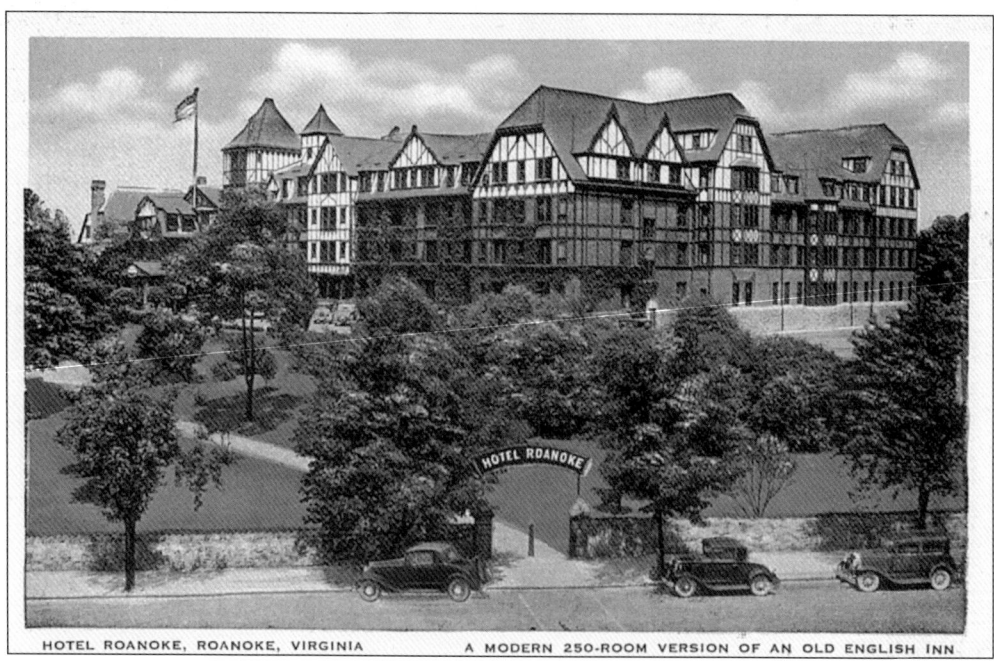

Hotel Roanoke, 1937. Known for its tudor-style architectural features, the Hotel Roanoke changed with the times. This postcard reminds recipients that the hotel is "a modern 250-room version of an old English inn." Further, the reverse side hailed the new 50-car garage that connected directly with the lobby.

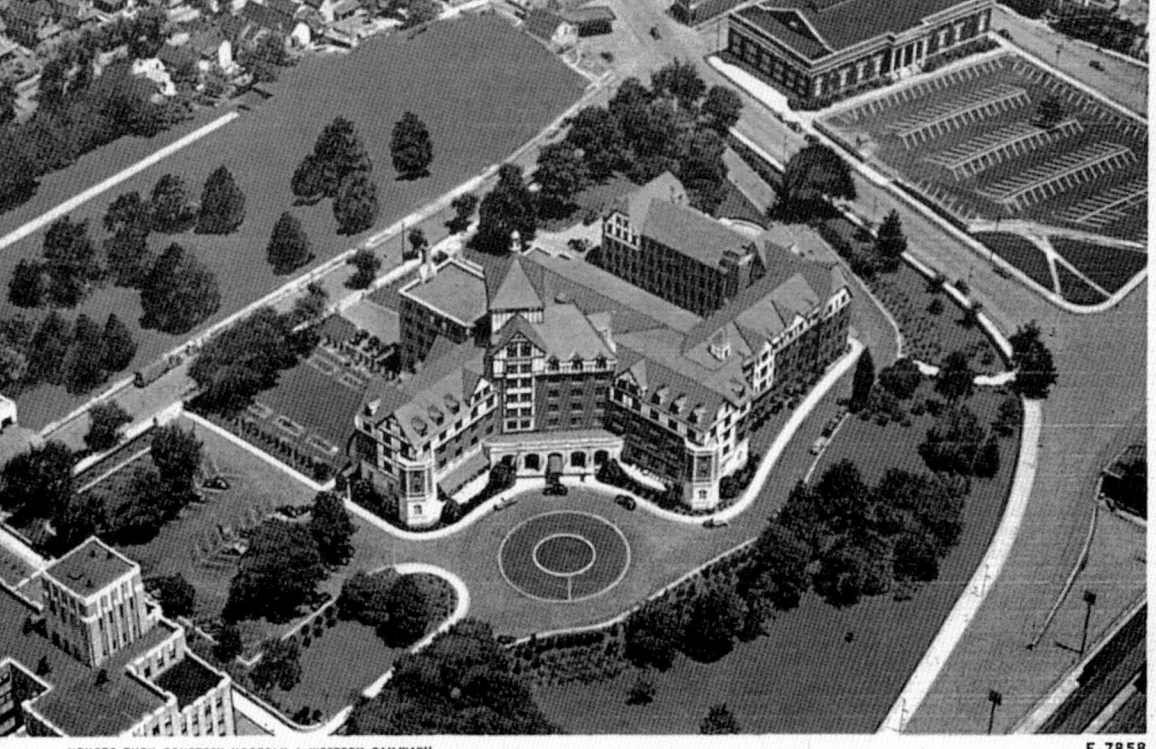

AIRPLANE VIEW OF HOTEL ROANOKE AND GROUNDS, 1950. By the time this postcard was printed, the lush lawn had disappeared to make room for travelers arriving more by automobile than train. While the hotel went through many changes, it always retained its tudor look. The structure in the top right is the city auditorium, no longer in existence.

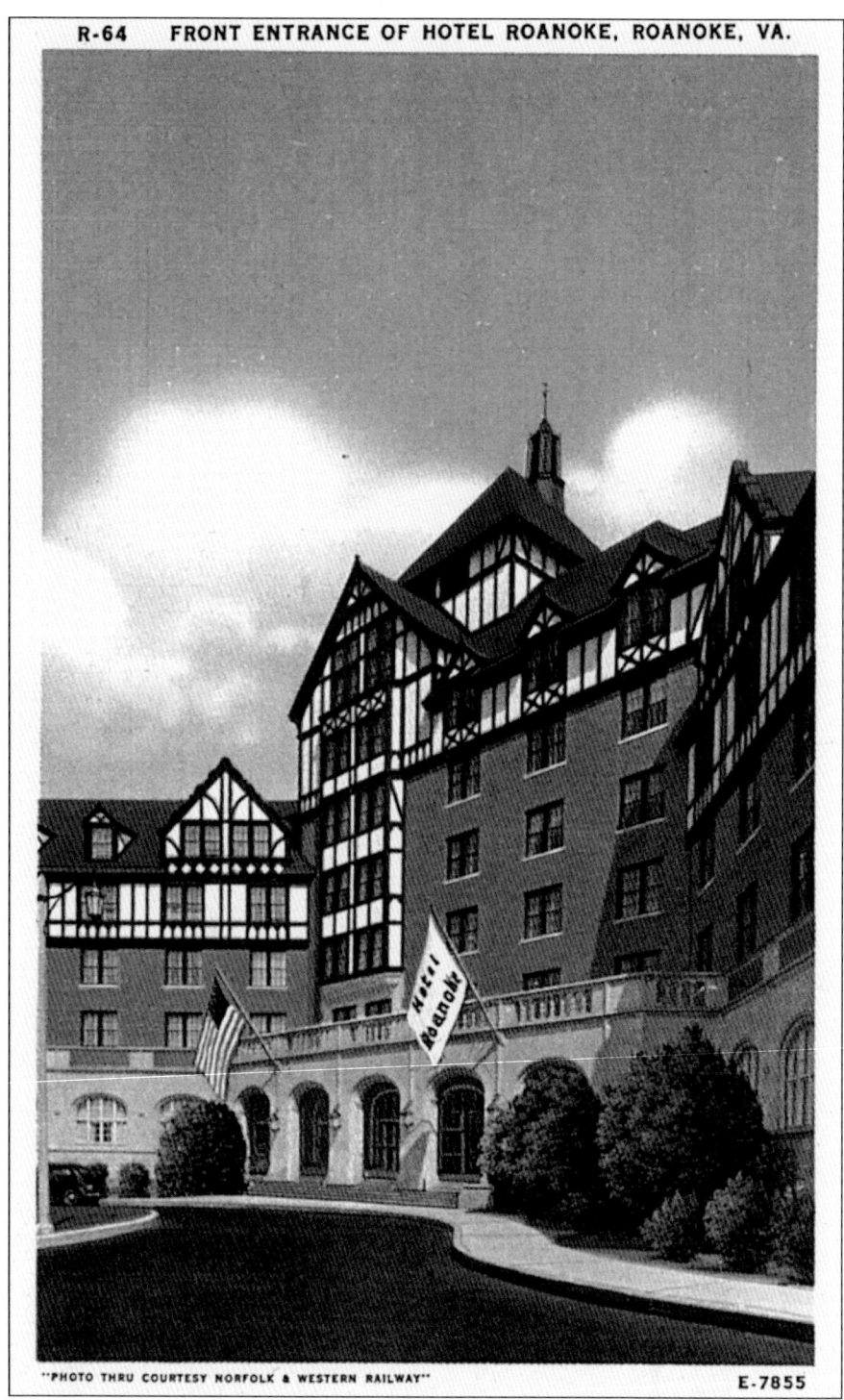

FRONT ENTRANCE OF HOTEL ROANOKE, 1950. One of the more popular cards of the hotel was this one from the 1950s showing the grand, flag-draped entrance of the hotel with its circular drive and arched lobby windows.

Two
Religion and Education

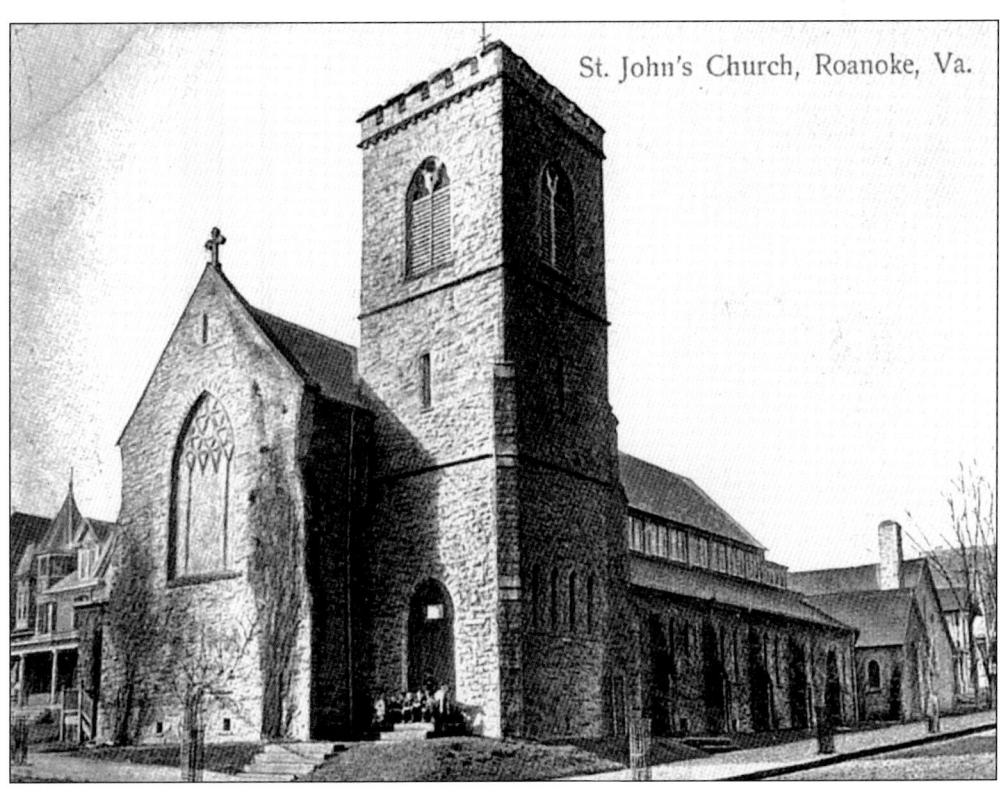

St. John's Episcopal Church, 1915. St. John's Episcopal Church, one of Roanoke's oldest congregations, has long stood at the corner of Elm Avenue and Jefferson Street.

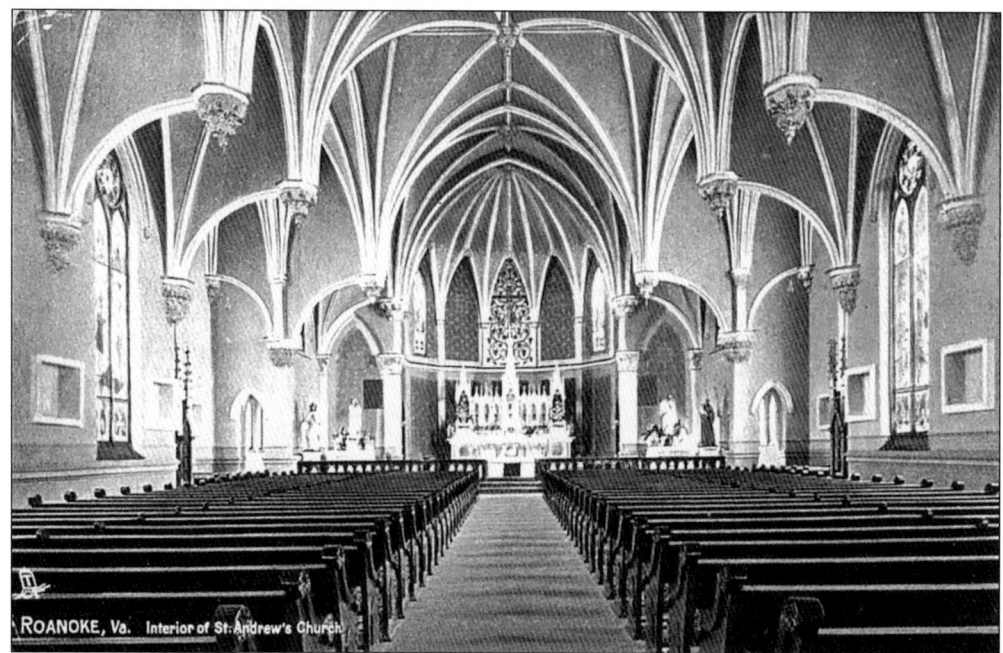

INTERIOR OF ST. ANDREWS CATHOLIC CHURCH, 1915. This card for St. Andrews states, "It is built of buff brick with trimmings of Ohio sandstone. The altar is beautiful and there are several fine memorial windows."

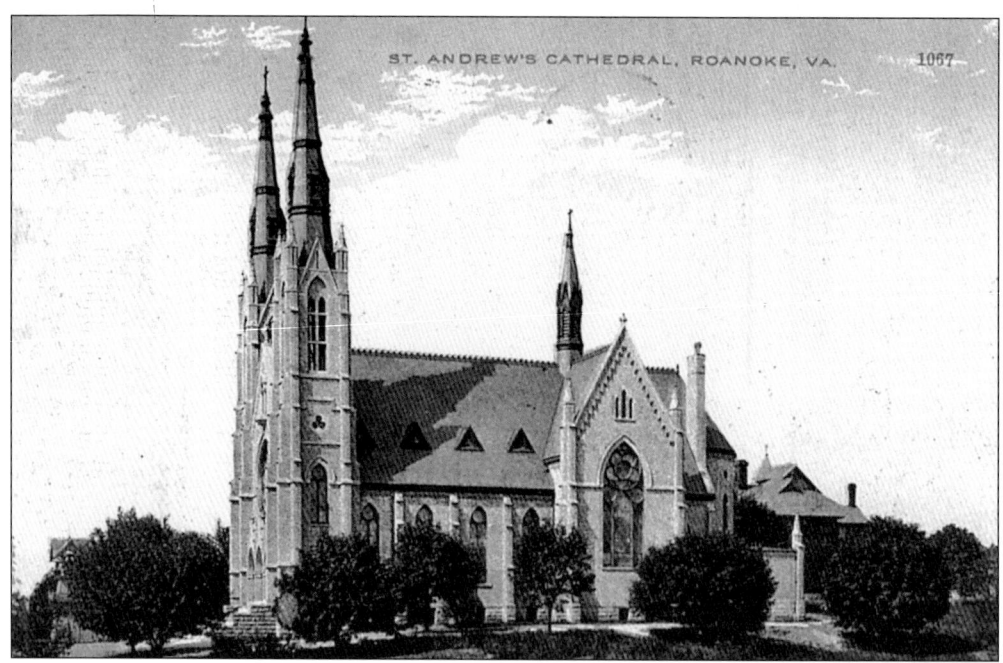

ST. ANDREWS CATHOLIC CHURCH, 1941. The spire of St. Andrews Church was at one time the highest structure in Roanoke. The structure remains one of the most elegant and beautiful in the city.

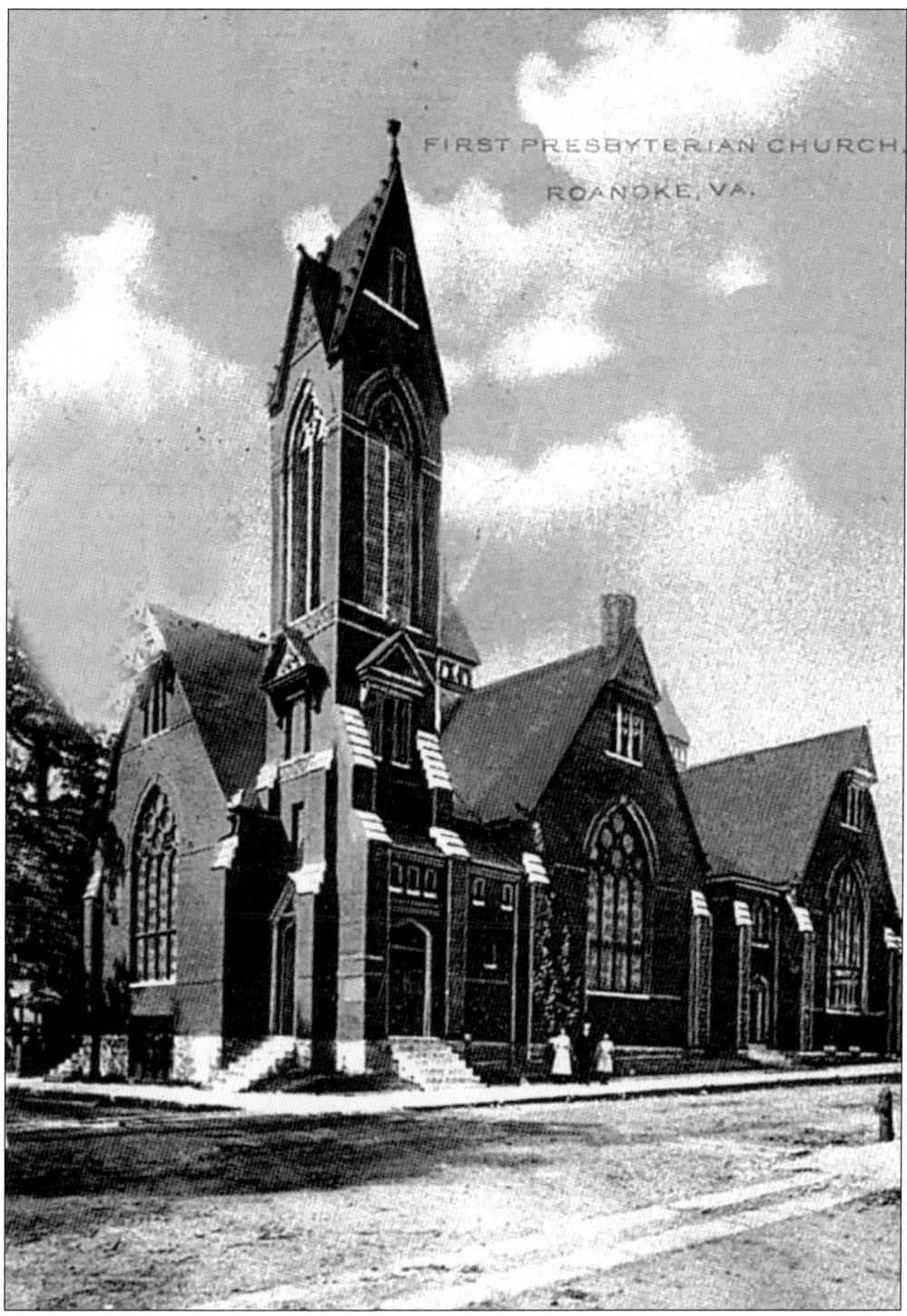

FIRST PRESBYTERIAN CHURCH, 1910. The First Presbyterian Church once stood in the downtown area of Roanoke, as shown on this card, before moving to its present location in South Roanoke in 1928. The most notable feature of the church was its tall bell tower.

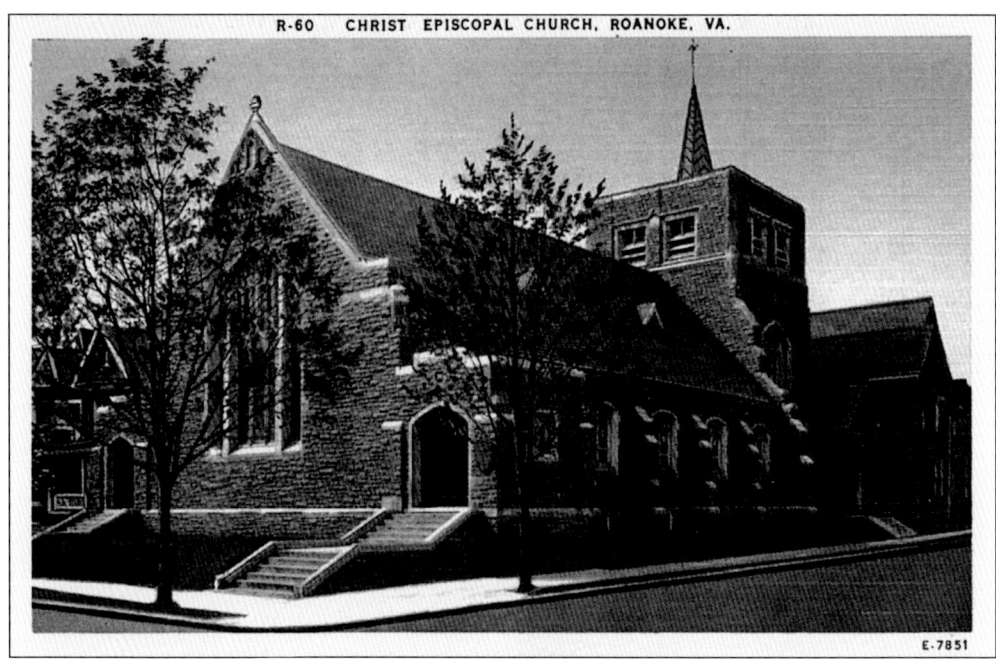

CHRIST EPISCOPAL CHURCH, 1950. Christ Episcopal Church was dedicated in 1918 and is located on Franklin Road in the "Old Southwest" neighborhood.

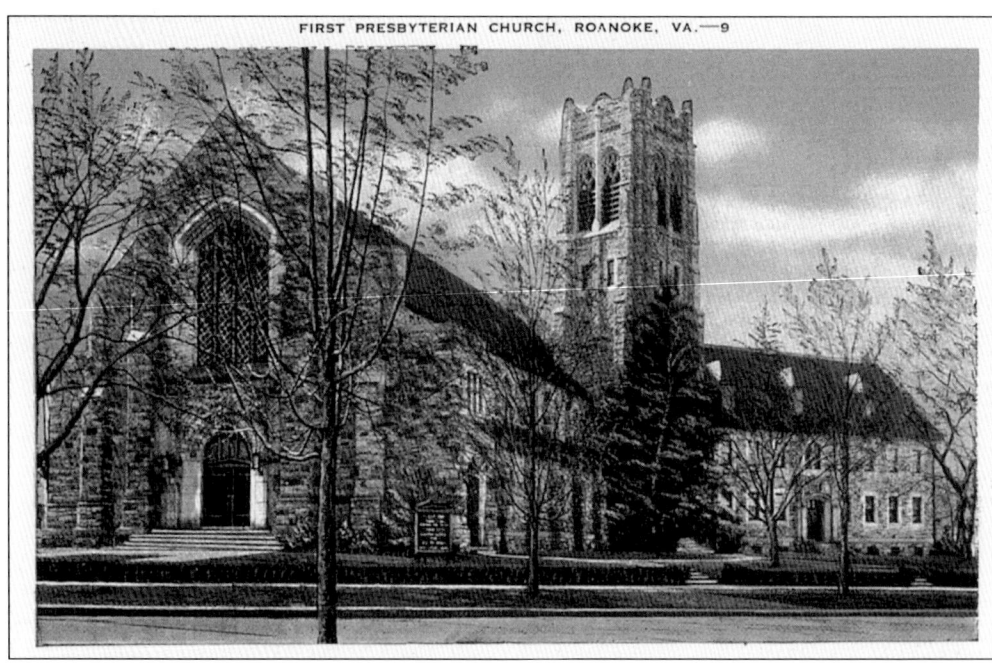

FIRST PRESBYTERIAN CHURCH, 1940. After moving from downtown, First Presbyterian Church built this sanctuary at the intersection of McClanahan Street and Jefferson Street.

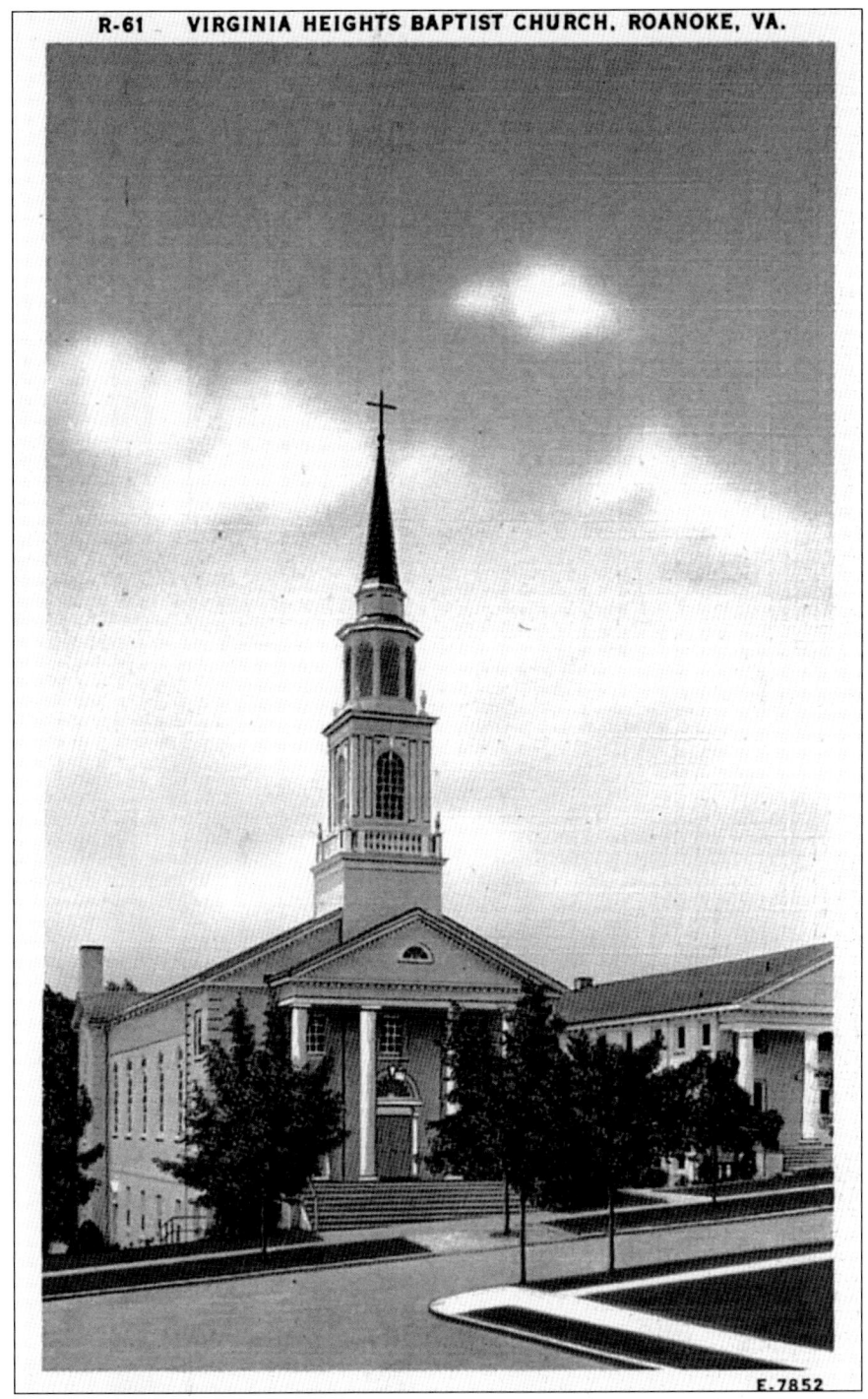

VIRGINIA HEIGHTS BAPTIST CHURCH, 1945. Virginia Heights Baptist Church began in 1919 but it was in 1938 that the sanctuary on this card was built at the intersection of Memorial Avenue and Grandin Road in Roanoke's Raleigh Court neighborhood.

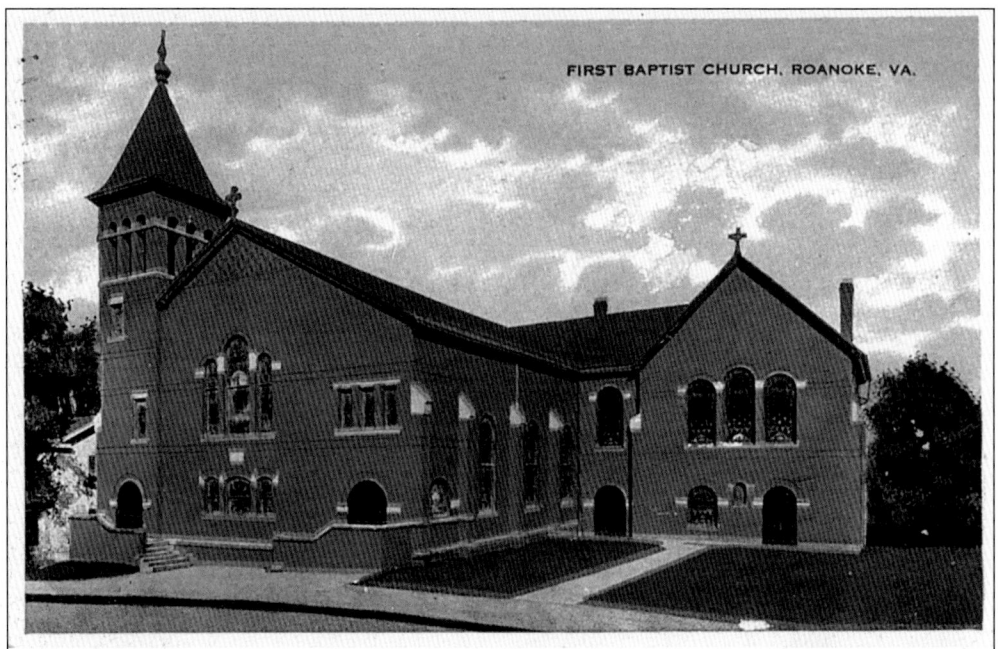

FIRST BAPTIST CHURCH, 1916. First Baptist Church is the largest congregation in Roanoke and shown here is the "old" sanctuary building. This sanctuary was directly across the street from the present church on property now occupied by Verizon. The structure was demolished around 1948.

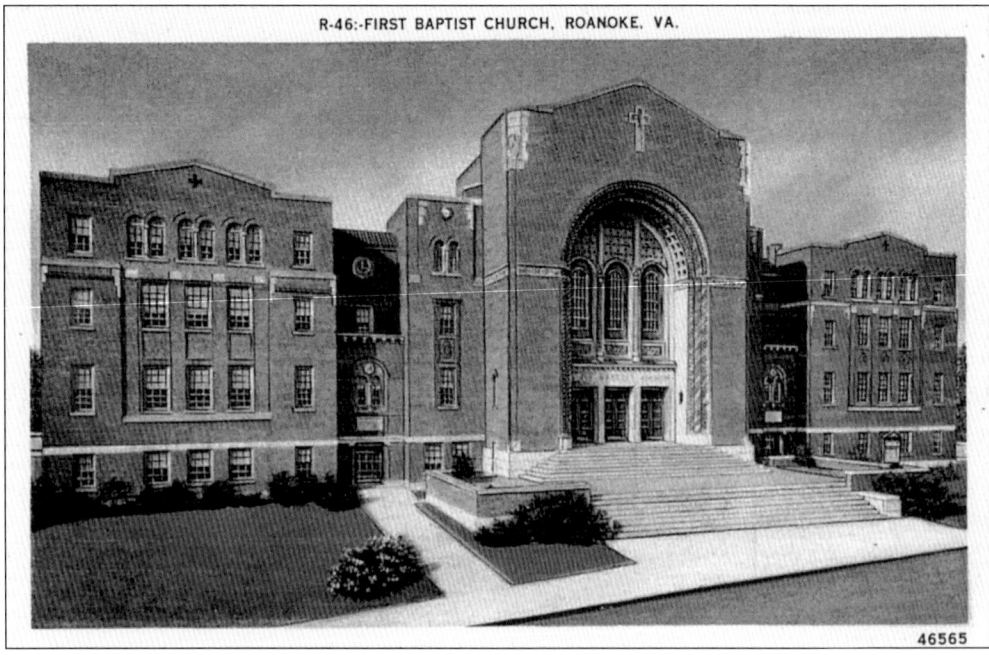

FIRST BAPTIST CHURCH, 1940. When First Church needed larger facilities, the congregation erected the sanctuary depicted on this card in 1929.

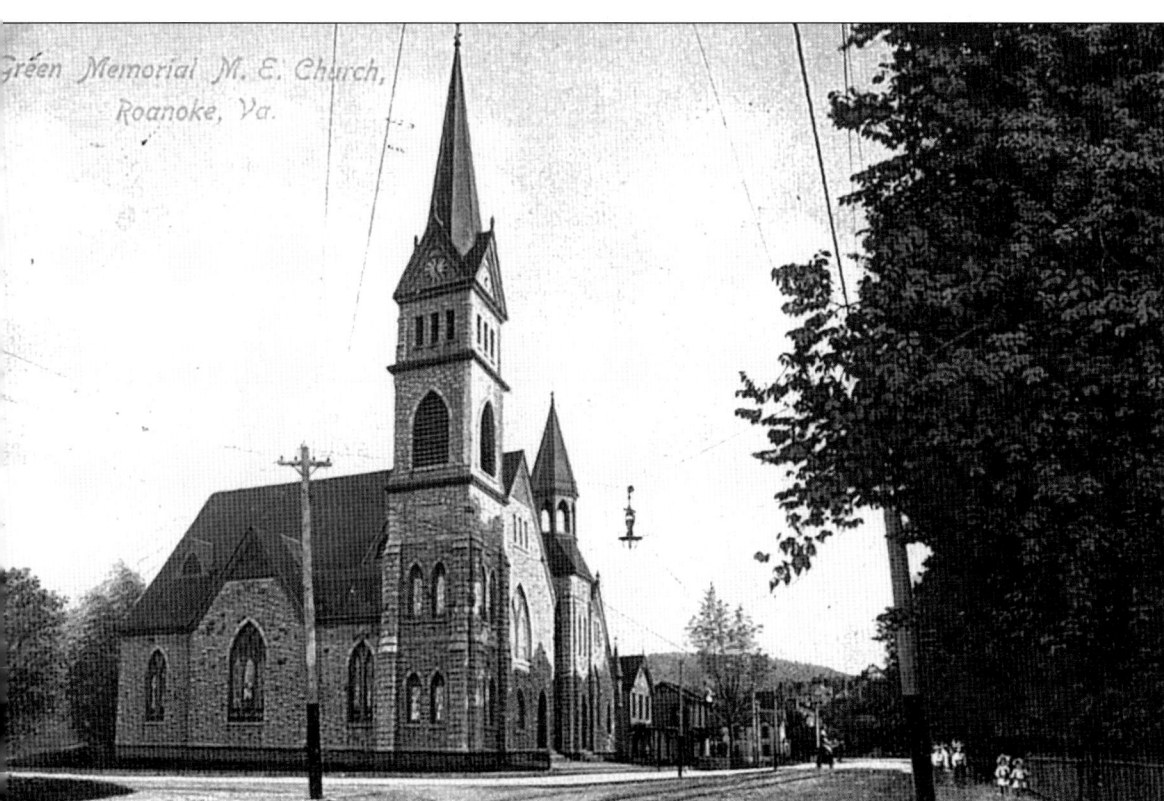

GREENE MEMORIAL METHODIST EPISCOPAL CHURCH, 1908. Green Memorial Methodist Church still retains much of its original look, although larger and without the smaller of the two steeples. Notice the brick streets with trolley tracks.

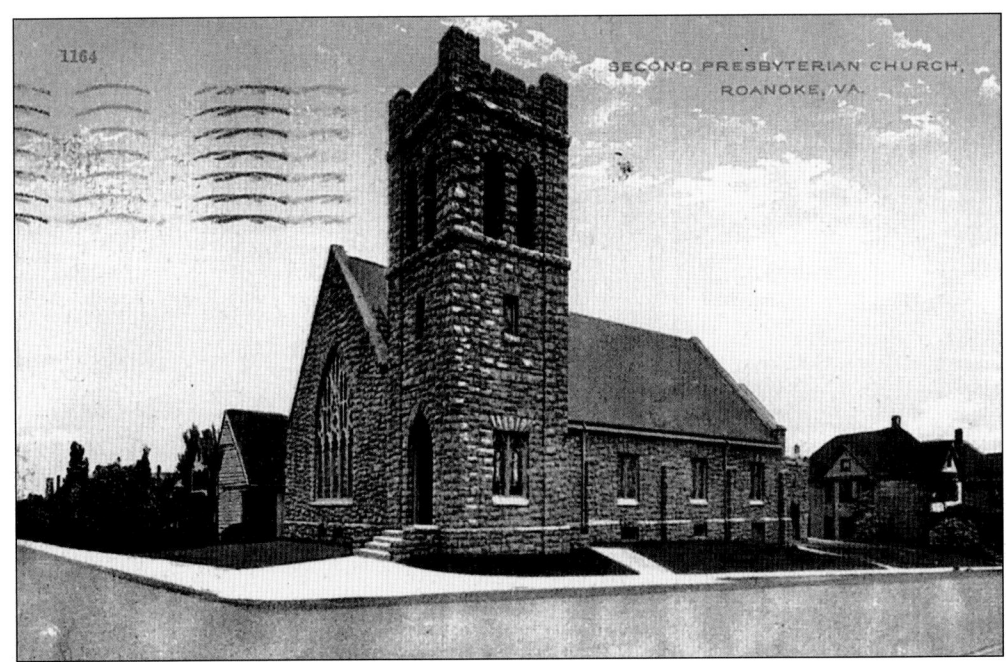

SECOND PRESBYTERIAN CHURCH, 1911. Second Presbyterian Church on Mountain Avenue in "Old Southwest" was started in 1891 as a mission of First Presbyterian. The sanctuary, built in 1905, is still in use today.

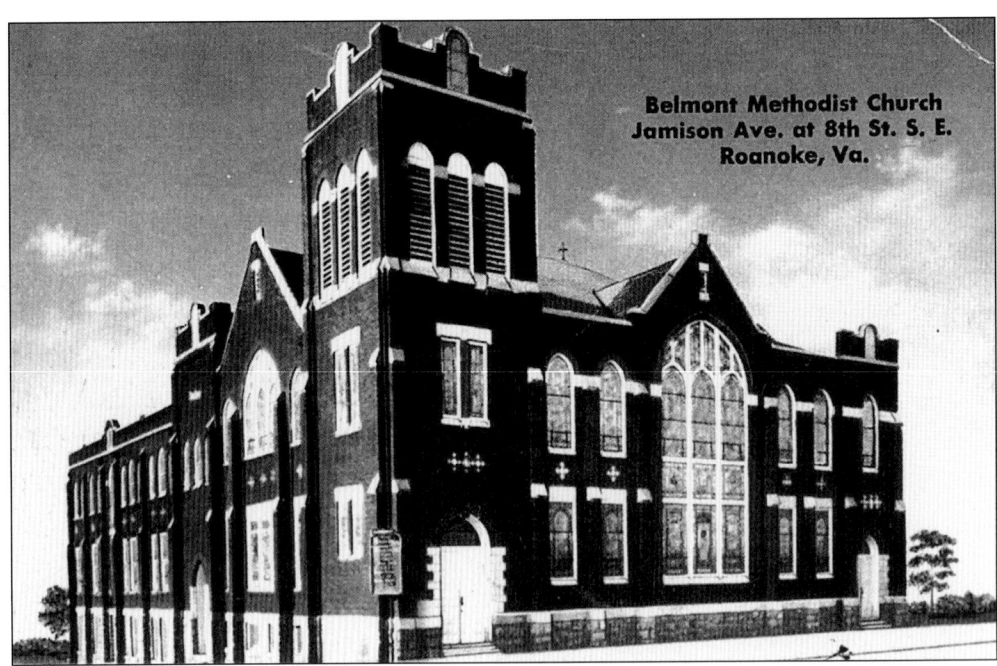

BELMONT METHODIST CHURCH, 1957. Belmont Methodist Church was organized in 1891 and the sanctuary was erected in 1917. The sender of this card was the minister newly appointed to serve Belmont Methodist in 1957, who mailed the card to show off his new assignment.

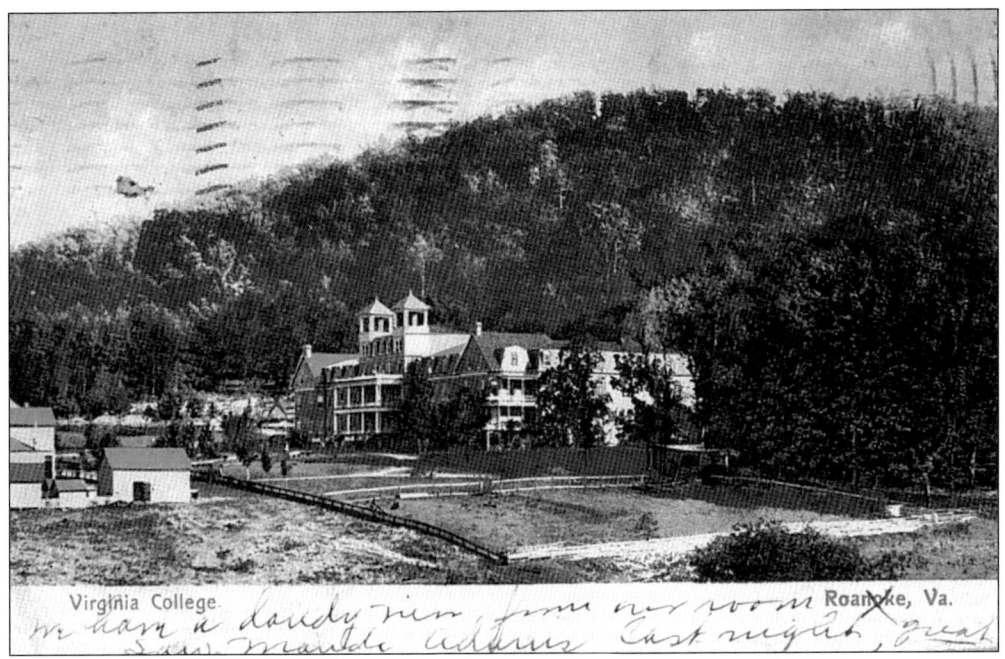

VIRGINIA COLLEGE, 1910. Virginia College was nestled at the foot of Stone Mountain, surrounded by gardens and pasture. A student sent this card with the following message: "Here is a picture of the college but it does not do it justice. This is a very pretty place, but gee I am tired of these old hills and mountains."

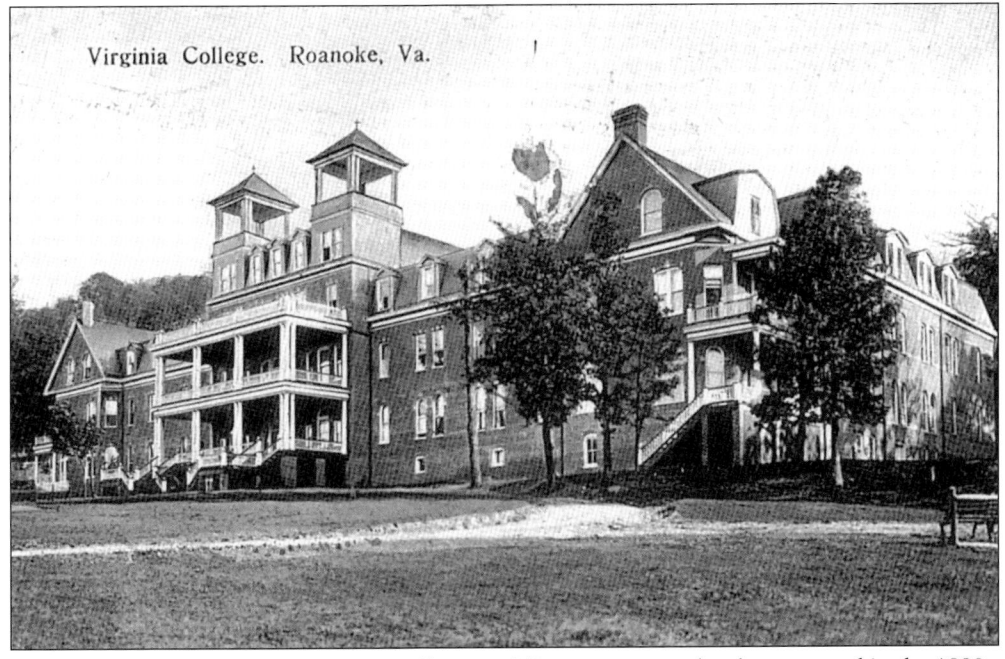

VIRGINIA COLLEGE, 1908. Virginia College, a girl's preparatory school, was started in the 1890s. Hit hard by the Depression, the college closed its doors permanently in 1934. It was later converted into apartments, caught fire, and was destroyed.

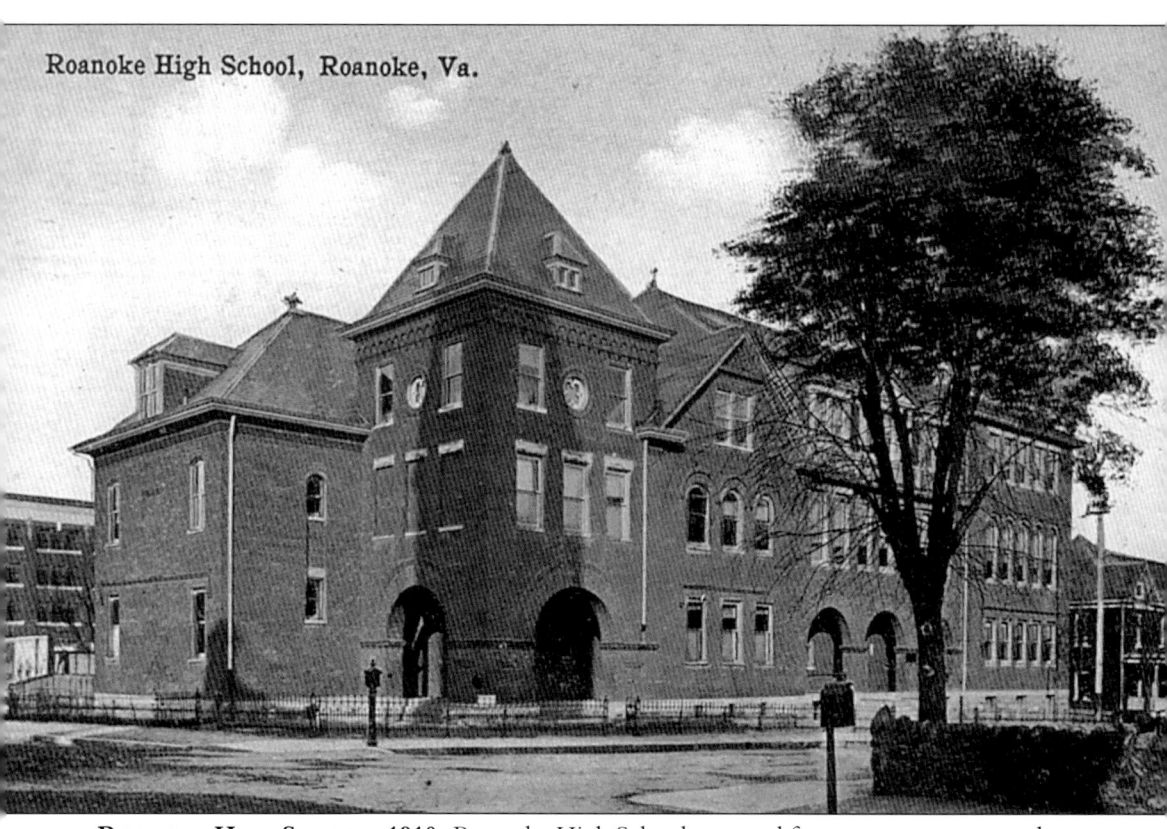

ROANOKE HIGH SCHOOL, 1910. Roanoke High School operated for a quarter century and was located across from the present-day Municipal Building. It closed with the opening of Jefferson High School in the 1920s.

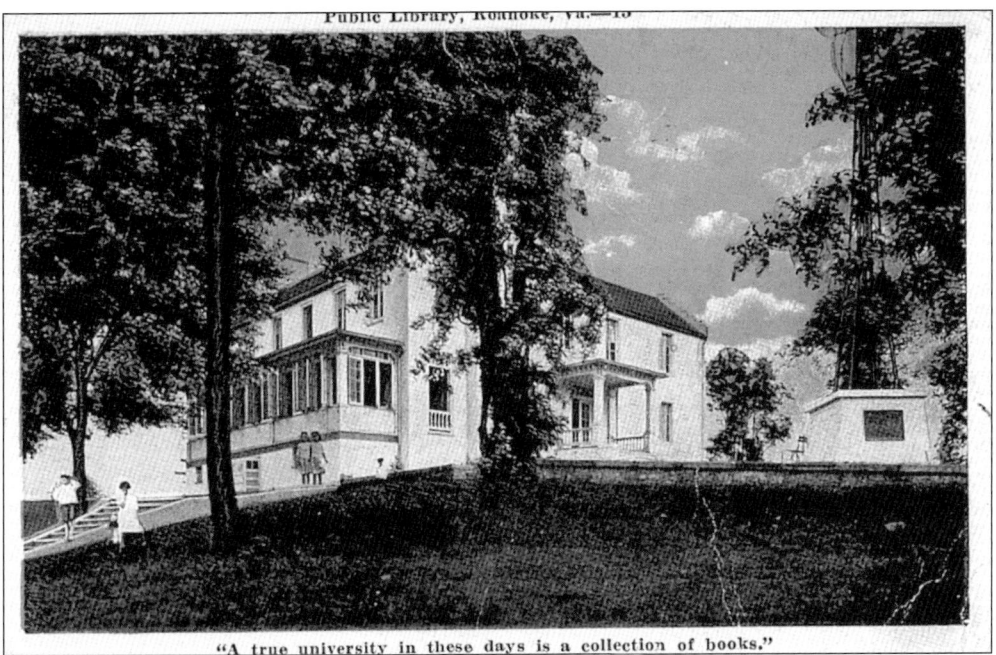

PUBLIC LIBRARY, 1924. The Elmwood home was the first location for Roanoke's public library and was located in Elmwood Park. The home no longer exists.

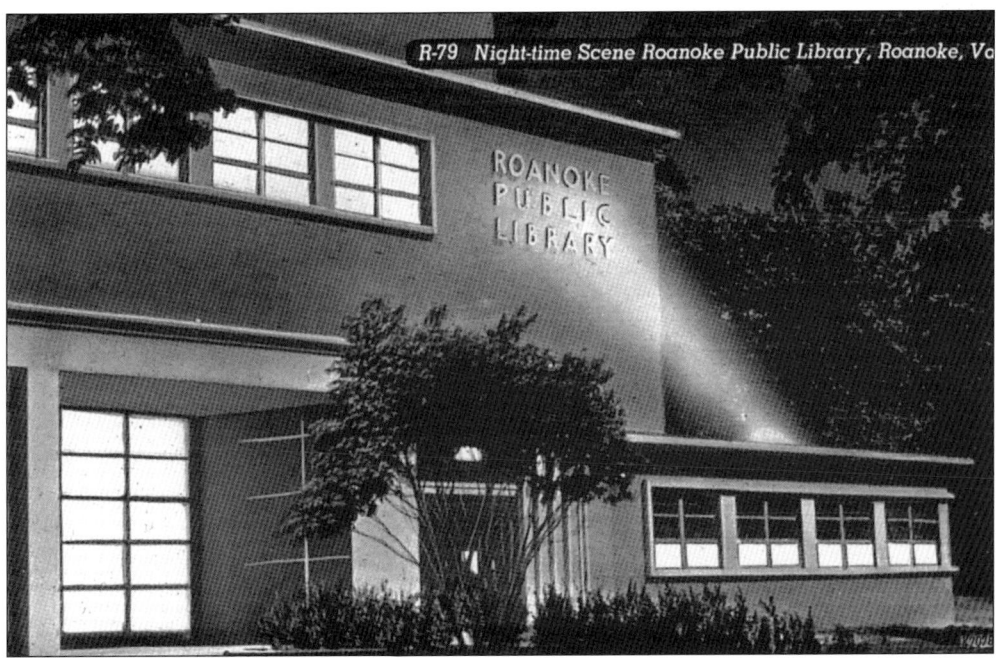

NIGHTTIME SCENE, ROANOKE PUBLIC LIBRARY, 1955. Roanoke's new main public library opened in 1952 with an initial capacity for 185,000 volumes.

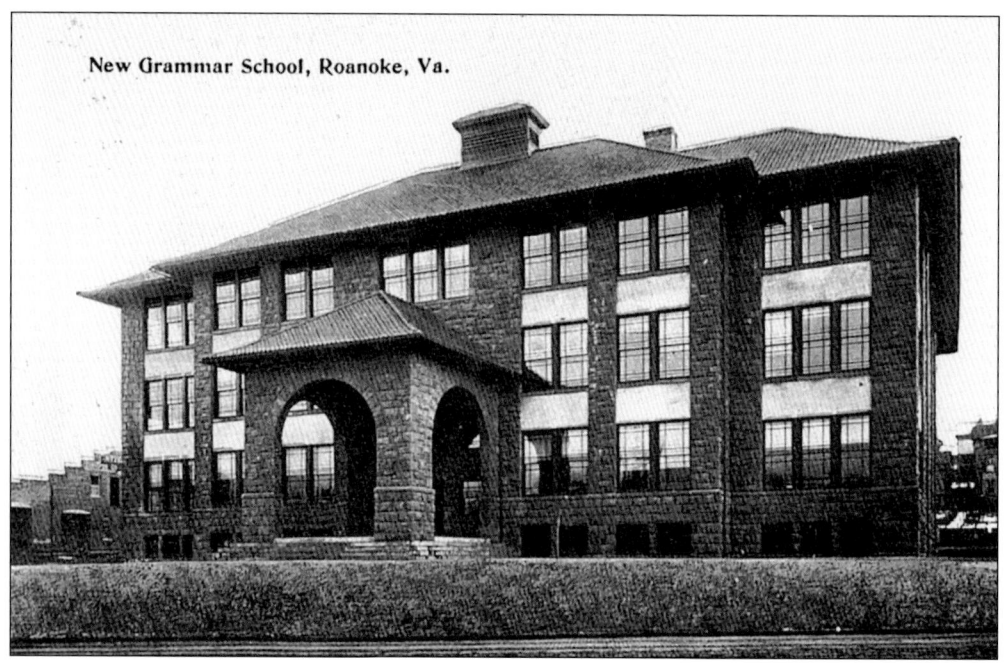

NEW GRAMMAR SCHOOL, 1913. Called the "New Grammar School" on this card, the image depicts what most Roanokers know to have been Lee Junior High School on Franklin Road. The school was torn down to make room for the Poff Federal Building.

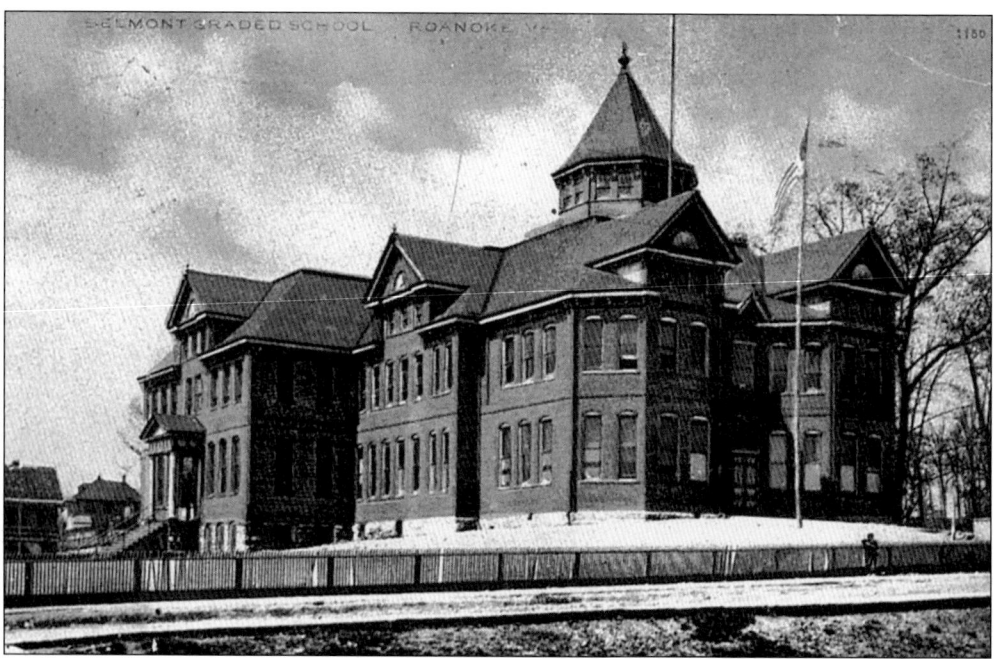

BELMONT GRADED SCHOOL, 1910. Belmont Graded Academy opened its doors in 1893 as one of the earliest school buildings erected by the city. The school no longer exists.

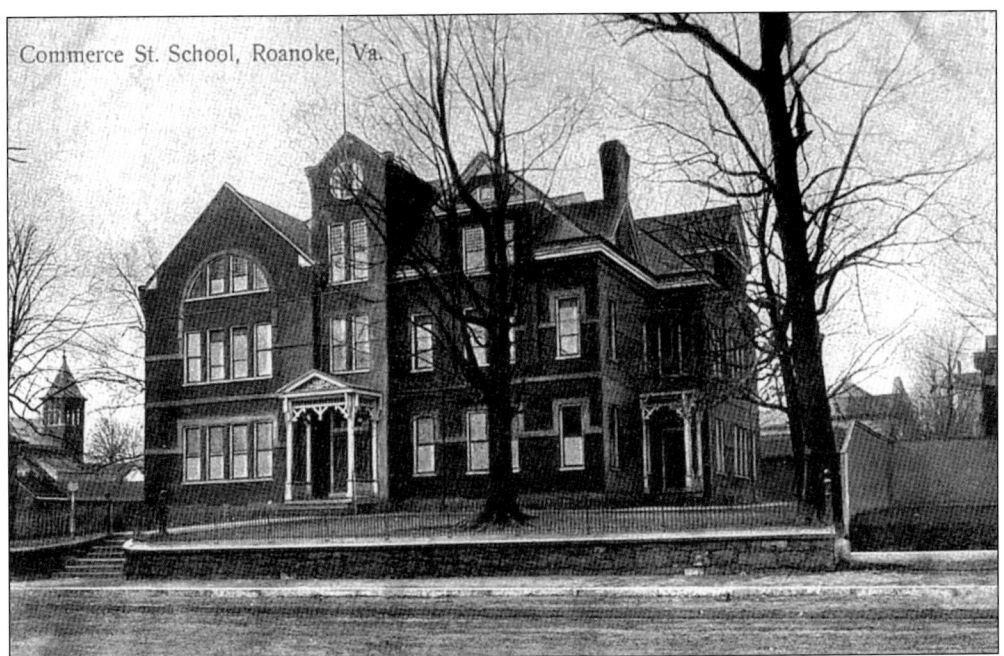

COMMERCE STREET SCHOOL, 1910. Commerce Street School was Roanoke's first school, originally built as a wooden structure in "Big Lick." Later encased in brick, the school served as the city's high school in 1891 and 1892. It was torn down to make room for a federal post office.

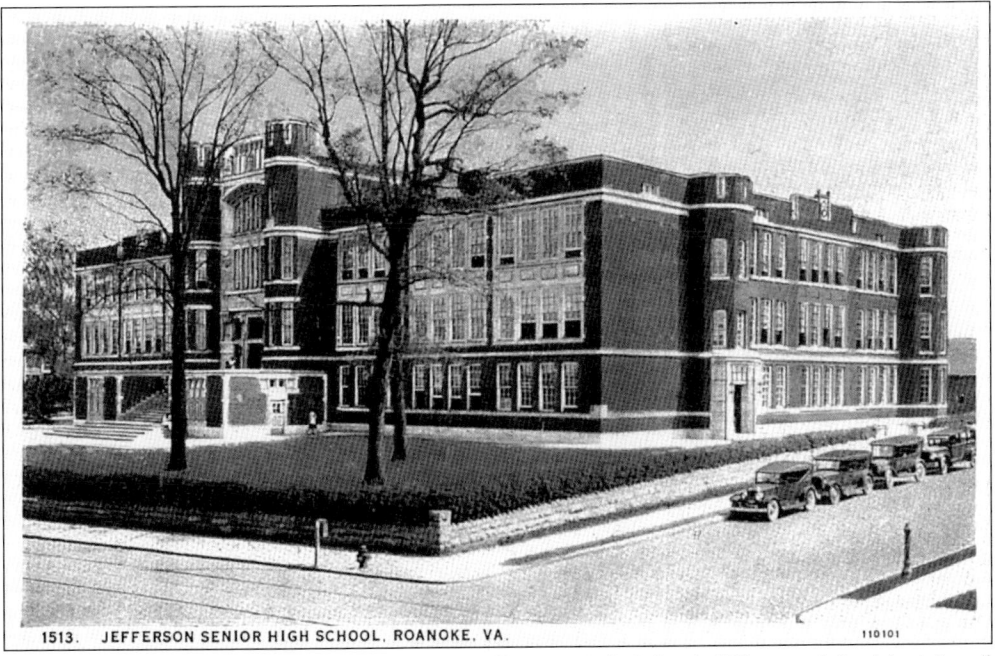

JEFFERSON SENIOR HIGH SCHOOL, 1934. Jefferson High School, "Home of the Magicians," had its cornerstone laid in 1923. Closed as a school, it is now Jefferson Center and home to many cultural and civic organizations.

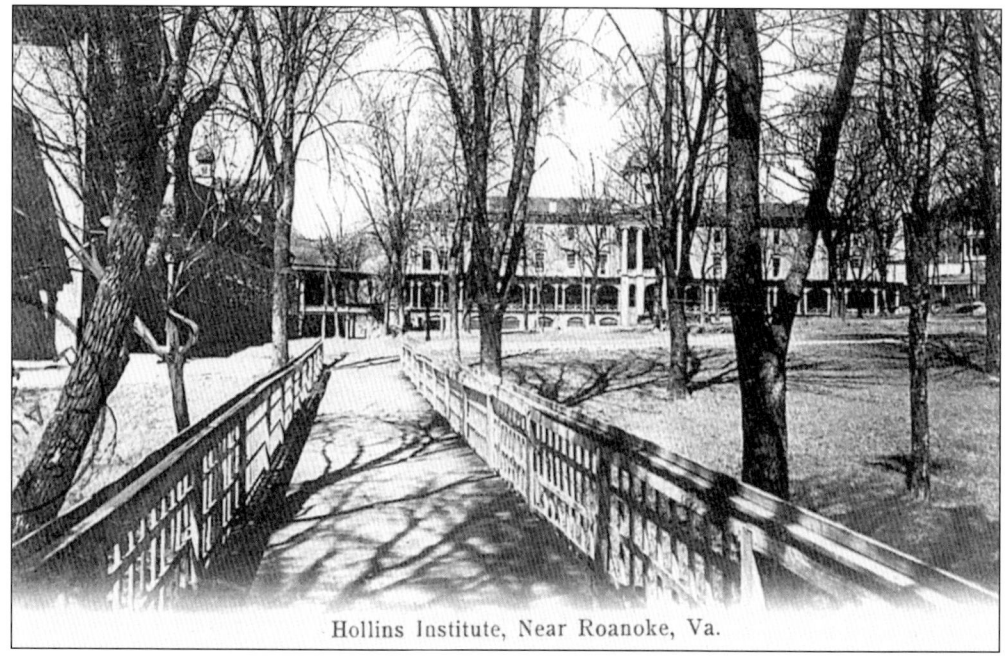

Hollins Institute, Near Roanoke, Va.

HOLLINS INSTITUTE, 1907. Hollins Institute is now Hollins University, an all-female school, located in north Roanoke County. The area on this postcard is the central lawn of the university.

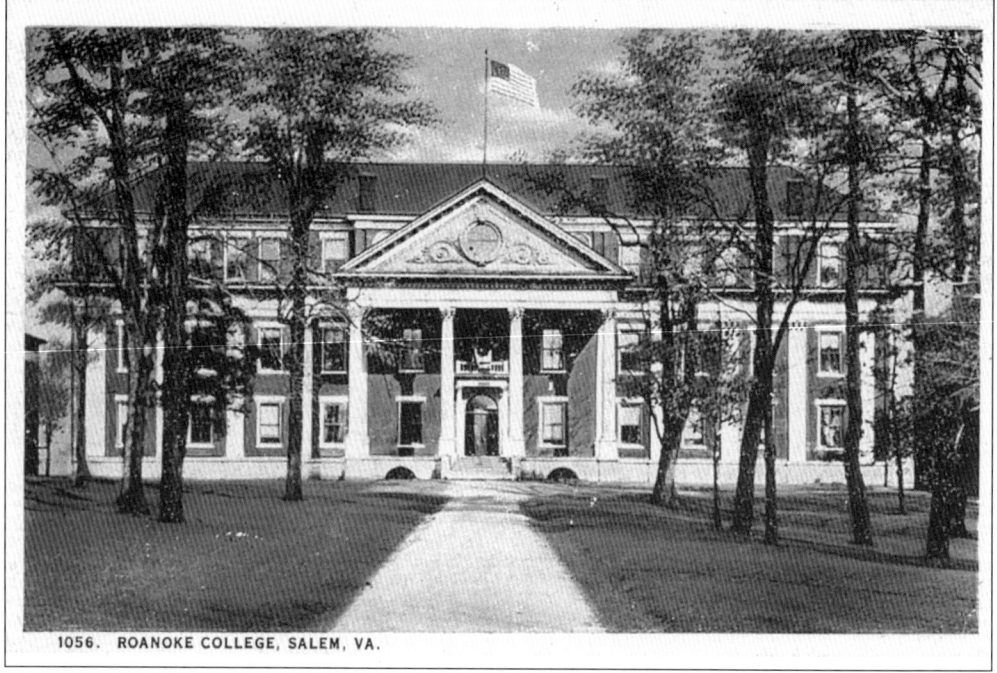

1056. ROANOKE COLLEGE, SALEM, VA.

ROANOKE COLLEGE, 1936. Roanoke College moved to Salem just before the Civil War and was one of the few schools to remain open during that period. It is a private, Lutheran-affiliated college. This postcard is of the central administration building.

Three
Government and Commerce

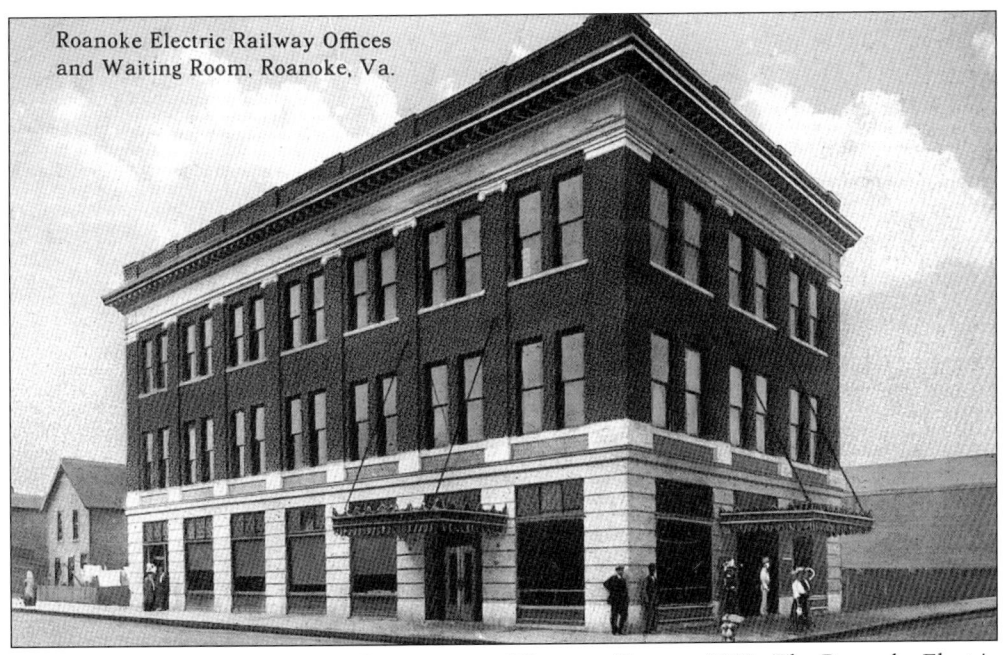

Roanoke Electric Railway Offices and Waiting Room, 1913. The Roanoke Electric Railway ran the city's trolley lines. While trolleys are long gone, the building is not. It remains today as a home for business and retail in downtown.

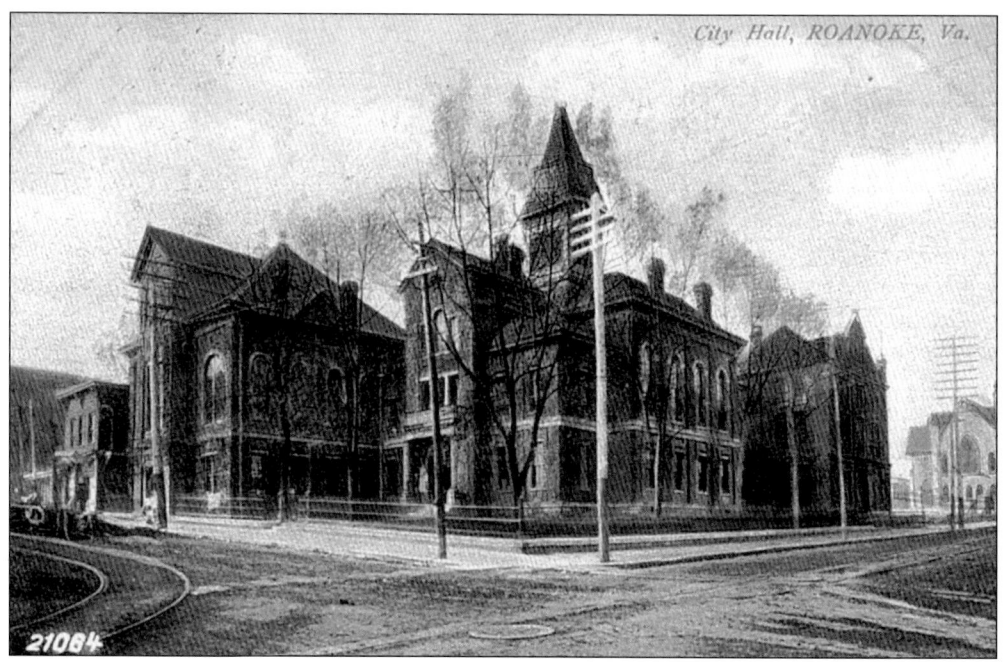

CITY HALL, 1908. Roanoke's first formal city hall was a stately resident of the city's early years. It was demolished after the new municipal building was erected in 1915.

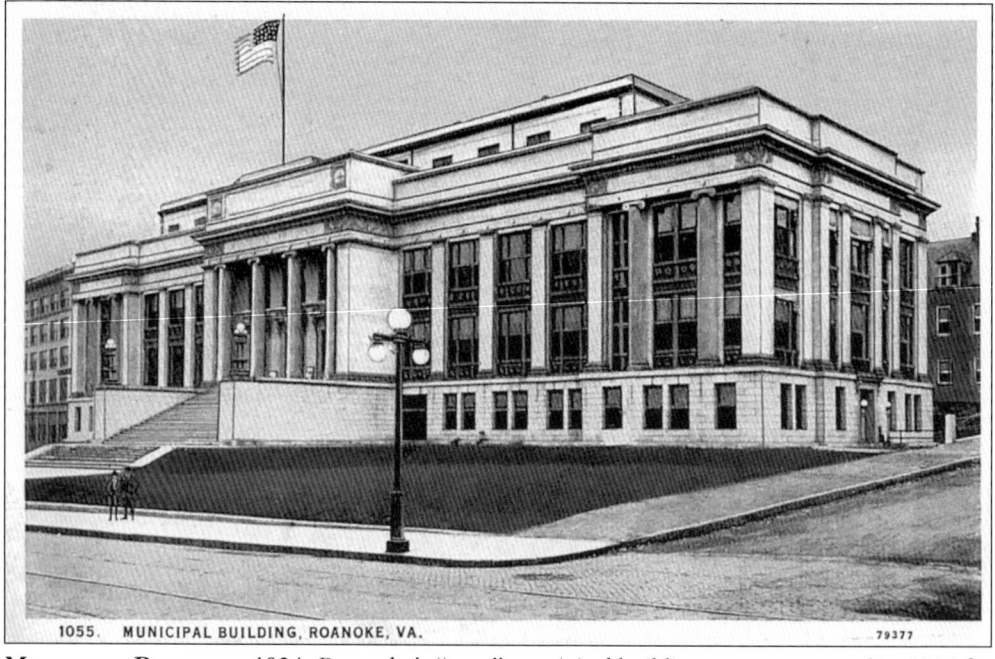

MUNICIPAL BUILDING, 1924. Roanoke's "new" municipal building was constructed in 1915 for a cost of $250,000. The building still operates as municipal offices on Campbell Avenue with a newer annex on Church Avenue.

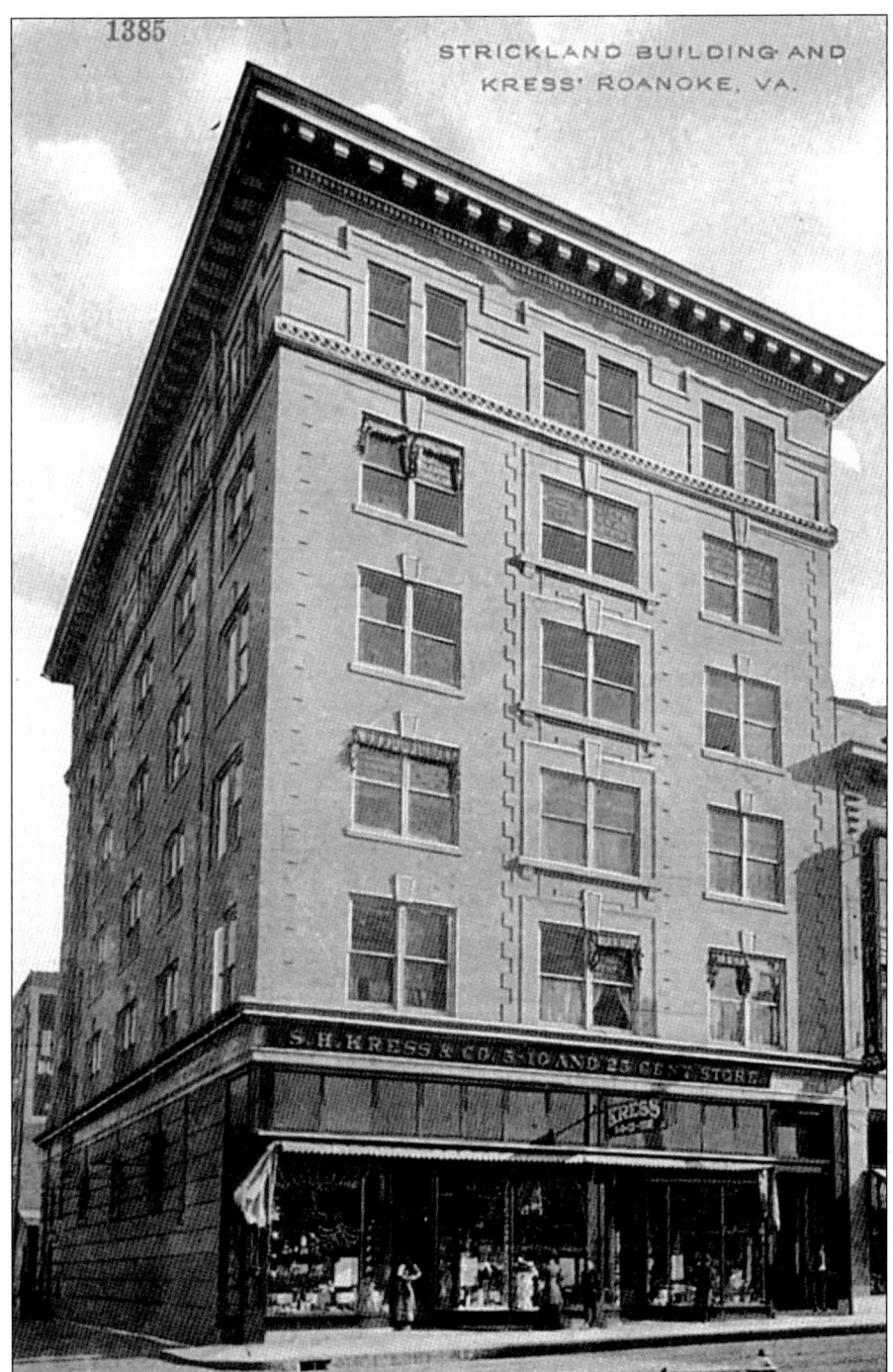

STRICKLAND BUILDING AND S.H. KRESS, 1910. The Strickland Building was one of the early office buildings in downtown Roanoke. The first floor contained S.H. Kress "5, 10 and 25 Cent Store." Kress moved from the building in 1913. In 1921, the building was purchased by Mountain Trust Bank. On their opening day that year, the bank gave all the ladies roses and the men, cigars.

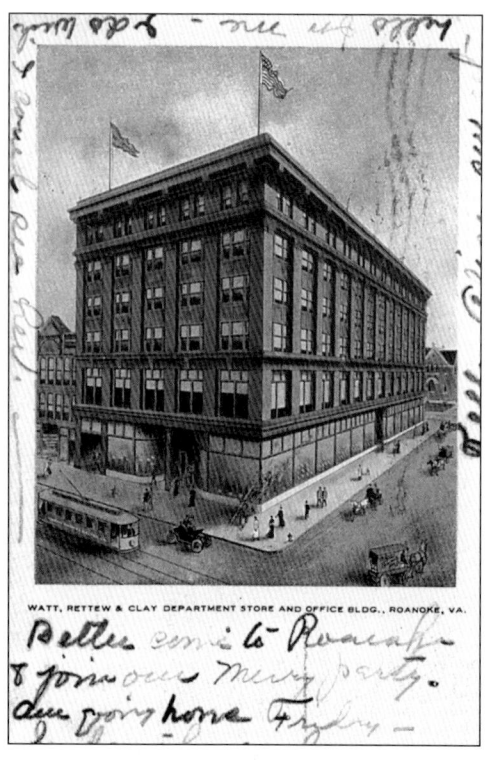

WATT, RETTEW, AND CLAY DEPARTMENT STORE AND OFFICE BUILDING, 1908. This was one of Roanoke's finest department stores in the 1890s. Located on the southeast corner of Campbell and First Streets, the department store and office complex was sold to George MacBain in 1913. In 1935 the MacBain Building became the new quarters for another department store, S.H. Heironimus.

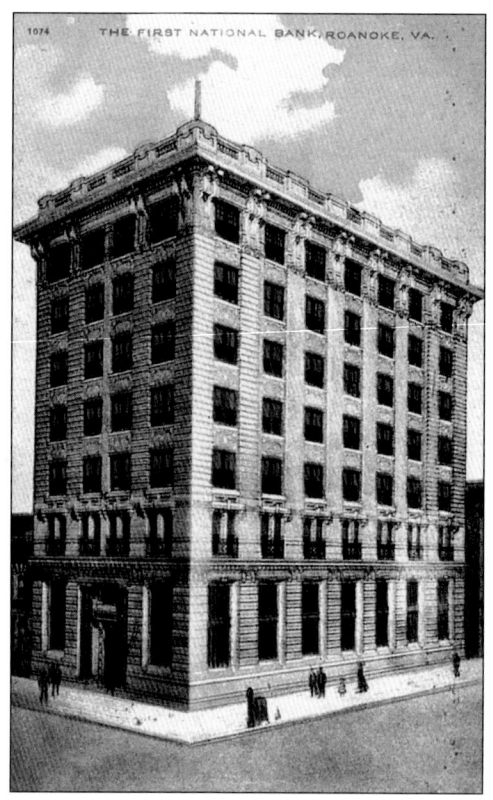

THE FIRST NATIONAL BANK, 1910. The First National Bank Building was constructed by Dr. J.D. Kirk on the southwest corner of Jefferson and First Streets.

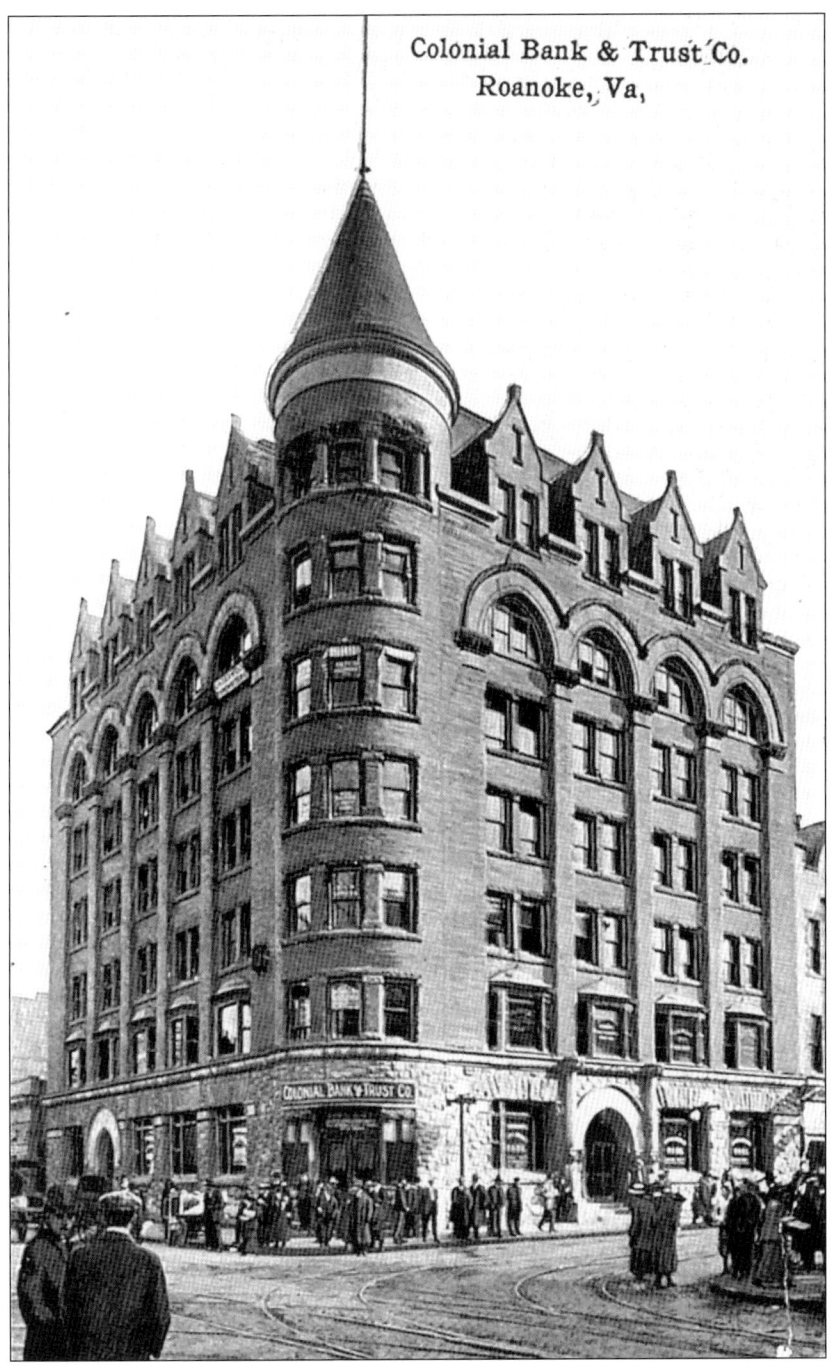

COLONIAL BANK AND TRUST COMPANY, 1911. Originally known as the Terry Building when it was constructed in 1892, this was the largest building in Roanoke and the first to be serviced by elevators. The Terry Building immediately increased the value of adjacent commercial property and took two years to construct. Purchased by Colonial Bank and Trust Co., the bank demolished the grand structure in 1926. It stood on the southeast corner of Campbell and Jefferson.

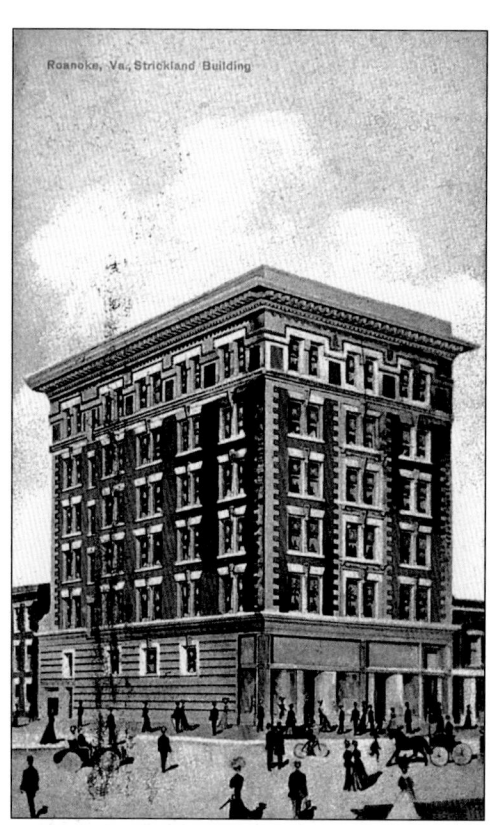

STRICKLAND BUILDING, 1909. Another view of the Strickland Building, this card shows the brick work of the buildings and period clothing of its shoppers.

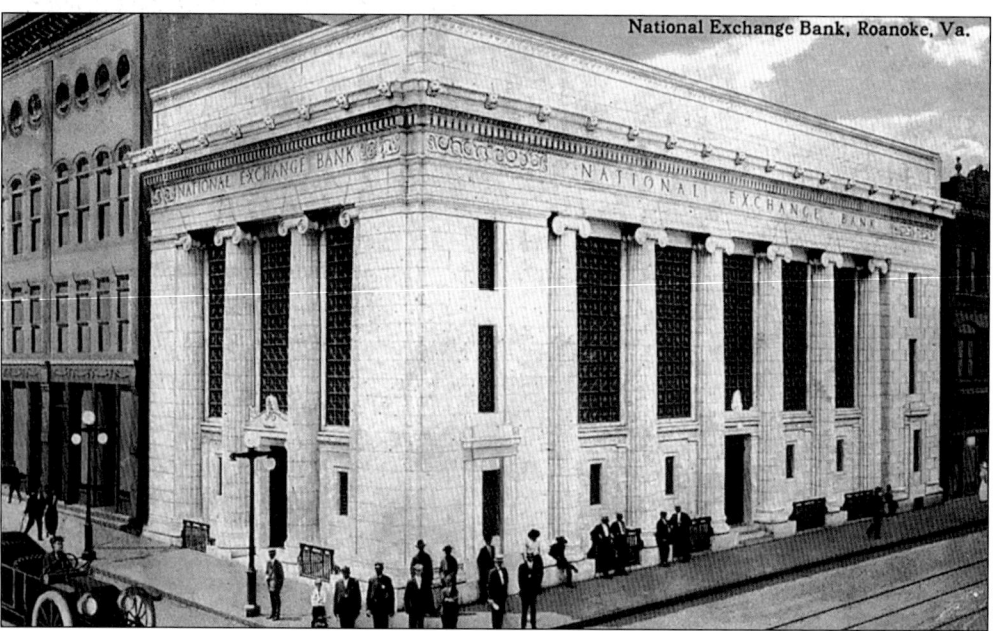

NATIONAL EXCHANGE BANK, 1915. The National Exchange Bank was built in two phases with the first phase, depicted here, completed in 1912. The bank building still remains at the corner of Campbell and Jefferson.

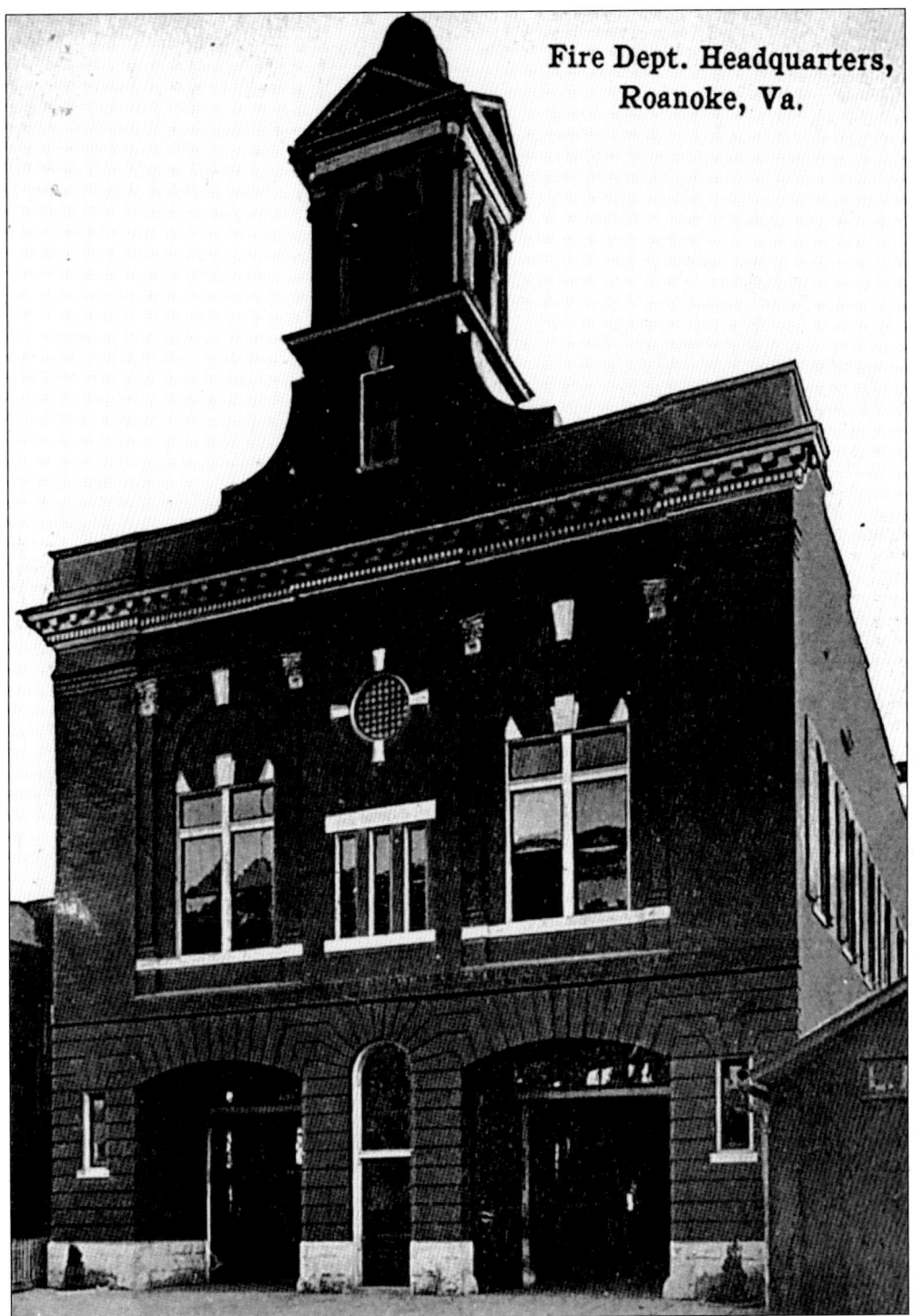

FIRE DEPARTMENT HEADQUARTERS, 1915. Known as Station No. 1, the downtown firehouse is one of Roanoke's most recognizable facilities. Built in 1906, the tower also served as a lookout for fires.

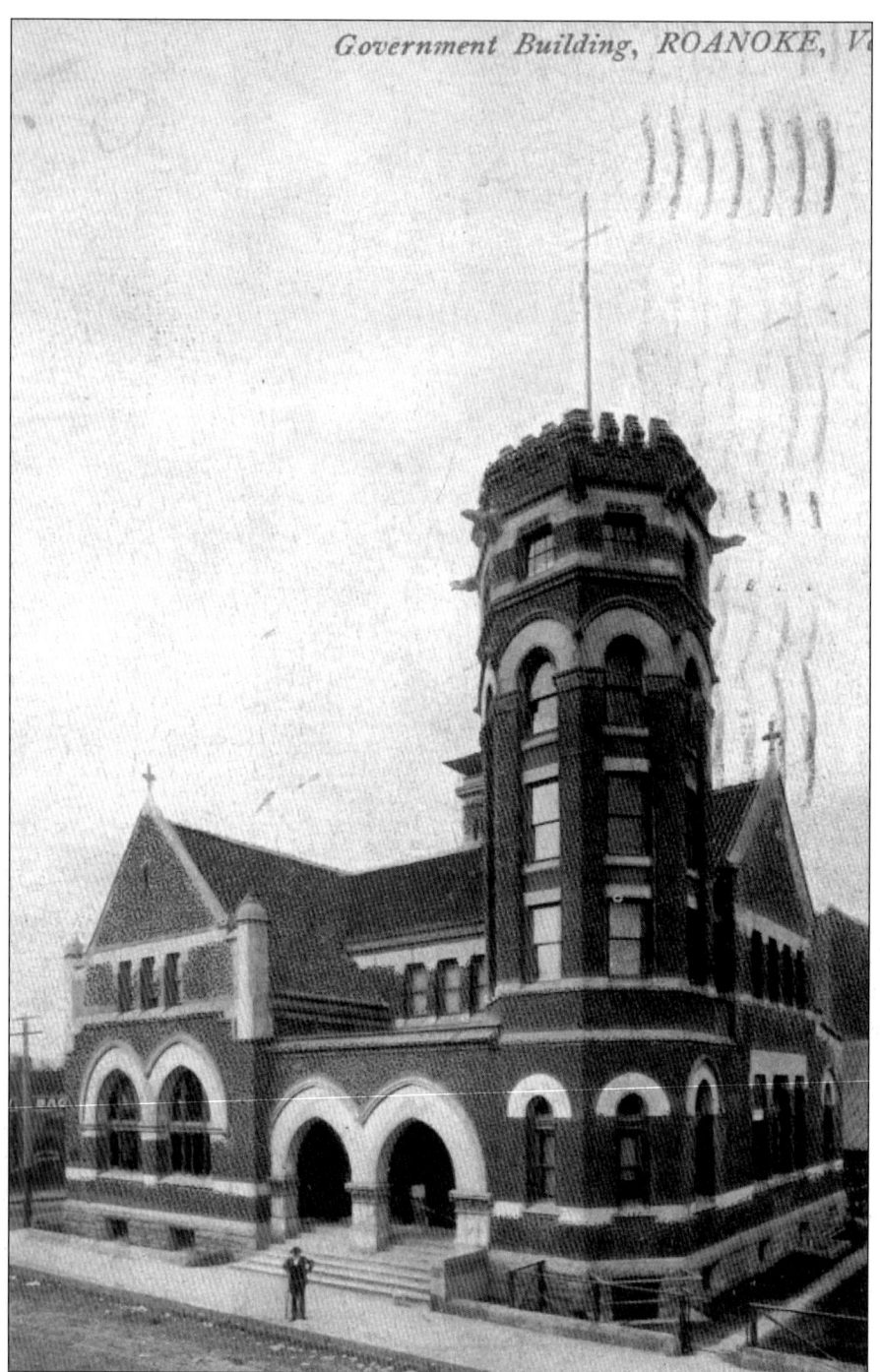

POST OFFICE, 1911. One of Roanoke's first federally-constructed post offices may have been its finest. The design won national recognition for its architect and was described as "the handsomest building South of Baltimore." Completed in 1897 for a cost of $75,000, the post office stood on the northeast corner of Church Avenue and First Street. The building was razed in the 1930s for a newer post office building.

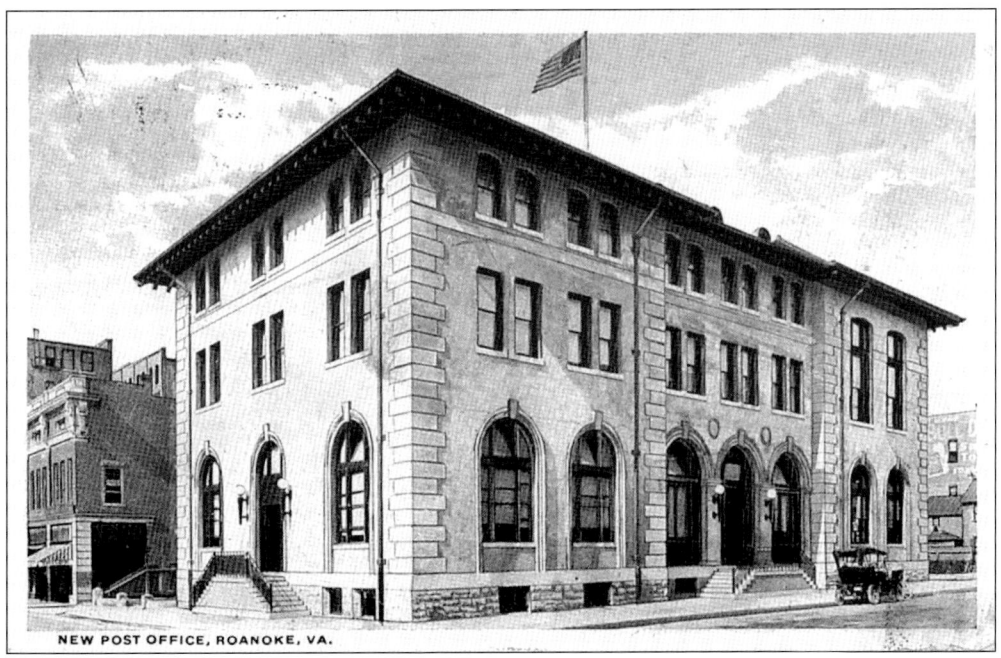

NEW POST OFFICE, 1931. Roanoke's second federally constructed post office was not nearly as architecturally ornate as its predecessor, but it was more practical for the postal service needs of a growing city.

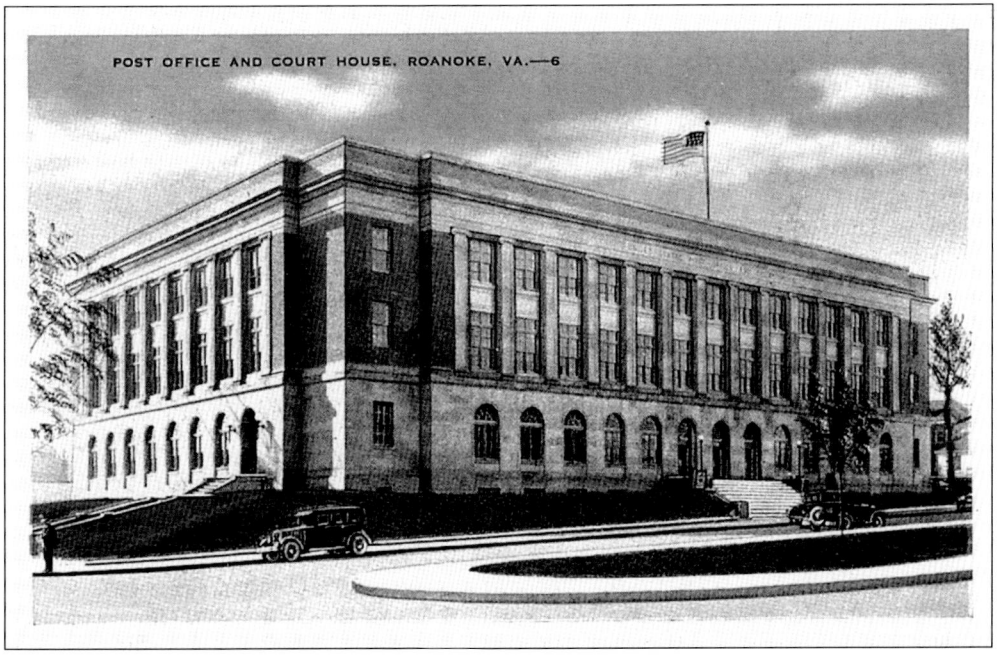

POST OFFICE AND COURT HOUSE, 1935. A new federal building was erected in 1931 complete with post office and court facilities.

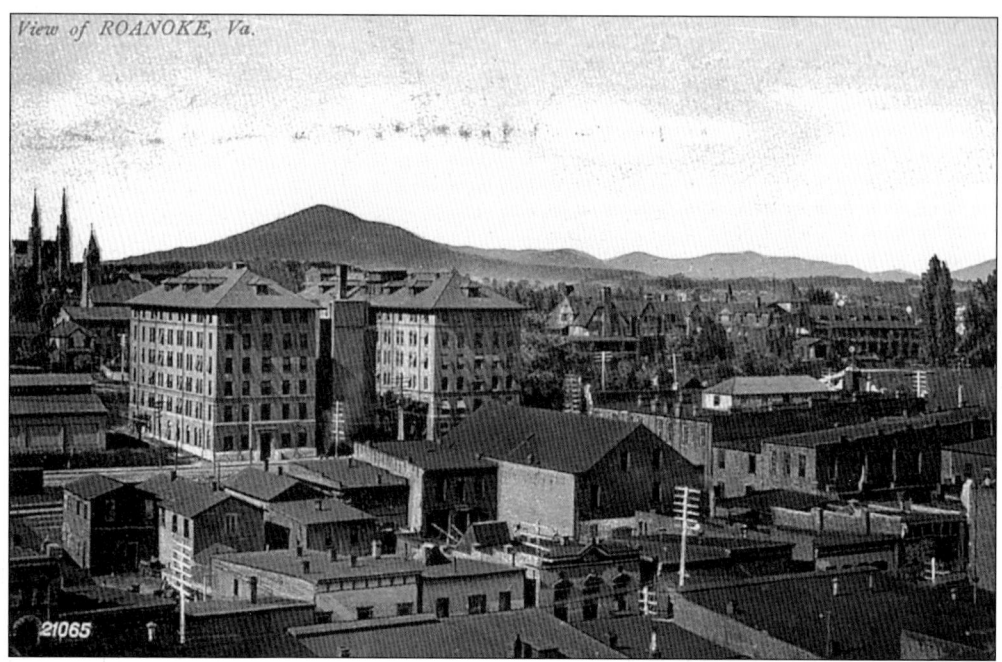

VIEW OF ROANOKE, 1908. The downtown skyline just after the turn of the century contained mostly small warehouses and a few office buildings, most notably those of the railroad.

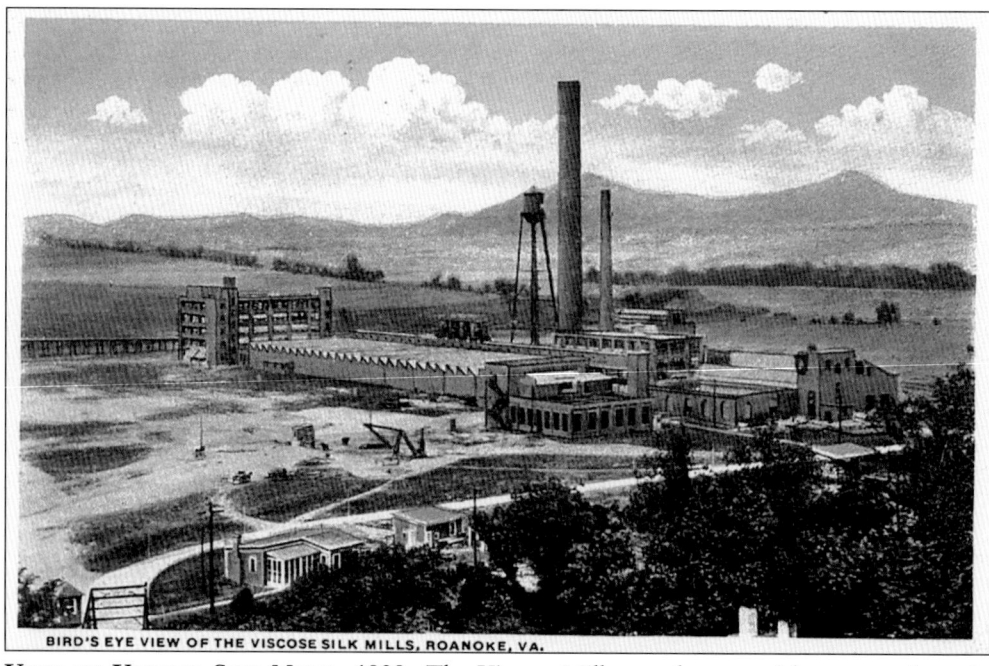

VIEW OF VISCOSE SILK MILLS, 1929. The Viscose Mills was the second-largest employer in Roanoke at one time. In fact, Southeast Roanoke's residential areas developed largely as housing for those employed at Viscose. Even dormitories were needed for workers. Though the Viscose Mills have since ceased operation, the buildings are now occupied by other businesses and industry.

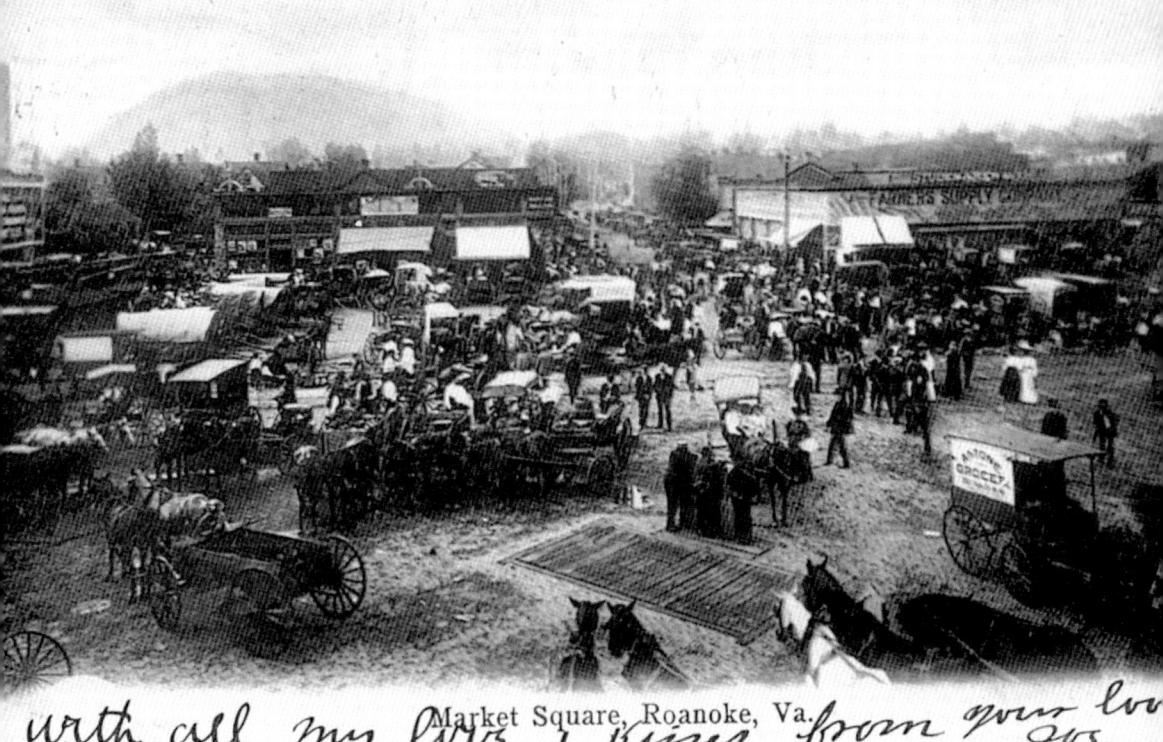

MARKET SQUARE, 1907. Roanoke's farmers' market was the center of goods and services at the turn of the century as this card indicates. Even today farmers and other merchants sell on the market which was recently honored as one of the South's top attractions. Signs within the postcard read "Farmers Supply Company" and "Antone Grocer."

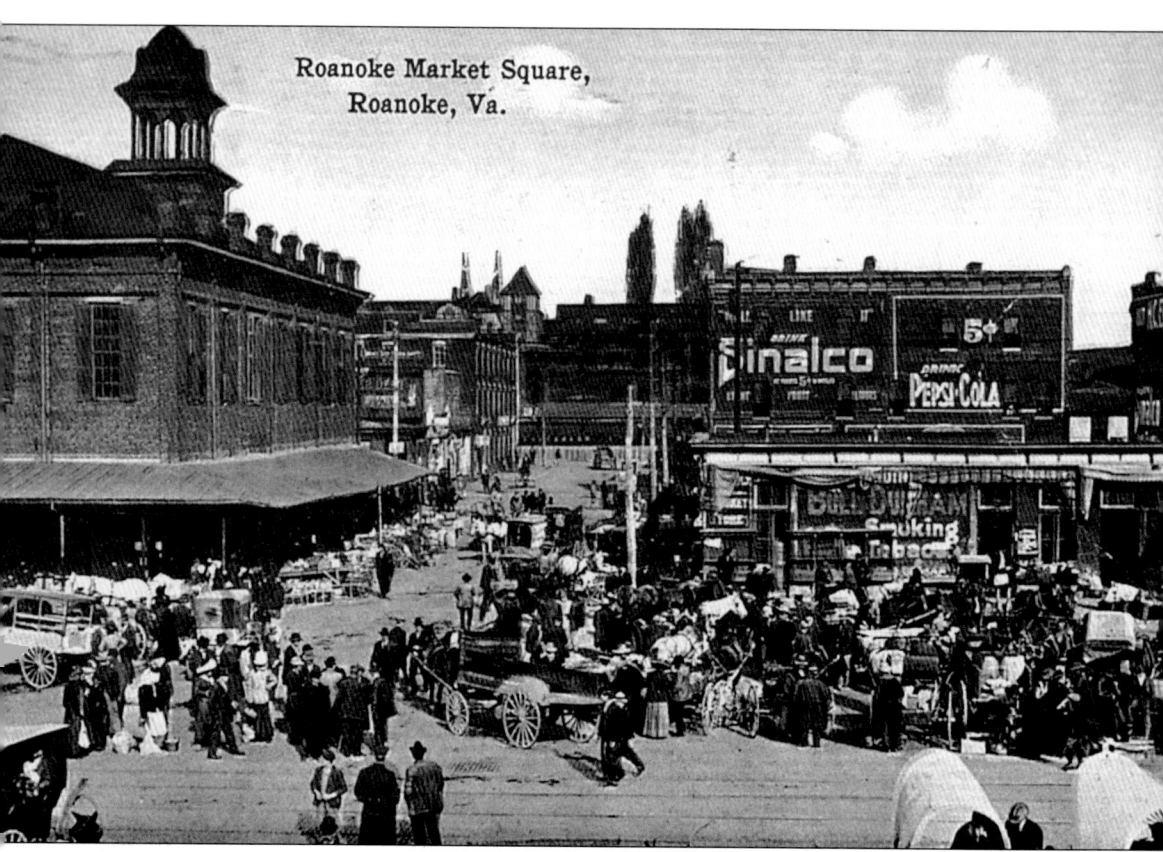

ROANOKE MARKET SQUARE, 1916. A closer view of the bustling market square shows the market building and advertisements for Bull Durham Smoking Tobacco, Pepsi-Cola, Sinalco, and H.C. Eller's Variety Store.

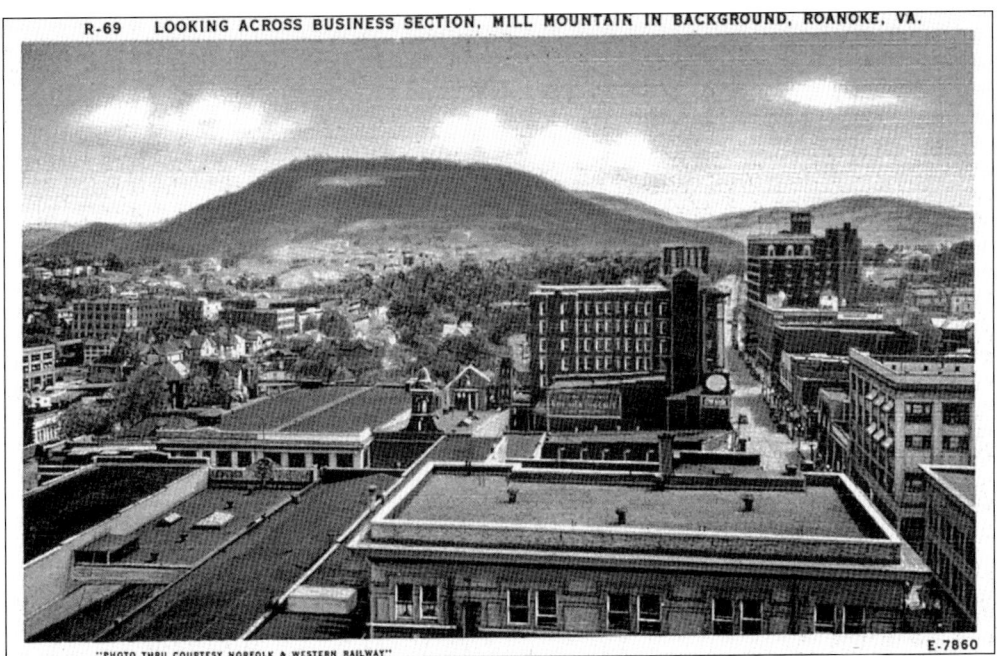

LOOKING ACROSS BUSINESS SECTION, 1940. Roanoke's business section began to broaden beyond the railroad yard and market square. By the 1940s, office buildings, new hotels, and retail stores began to emerge.

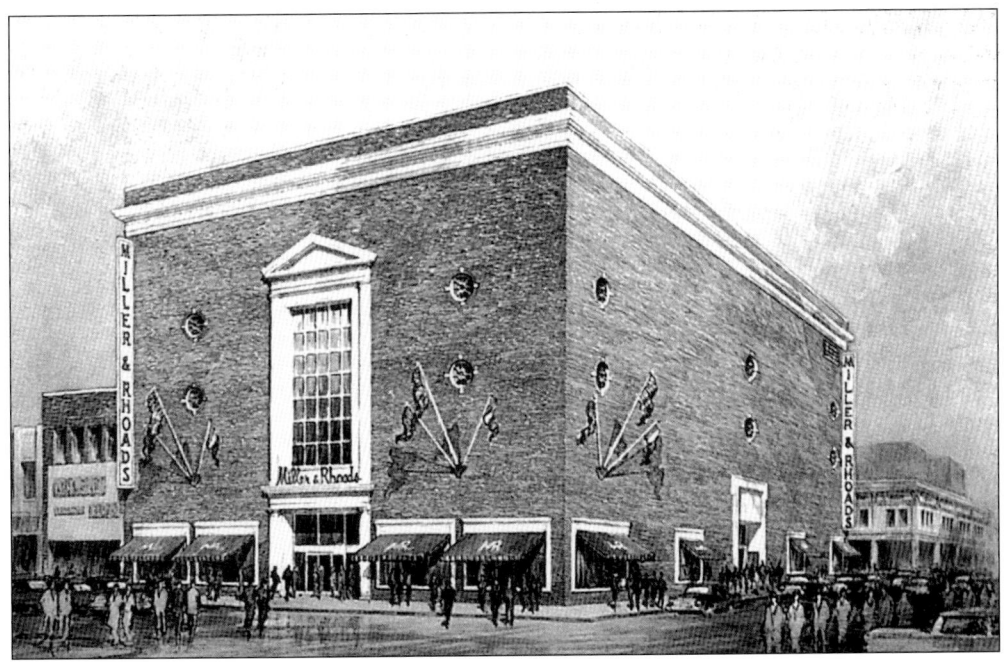

MILLER AND RHOADES, 1960. Before the arrival of malls, multi-level department stores flourished, such as Miller and Rhoades in downtown Roanoke. The card advertises "a great department store distinctively Virginian in appearance, atmosphere and service."

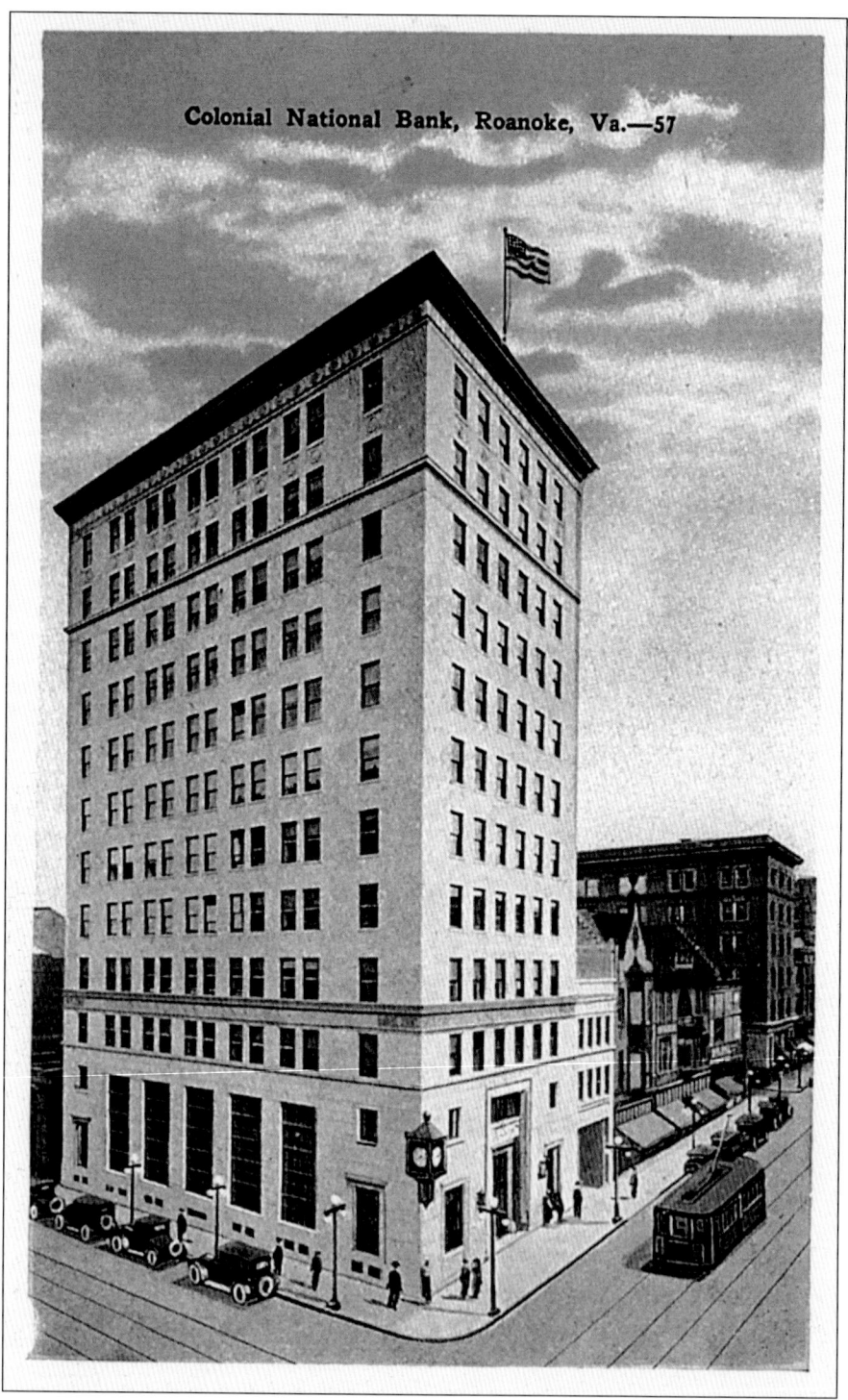

COLONIAL NATIONAL BANK, 1938. The new building for Colonial National Bank opened on April 30, 1927 and was built on the same spot where Colonial Bank had demolished the Terry Building.

Four
STREETS AND BRIDGES

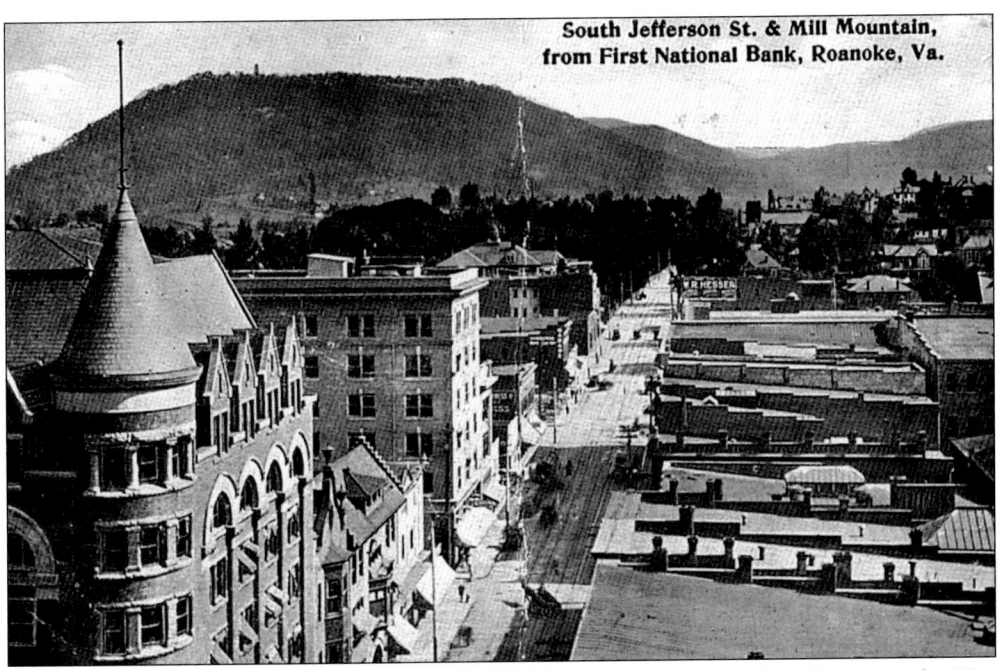

SOUTH JEFFERSON STREET AND MILL MOUNTAIN, 1913. This view taken from atop the First National Bank Building shows the Terry Building in the left foreground with several other business and retail properties lining Jefferson Street.

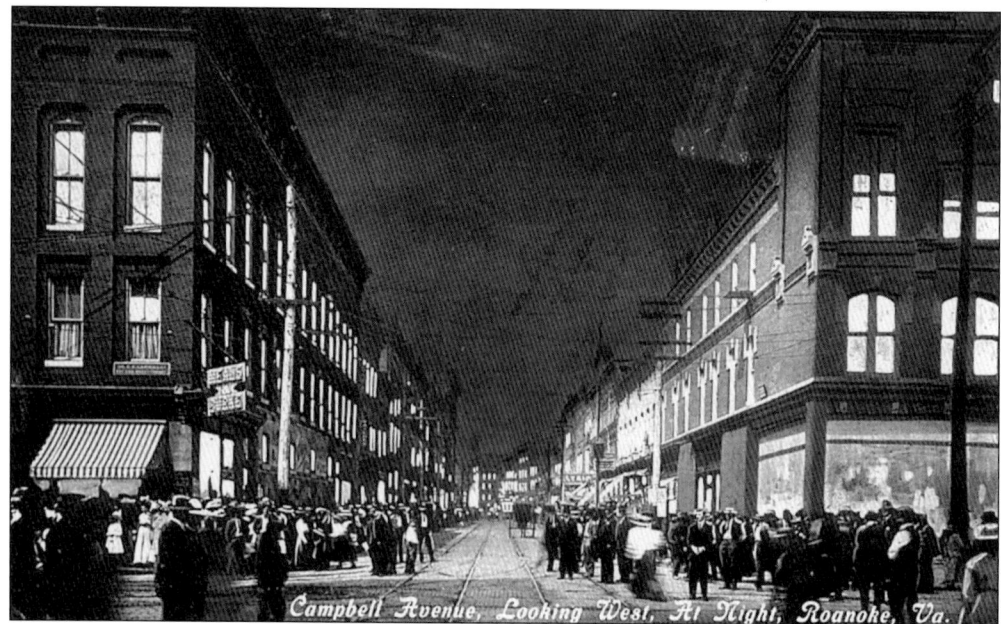

CAMPBELL AVENUE AT NIGHT, 1912. This postcard shows Campbell Avenue looking west. The small sign under the lighted window at left reads, "Dr. A.R. Cannady, Eye, Ear Nose & Throat."

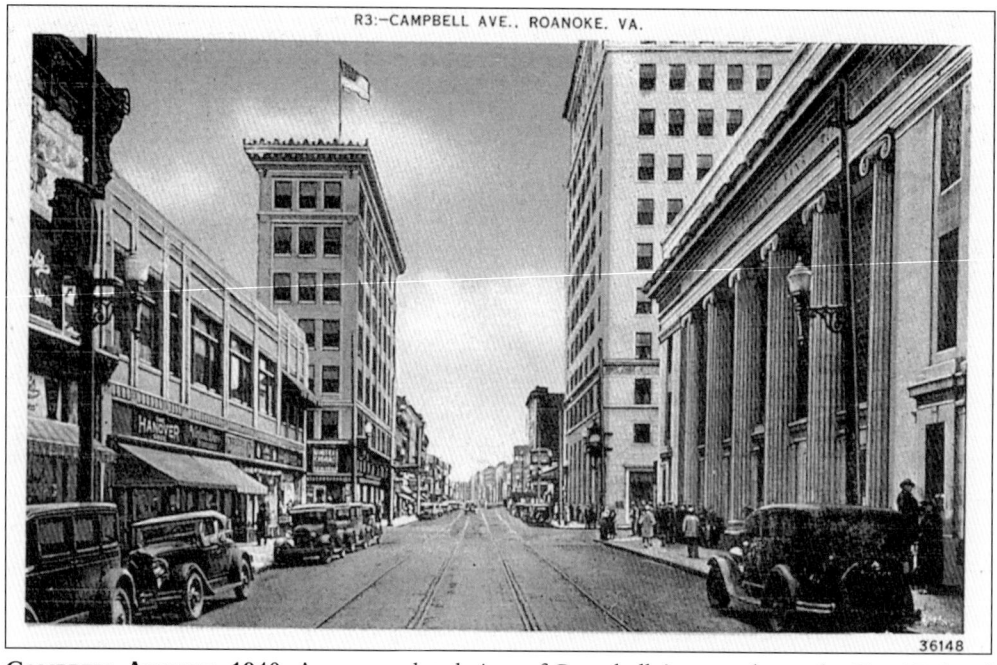

CAMPBELL AVENUE, 1940. A more updated view of Campbell Avenue shows the First National Bank building in right foreground and shops on the left, including Hanover Shoes.

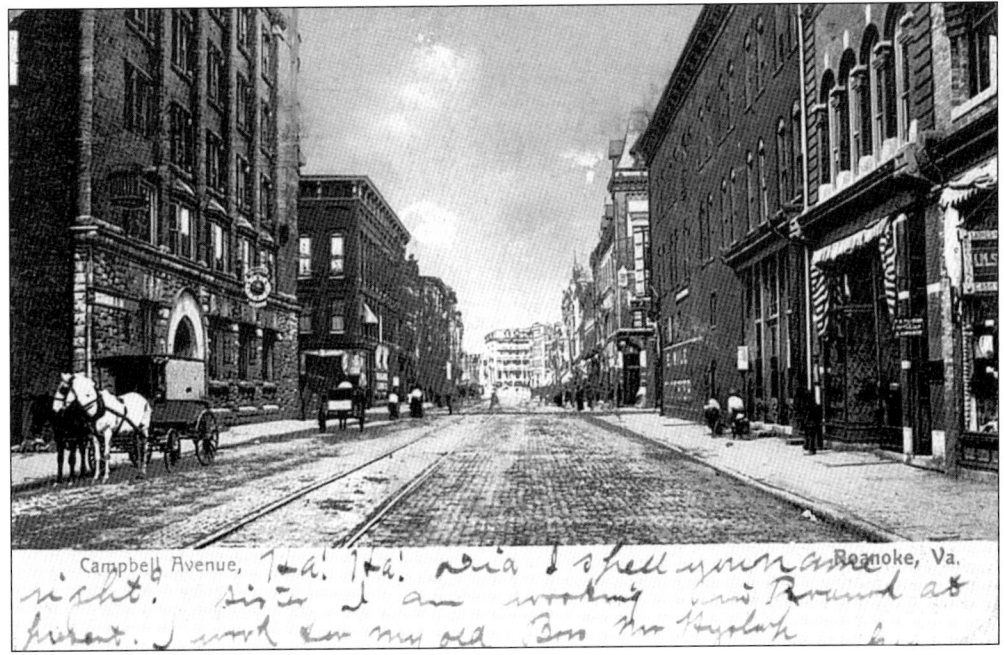

CAMPBELL AVENUE, 1910. This shot of Campbell Avenue has a horse and carriage and trolley tracks leading to the Ponce de Leon Hotel in the far background.

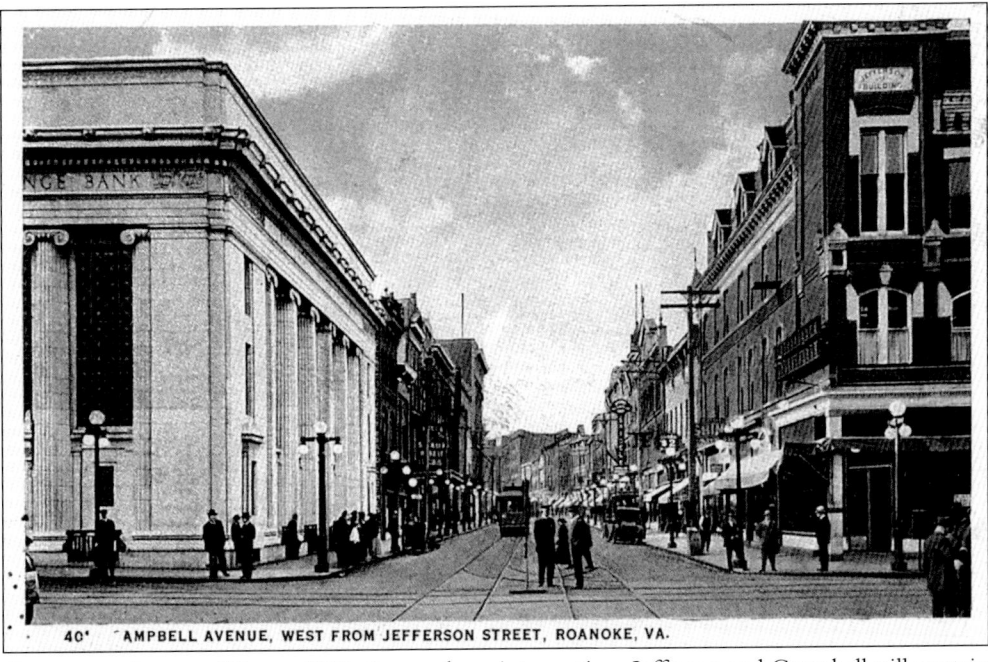

CAMPBELL AVENUE WEST, 1921. Long a busy intersection, Jefferson and Campbell still contain many of the same buildings shown here.

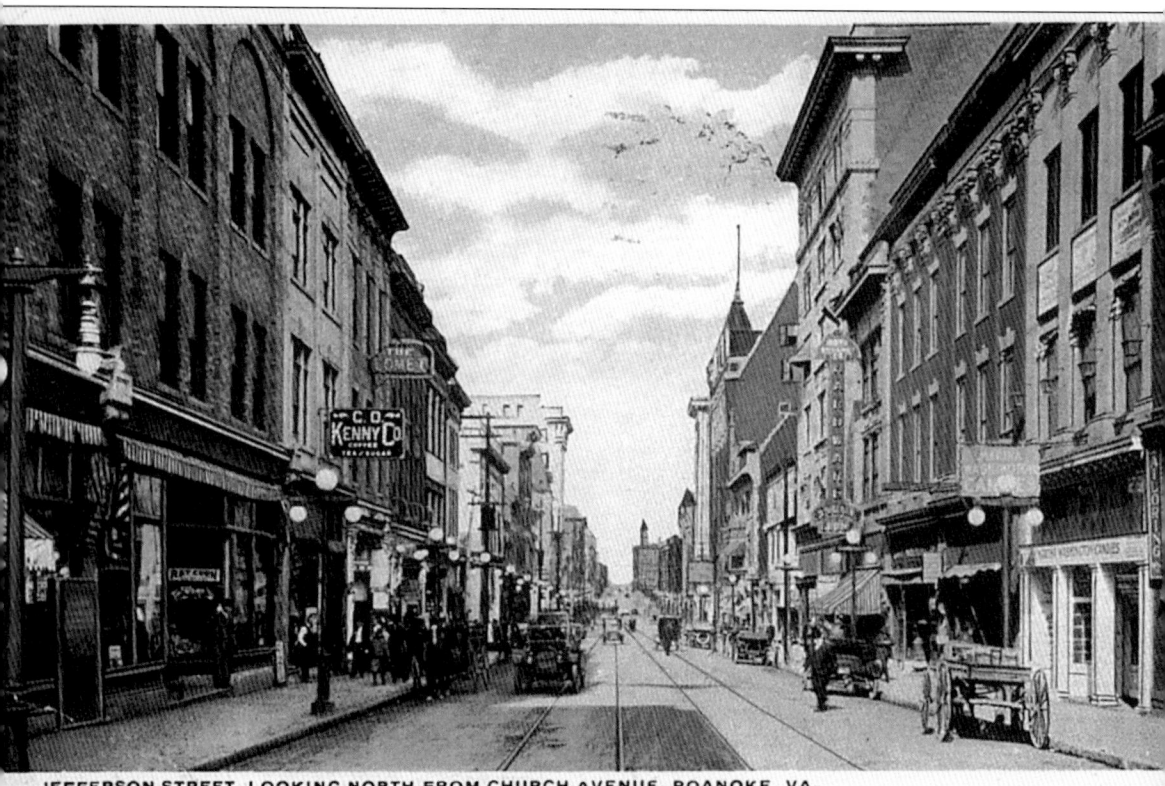

JEFFERSON STREET, LOOKING NORTH FROM CHURCH AVENUE, ROANOKE, VA.

JEFFERSON STREET, 1918. Jefferson Street, shown here looking north from Church Avenue, contained the C.D. Kenney Co. for coffee, tea, and sugar; the Comet Theater; and Martha Washington Candies.

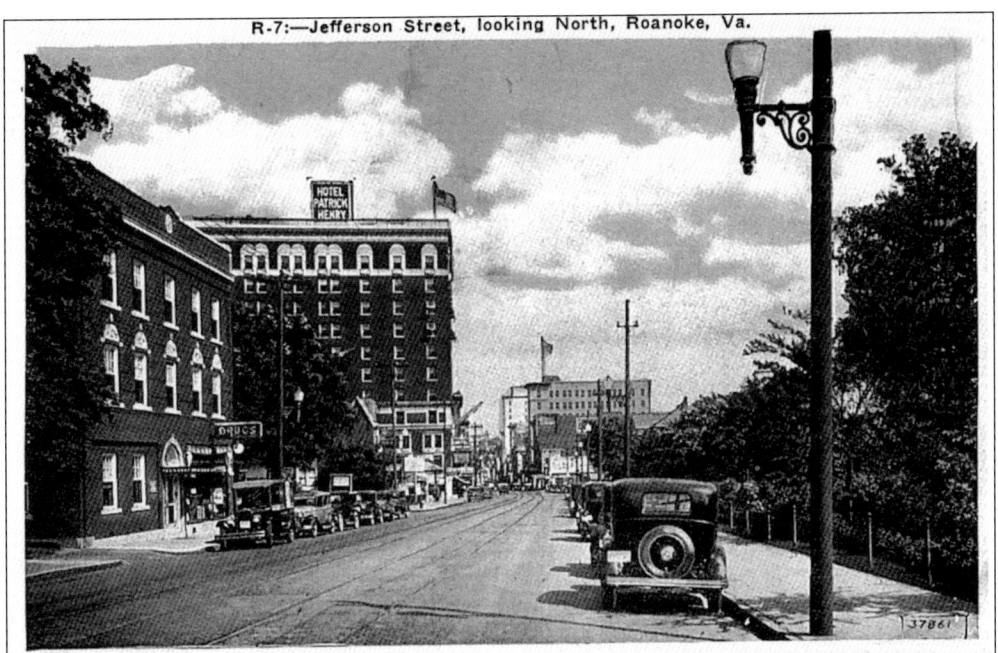

JEFFERSON STREET, 1930. Jefferson Street looking north shows the Hotel Patrick Henry and the corner of Elmwood Park on the right.

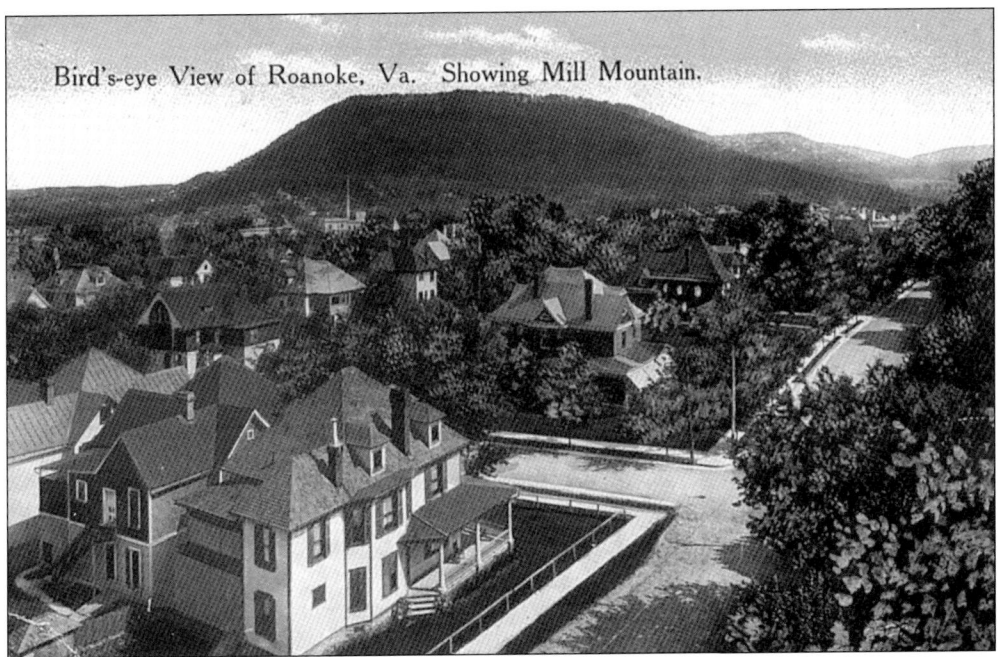

BIRD'S EYE VIEW OF ROANOKE, 1916. This postcard illustrates how Roanoke's residential quality had begun to develop with large homes and broad streets.

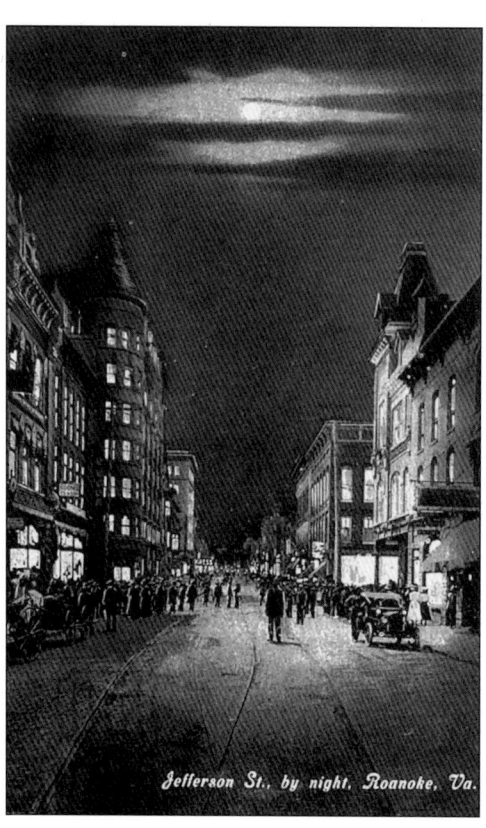

JEFFERSON STREET BY NIGHT, 1911. Jefferson Street is lit up by night activities emanating from stores, theaters, and hotels.

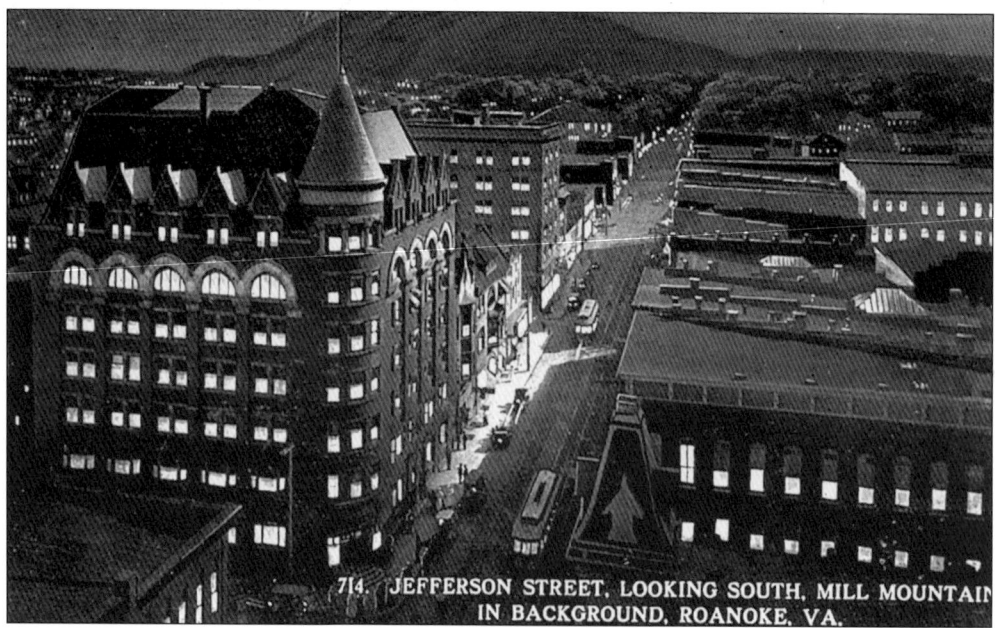

JEFFERSON STREET AT NIGHT, 1913. The Terry Building stands illuminated with Mill Mountain in the background in this moonlit scene. This is Jefferson Street looking south.

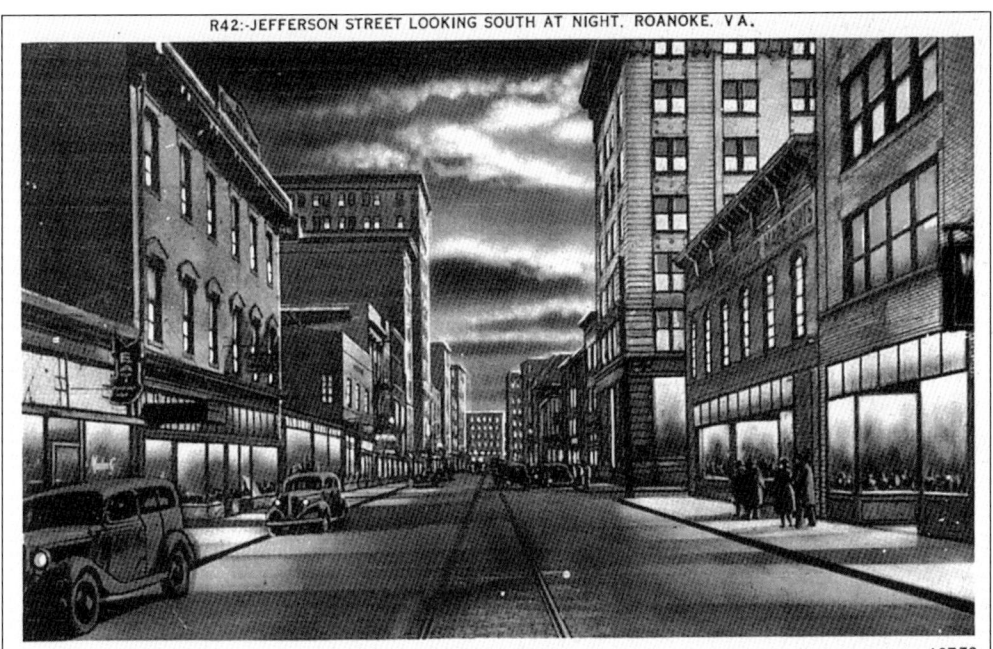

JEFFERSON STREET LOOKING SOUTH, 1940. Jefferson Street at night shows a few shoppers and patrons, quite different from the scenes of earlier days.

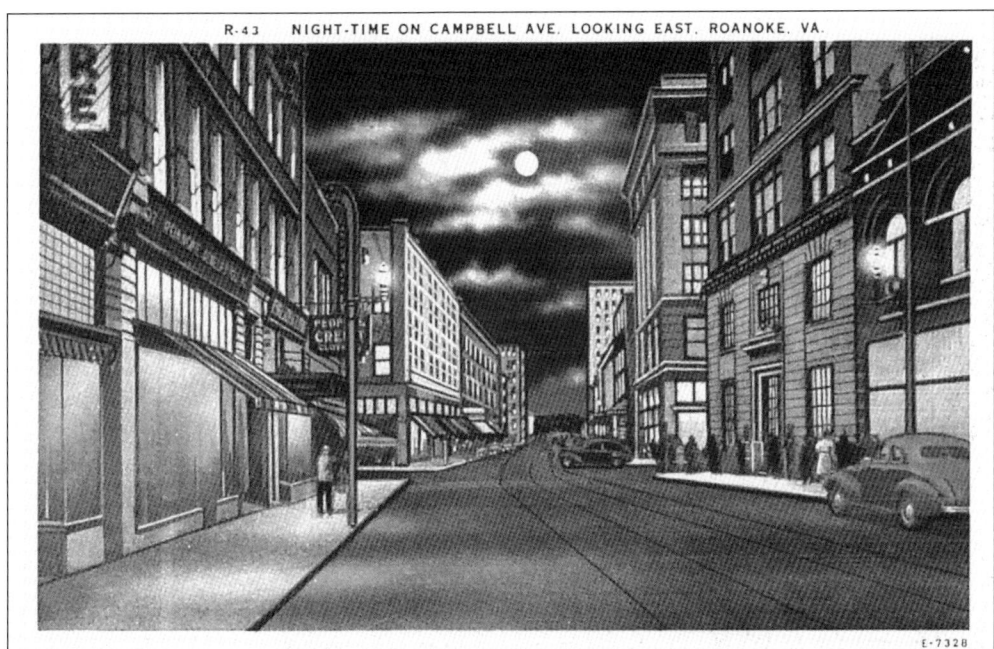

CAMPBELL AVENUE AT NIGHT, 1940. This is Campbell Avenue looking east with shops and stores still open.

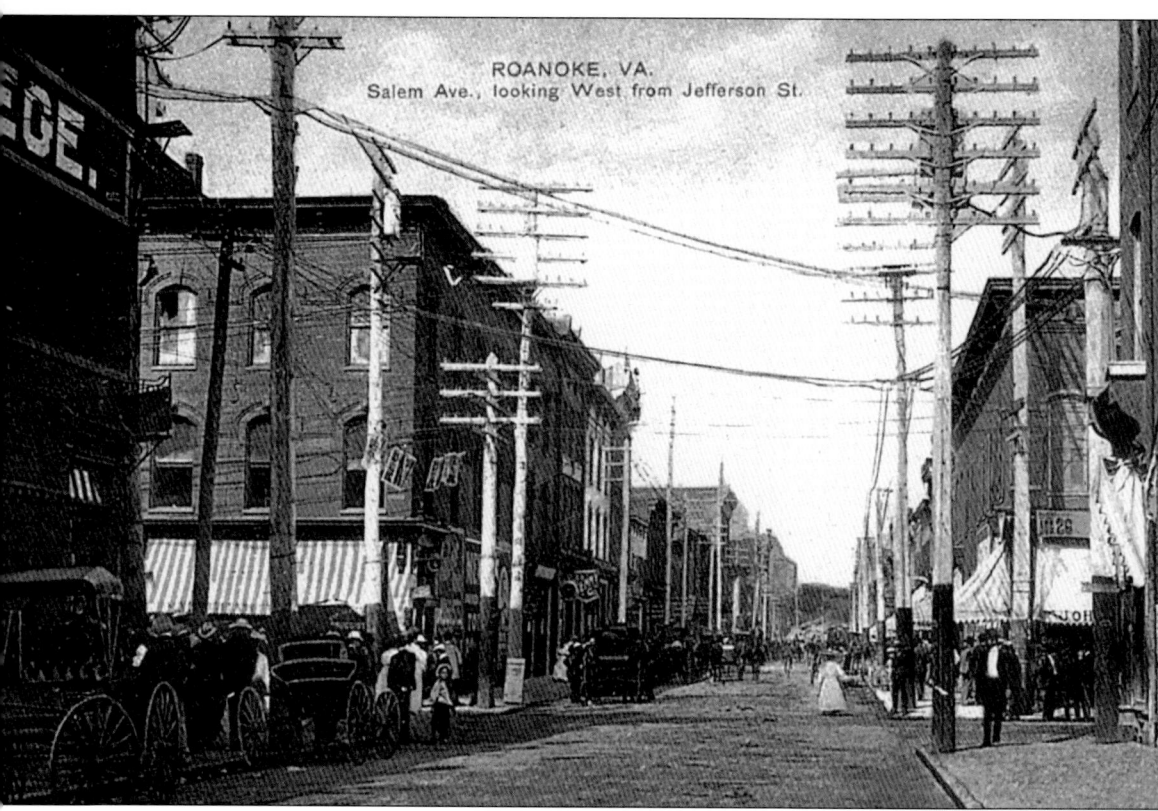

SALEM AVENUE, 1915. Salem Avenue is shown here looking west from Jefferson Street in a different era. Notice the total lack of automobiles as carriages line the street.

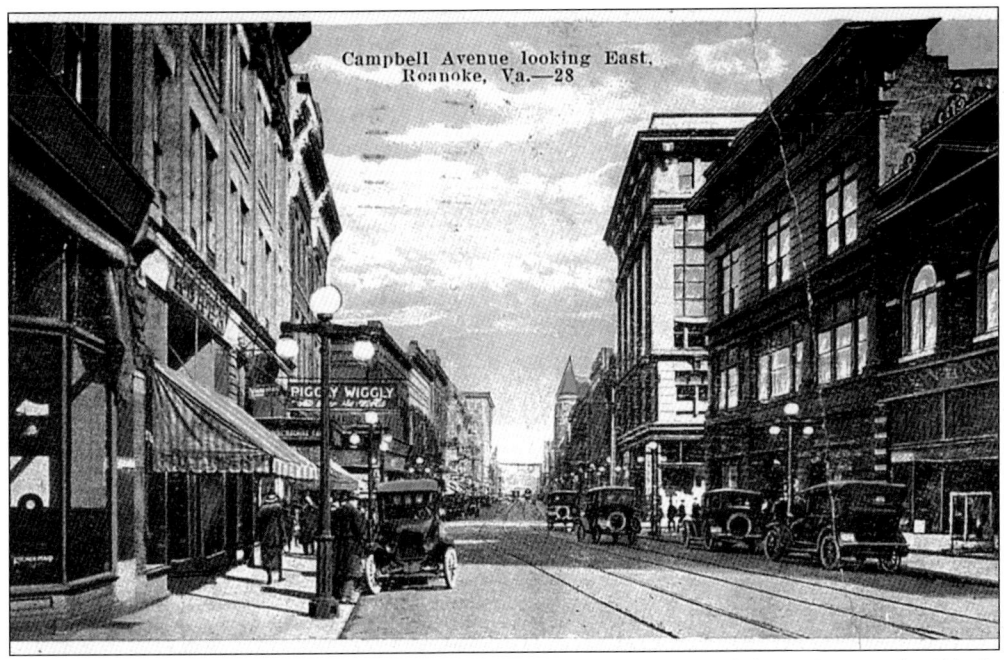

CAMPBELL AVENUE LOOKING EAST, 1929. Along the left side of the street are the Piggly Wiggly grocery and Kohen Dry Goods (with the protruding awning).

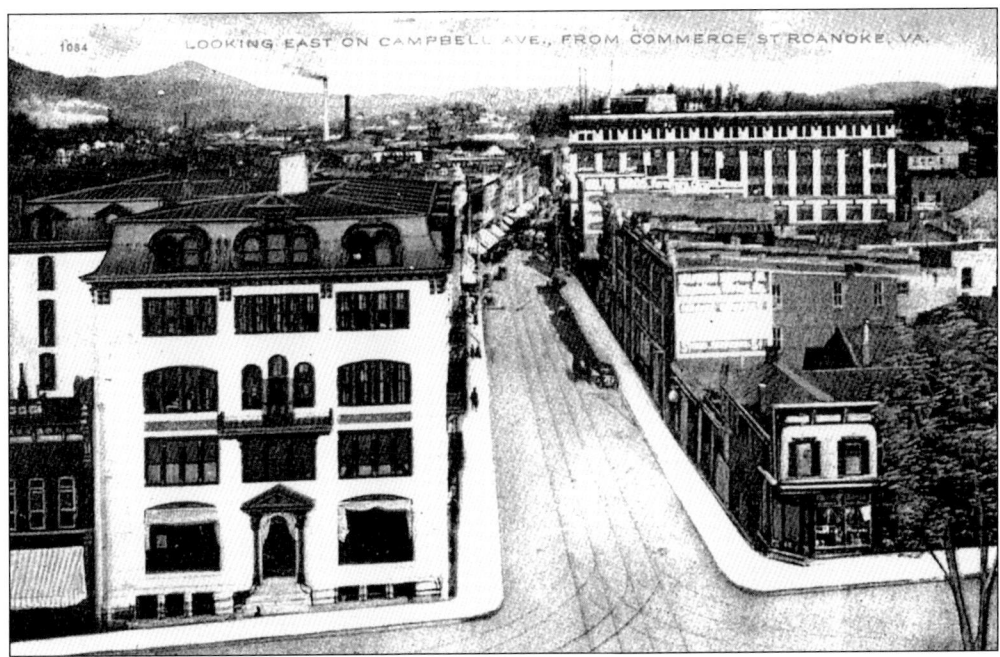

LOOKING EAST ON CAMPBELL AVENUE, 1917. This is the intersection of Campbell and Second Street (formerly Commerce Street) with the Ponce de Leon Hotel in the foreground.

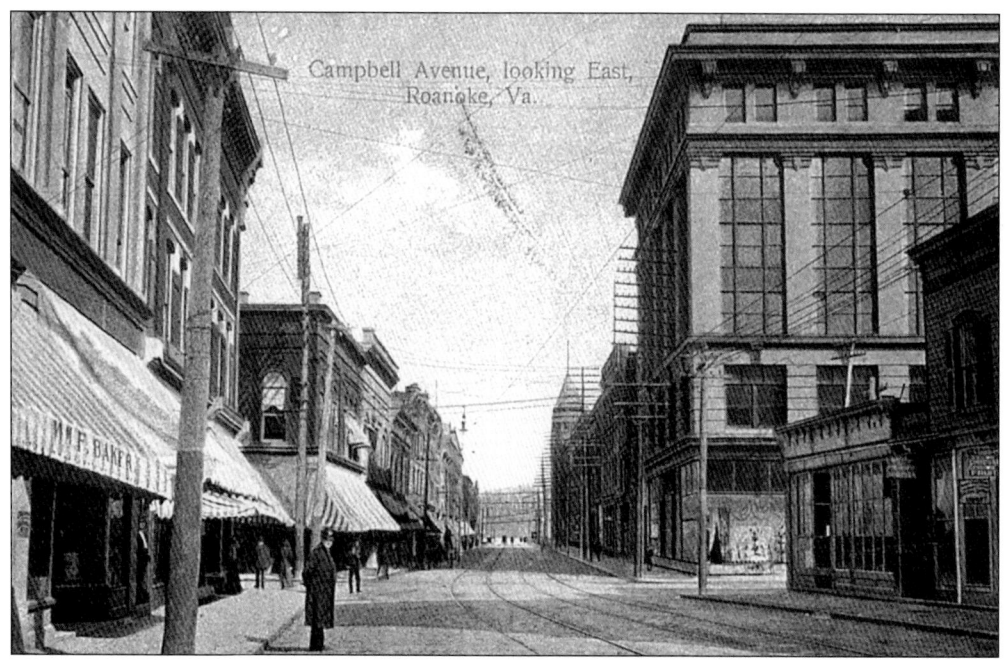

CAMPBELL AVENUE LOOKING EAST, 1909. In this picture of Campbell Avenue, a policeman walks the beat in front of William F. Baker's dry goods store.

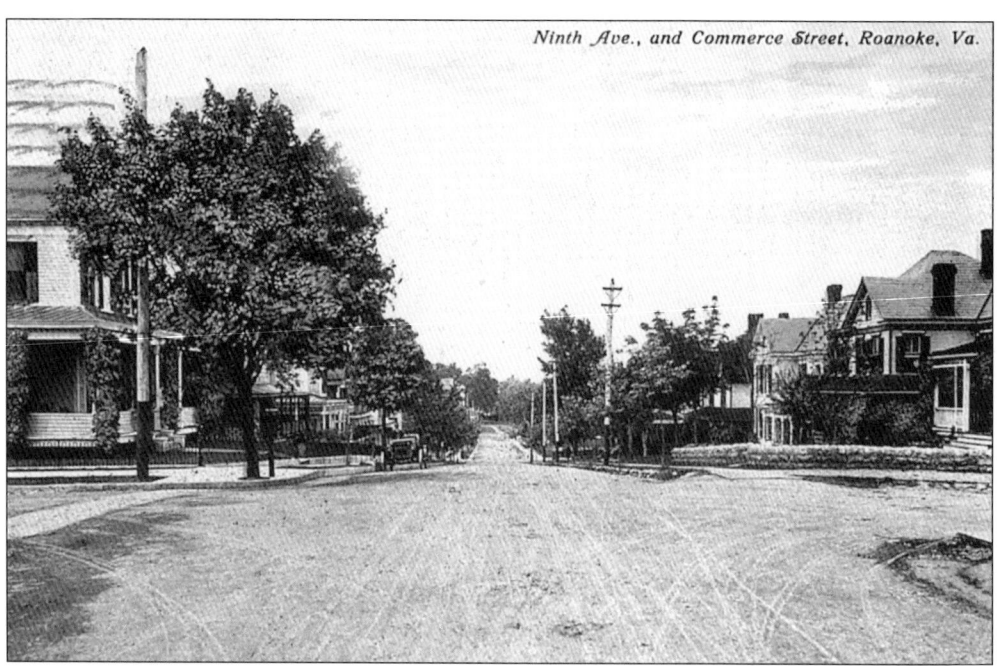

NINTH AVENUE AND COMMERCE STREET, 1911. Roanoke's residential development began booming after the turn of the century with the creation of neighborhood development corporations. This card shows one such residential section.

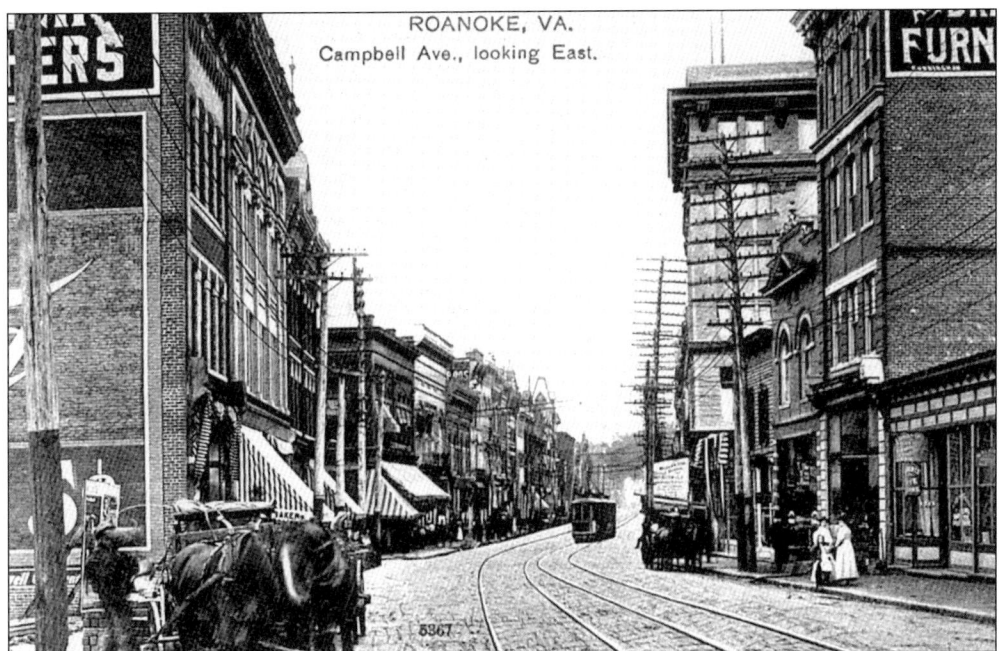

CAMPBELL AVENUE, LOOKING EAST, 1908. This is an early photo-postcard of Campbell Avenue. The Baker Dry Goods store is on the left and a dye works is on the right with a billboard for Watt, Rettew, and Clay's office building mid-block.

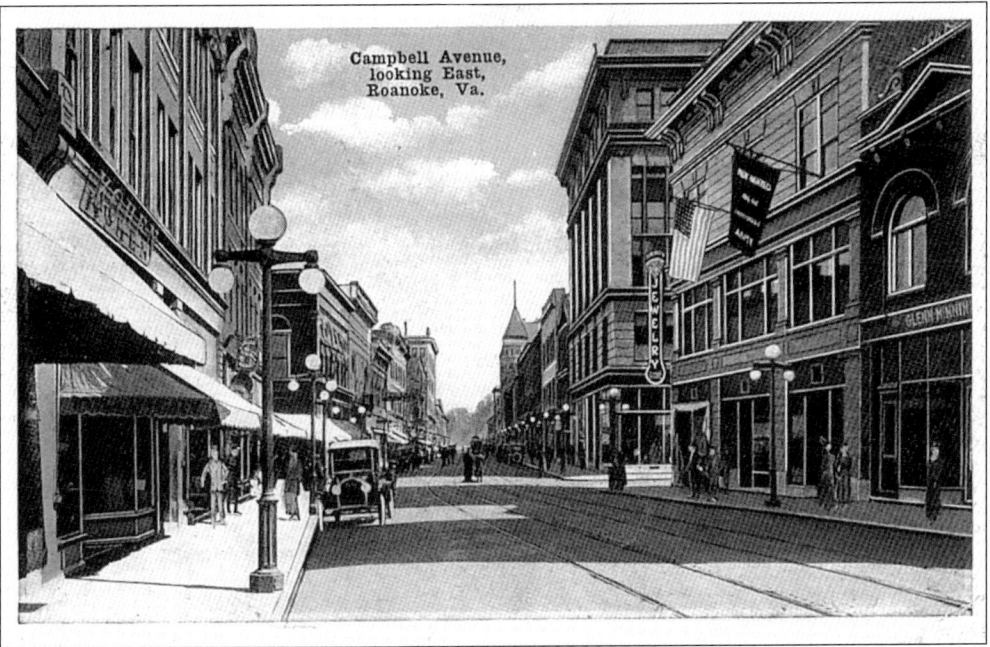

CAMPBELL AVENUE, LOOKING EAST, 1919. This look down Campbell Avenue conveys the times. The black flag hanging beside the American flag reads, "Men wanted for the United States Army." The first store on the right is the Glenn Minnich Clothing Co. and across the street, Kohen Dry Goods.

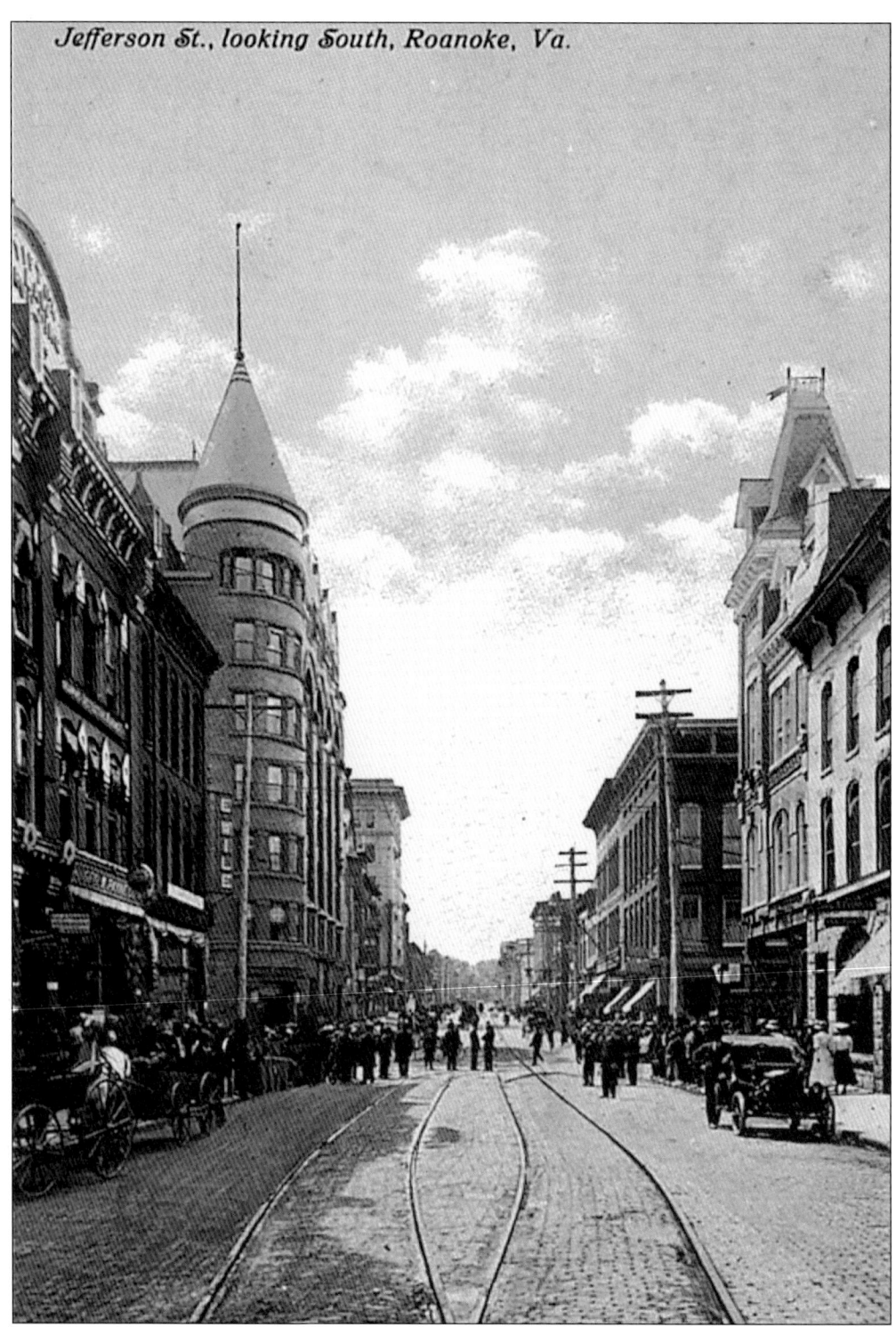

JEFFERSON STREET LOOKING SOUTH, 1915. Distinct as always in early cards of Jefferson Street is the Terry Building. In the left foreground is the business of George W. Payne.

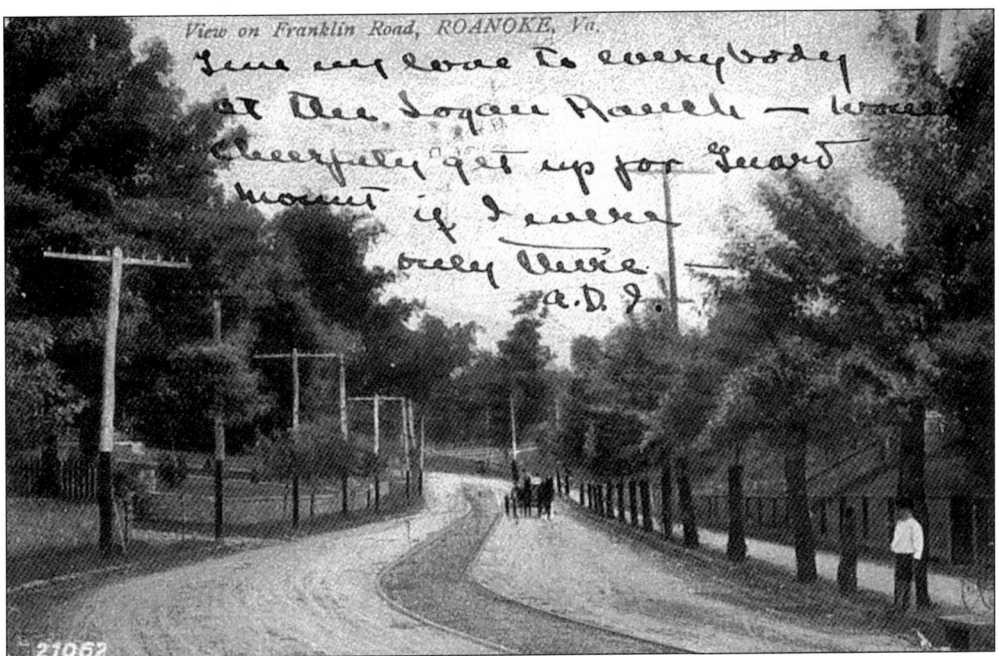

VIEW ON FRANKLIN ROAD, 1910. This rather agrarian view of early Franklin Road bears no resemblance to the commercialized Franklin Road of today.

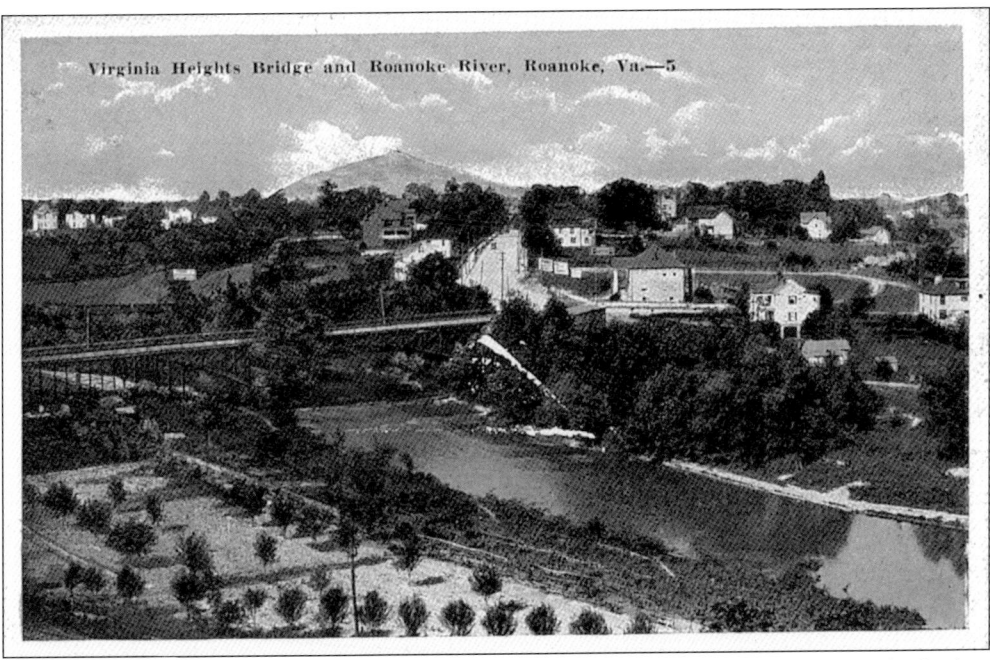

VIRGINIA HEIGHTS BRIDGE AND ROANOKE RIVER, 1919. An early postcard of the bridge, known as the Virginia Avenue Bridge, leading into the Virginia Heights section before the creation of Memorial Bridge, shows sparse housing and farm land.

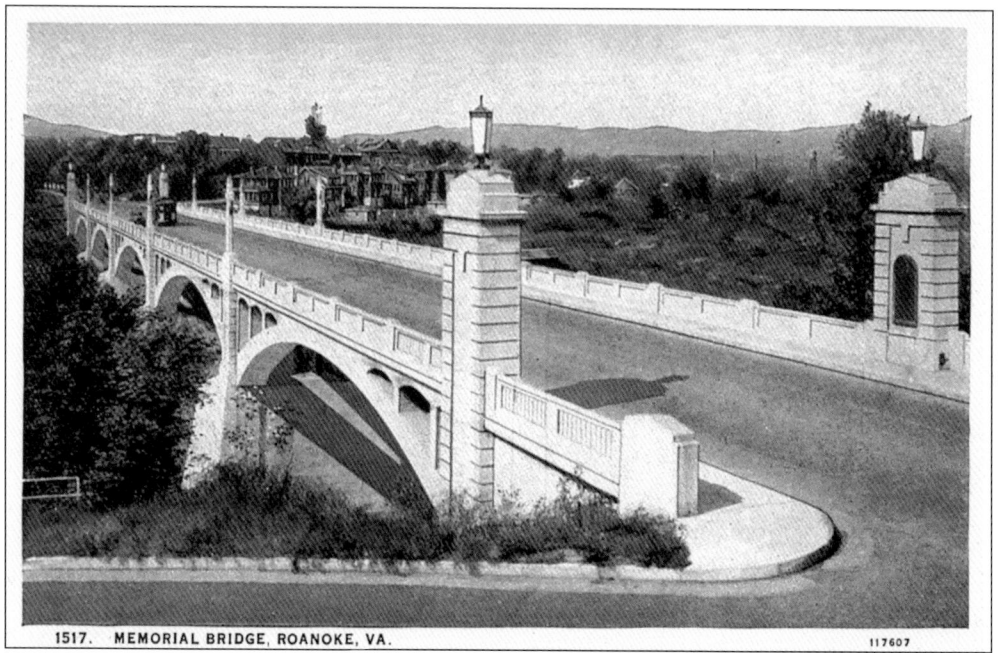

MEMORIAL BRIDGE, 1932. Memorial Bridge, erected in the early 1920s, provided the needed traffic flow ability and gateway entrance into the newly developed Virginia Heights and Ghent neighborhoods.

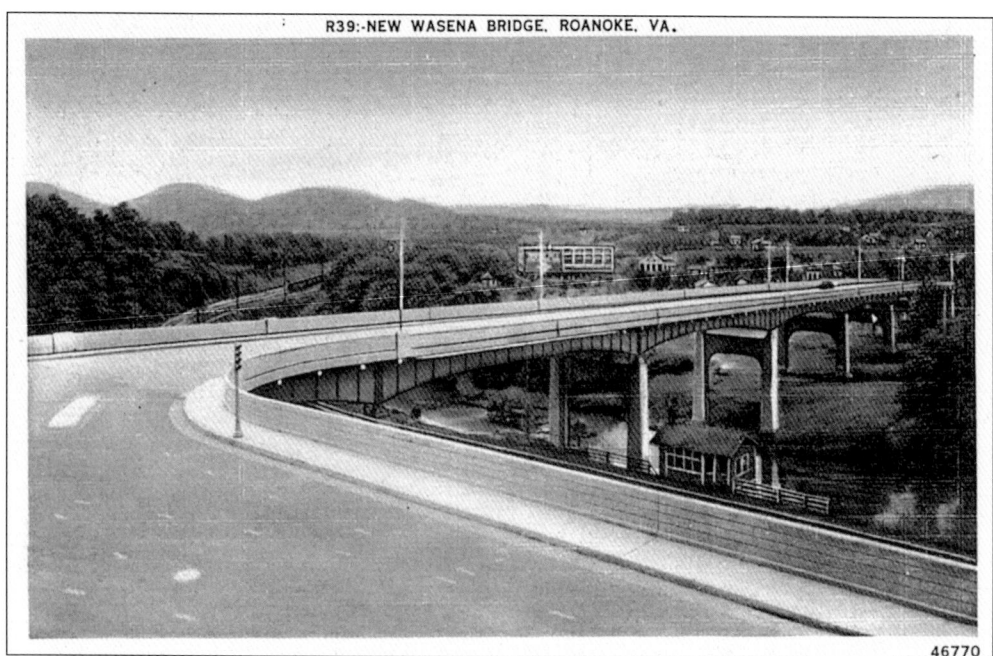

WASENA BRIDGE, 1940. The Wasena Bridge was constructed in 1938, replacing an old steel bridge erected by the Wasena Land Co. in 1912.

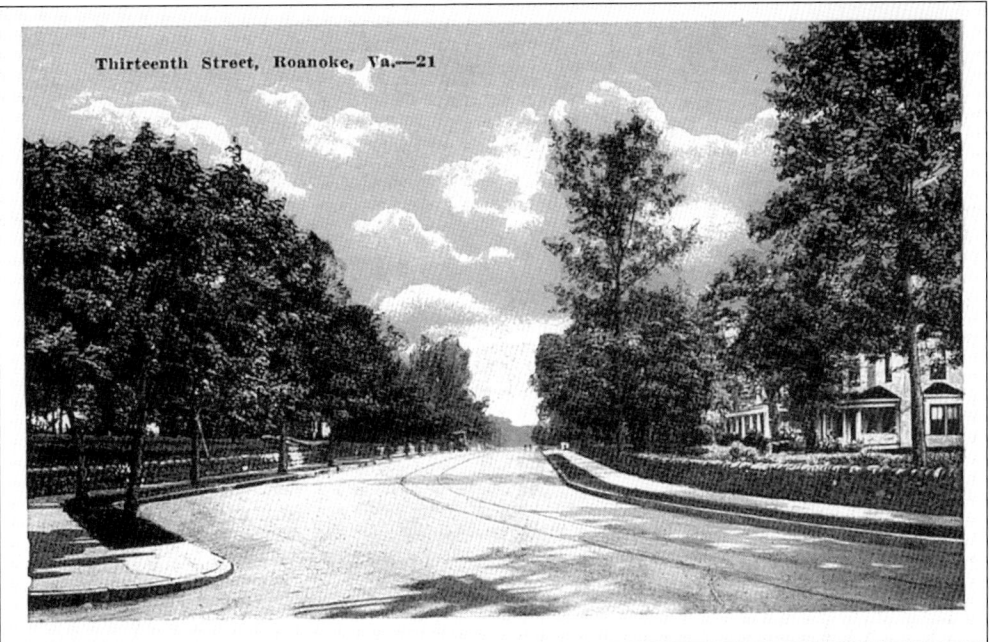

THIRTEENTH STREET, 1922. This postcard highlights the many amenities land development companies put into their residential developments, including sidewalks, wide streets, stone walls, curbs and gutters, and large homes on large lots.

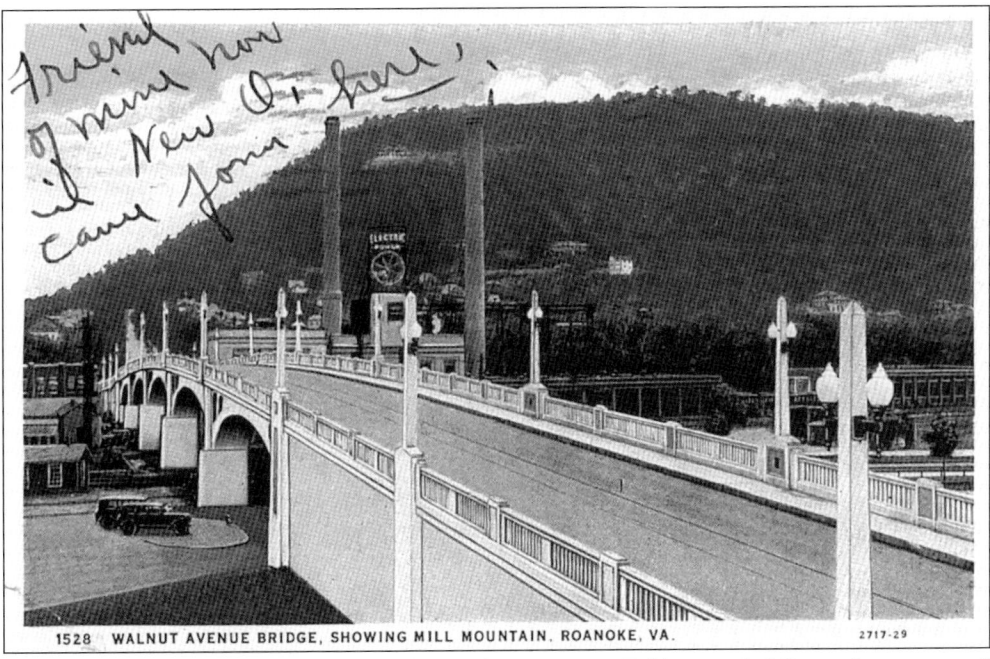

WALNUT AVENUE BRIDGE, 1943. The Walnut Avenue Bridge carried Roanokers over rail track and into the residential section at the foot of Mill Mountain. The bridge opened on November 21, 1927.

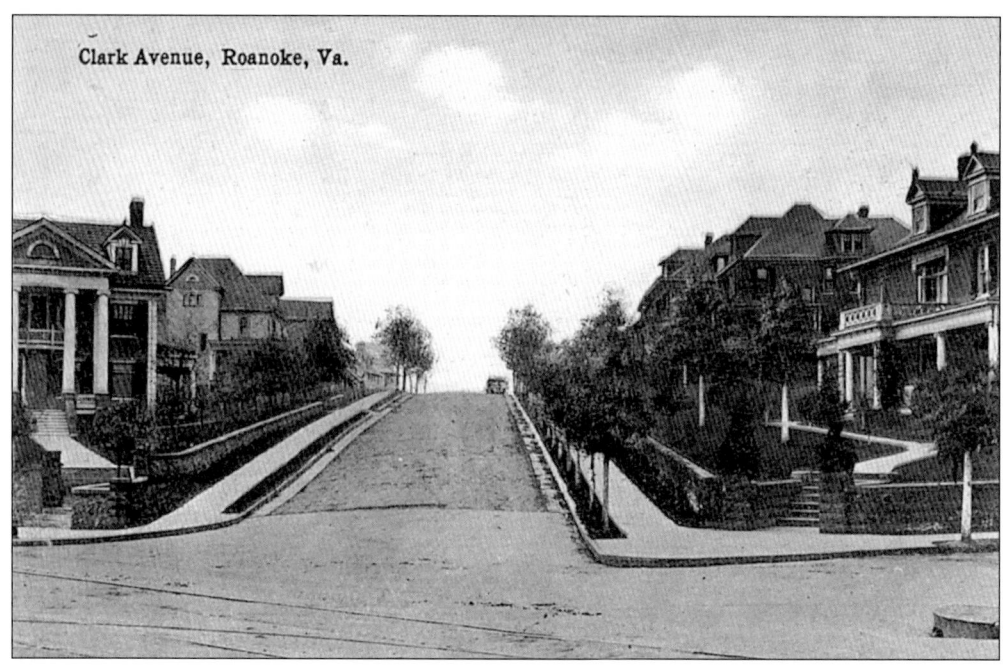

CLARK AVENUE, 1920. Clark Avenue represented one of the more prestigious addresses for Roanokers as denoted by the homes depicted in this postcard.

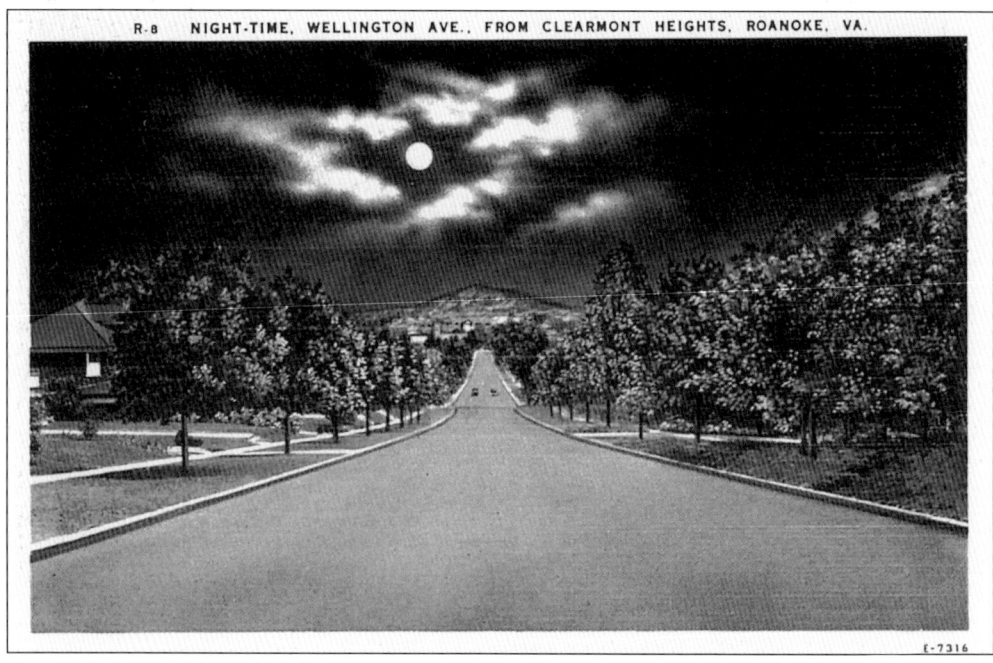

WELLINGTON AVENUE FROM CLEARMONT HEIGHTS, 1940. Wellington Avenue in South Roanoke, now Jefferson, was an early gateway into the South Roanoke neighborhood.

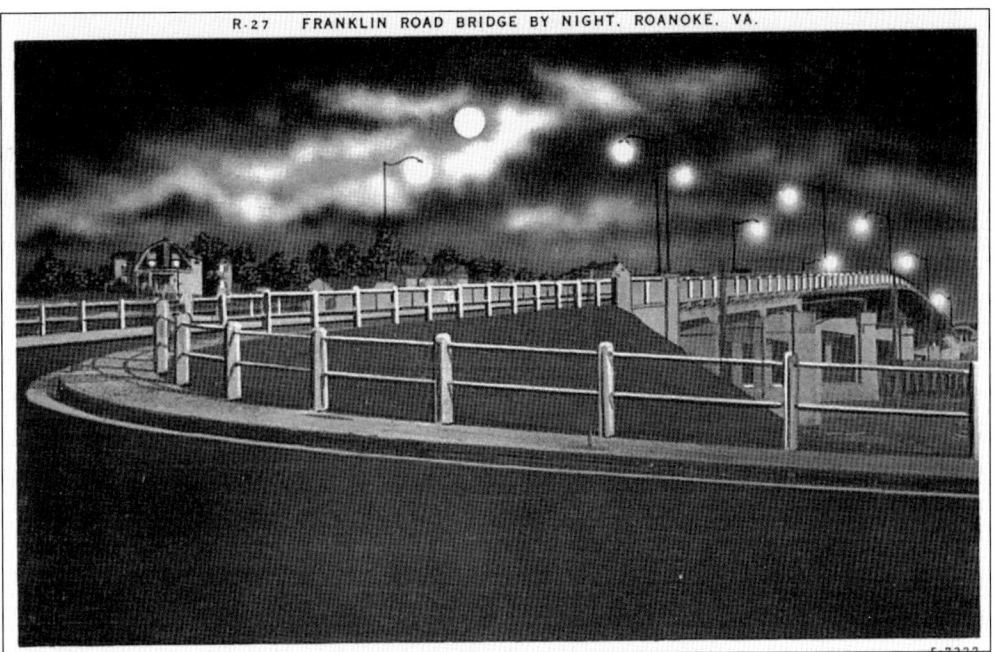

FRANKLIN ROAD BRIDGE BY NIGHT, 1940. The Franklin Road Bridge over the former Virginian Railroad officially opened for traffic on November 27, 1936.

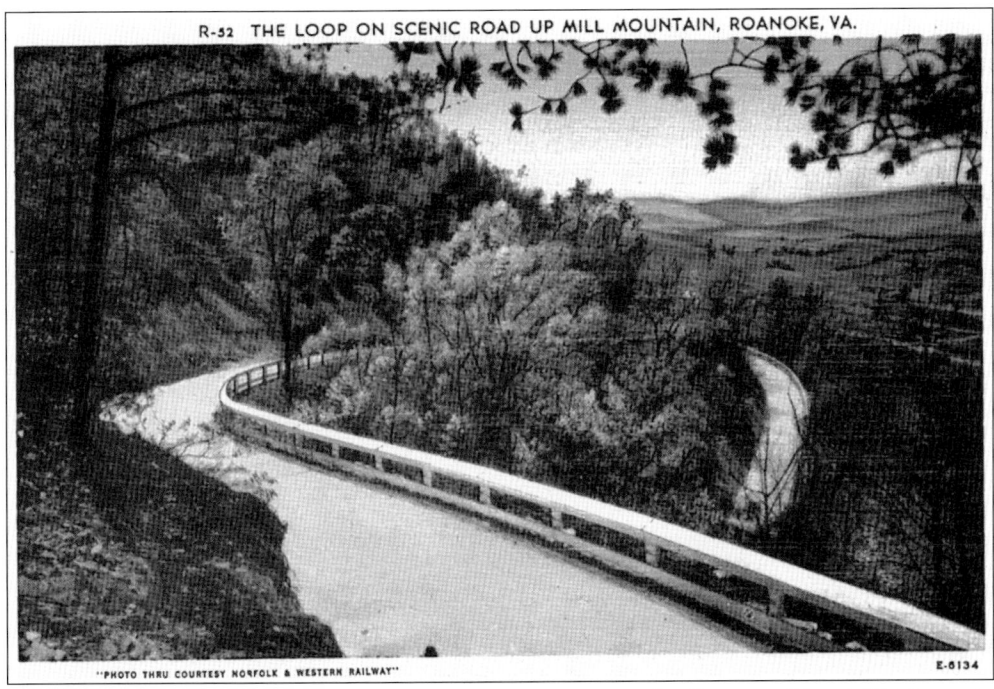

THE LOOP ON SCENIC ROAD UP MILL MOUNTAIN, 1940. The "loop road" up Mill Mountain was certainly one of the most scenic drives for Roanokers. Well before the Blue Ridge Parkway opened, the loop road provided the best views of the city and valley.

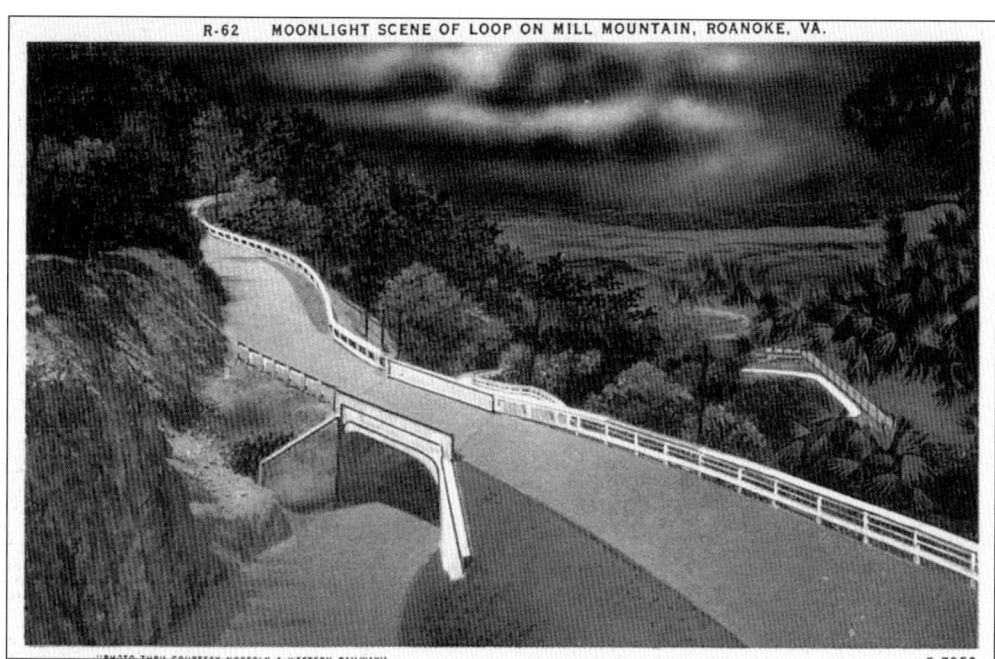

MOONLIGHT SCENE OF LOOP ON MILL MOUNTAIN, 1940. Because of the mountain terrain, the loop road actually crossed itself at one point in its meandering path up to the top.

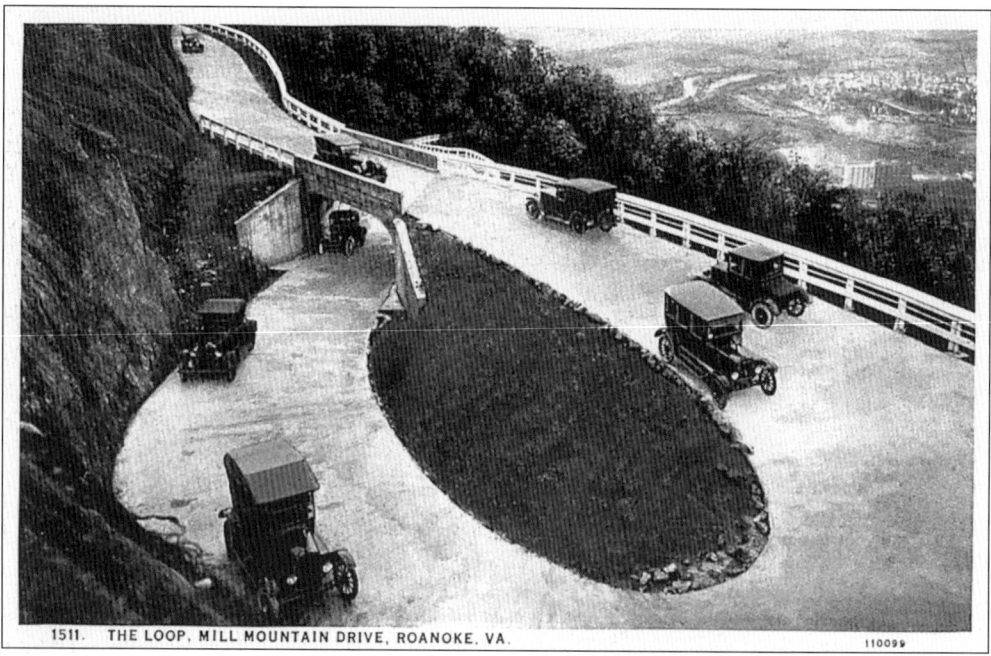

THE LOOP, MILL MOUNTAIN DRIVE, 1925. The drive up Mill Mountain was quite popular. For atop the mountain was an inn, a watch tower, and incline—attracting tourists and Roanoke citizens alike. Today, the loop road is closed to through traffic.

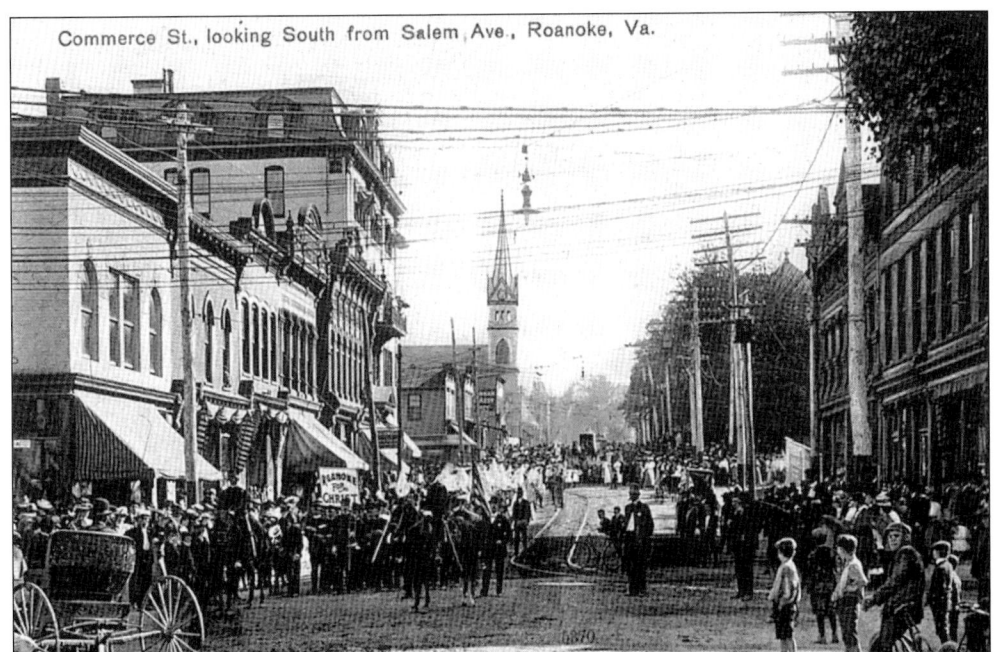

COMMERCE STREET, LOOKING SOUTH, 1911. This card shows the present-day intersection of Second Street and Salem Avenue. Apparently, there was a religious crusade in progress as the crowd shown is gathered in front a banner reading, "Roanoke for Christ."

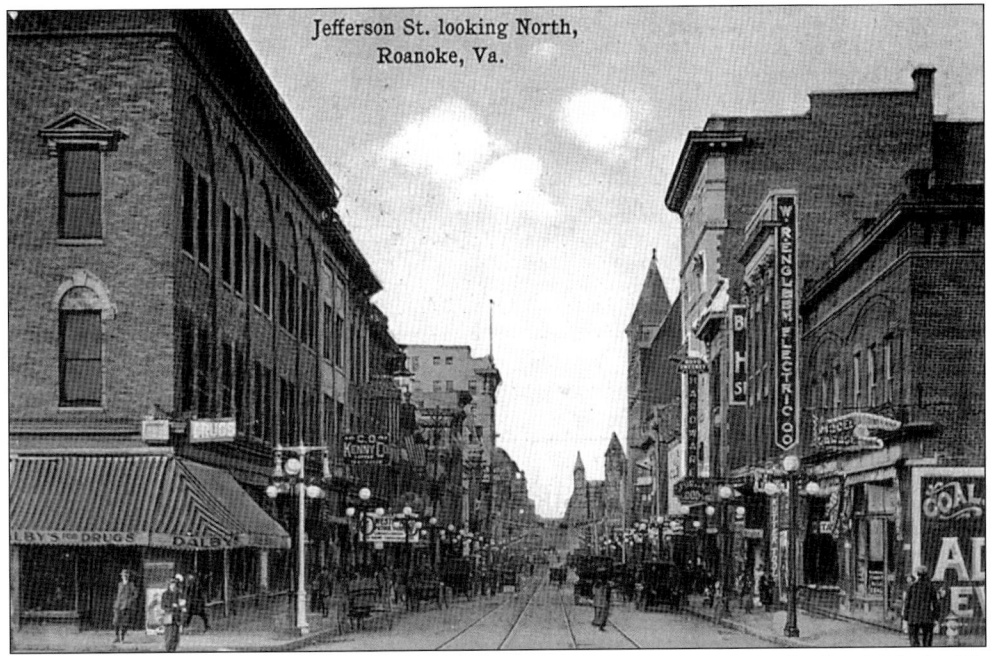

JEFFERSON STREET, LOOKING NORTH, 1915. Signs and store fronts are clearly visible in this card—W. Rengleem Electric Co., Model T Garage, C.D. Kenney Co., Dalby's Drugs, Comet Theater, and Boyd-Sweeney Hardware.

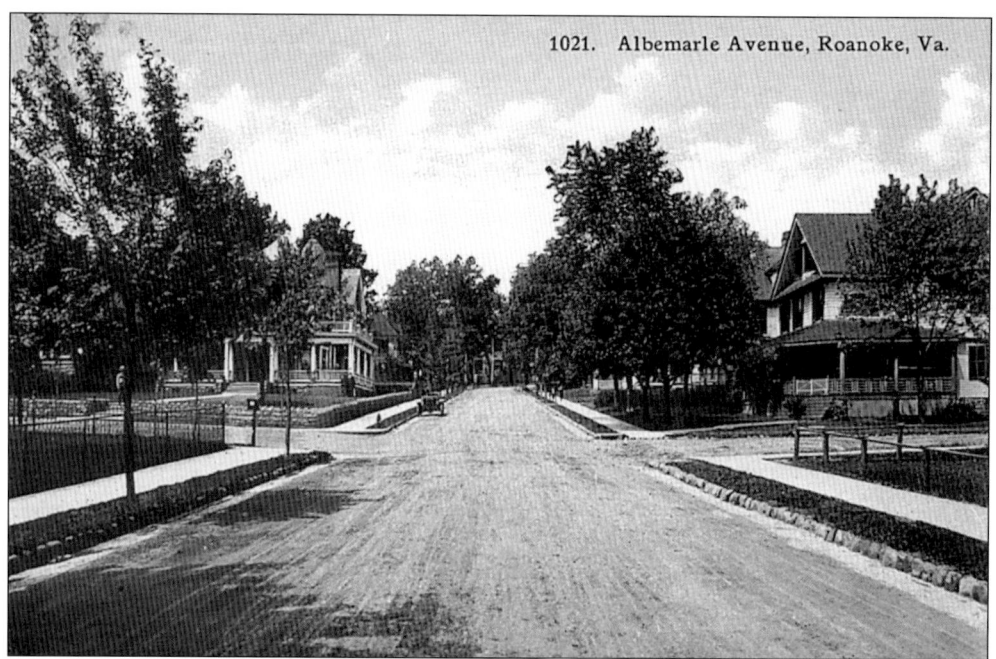

ALBEMARLE AVENUE, 1913. Another example of one of Roanoke's early neighborhood streets, Albemarle Avenue boasted many fine homes.

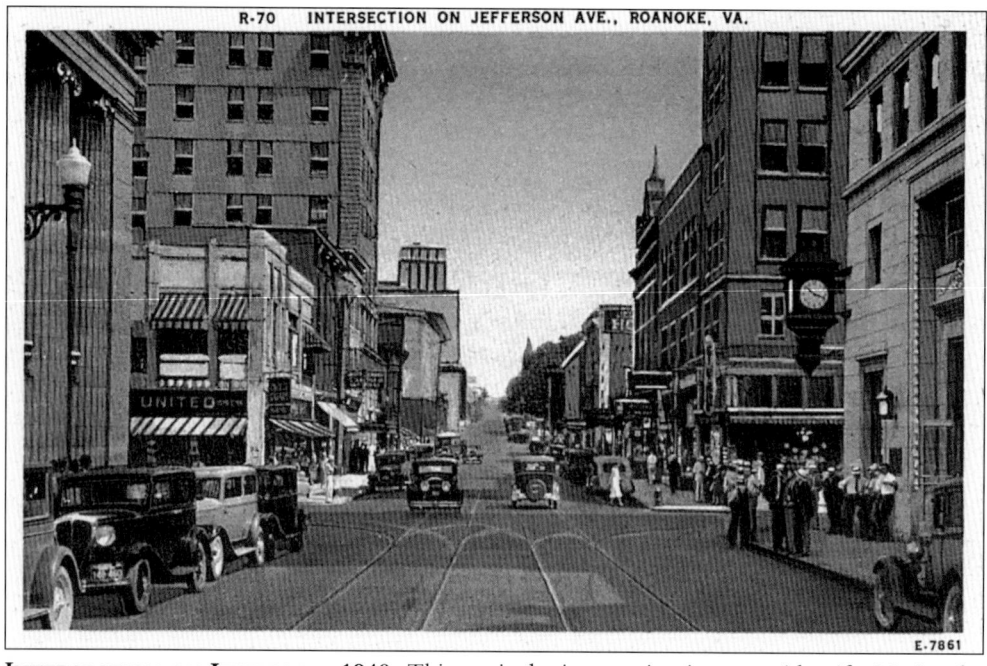

INTERSECTION ON JEFFERSON, 1940. This particular intersection is easy to identify. Notice the protruding clock attached to the Colonial National Bank building. The time is 10:20.

Five
RECREATION AND LEISURE

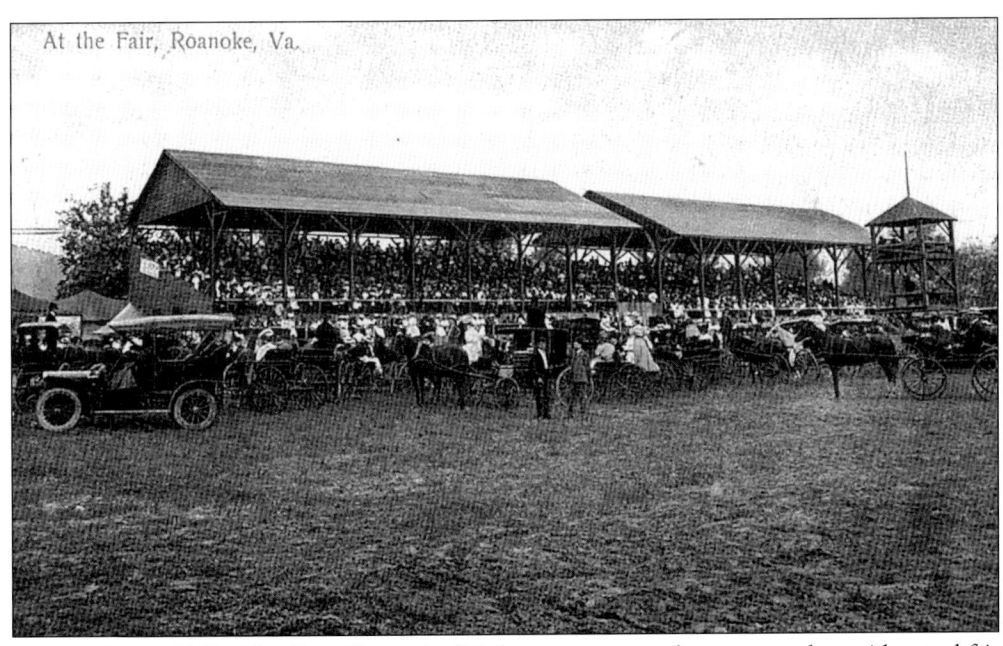

AT THE FAIR, 1913. The Great Roanoke Fair became an annual event complete with actual fair grounds designed for the event.

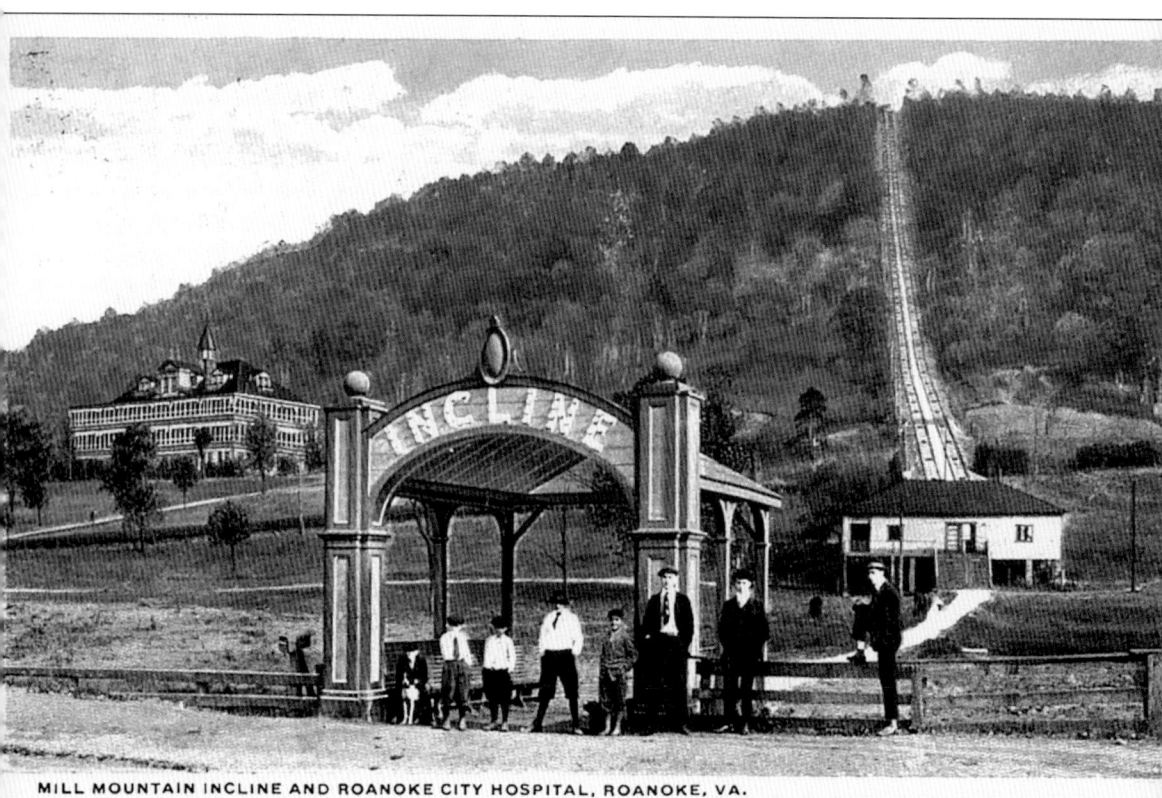

MILL MOUNTAIN INCLINE AND ROANOKE CITY HOSPITAL, ROANOKE, VA.

MILL MOUNTAIN INCLINE, 1917. The Mill Mountain Incline was one of Roanoke's earliest and most successful attractions. The message written on the back this card reads, "I have been up here. I am afraid the string will break. Roanoke Fair was just in front of where these men are standing." The Incline Railway opened on August 14, 1910, and 1,500 passengers were accommodated that first day.

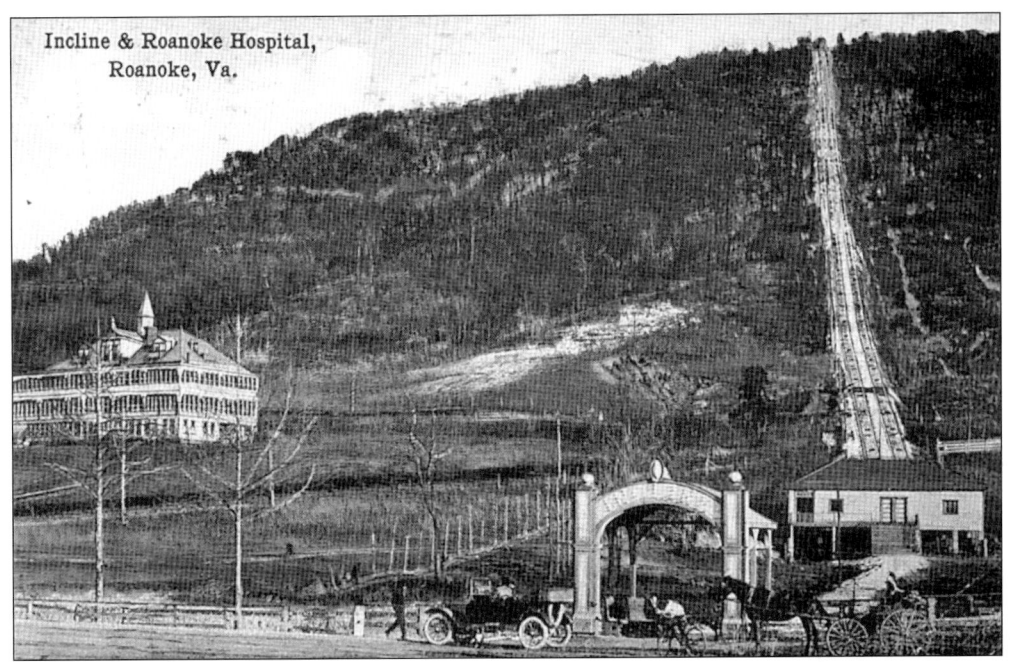

INCLINE AND ROANOKE HOSPITAL, 1914. The Incline operated on two steel tracks and was pulled by cable. Fare for the four-minute round trip was 25¢.

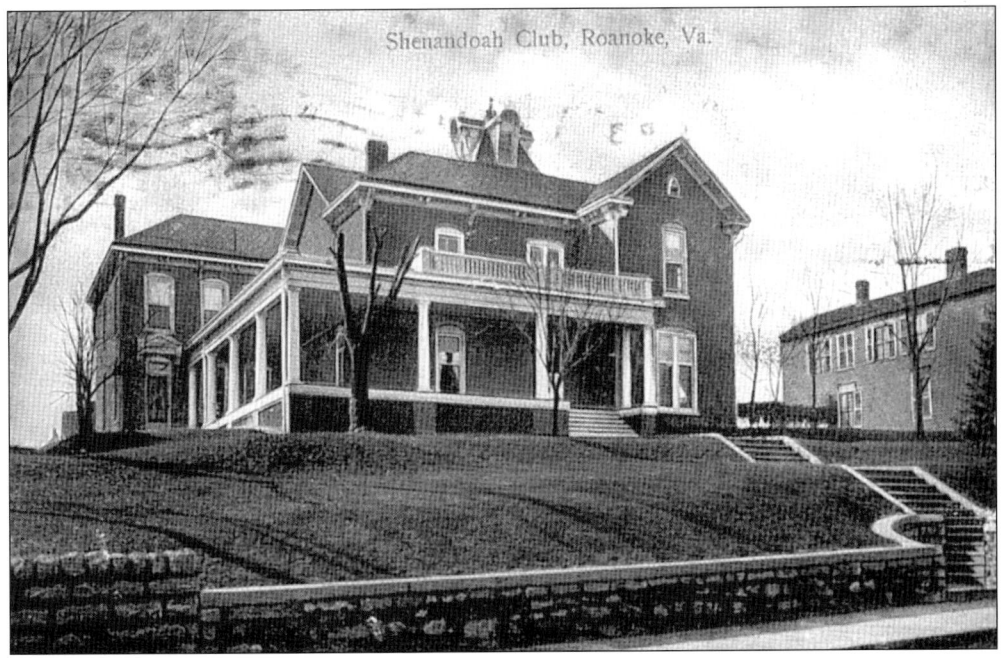

SHENANDOAH CLUB, 1912. The Shenandoah Club, organized in 1893, originally purchased a home (shown here) for their club meetings on Franklin Road.

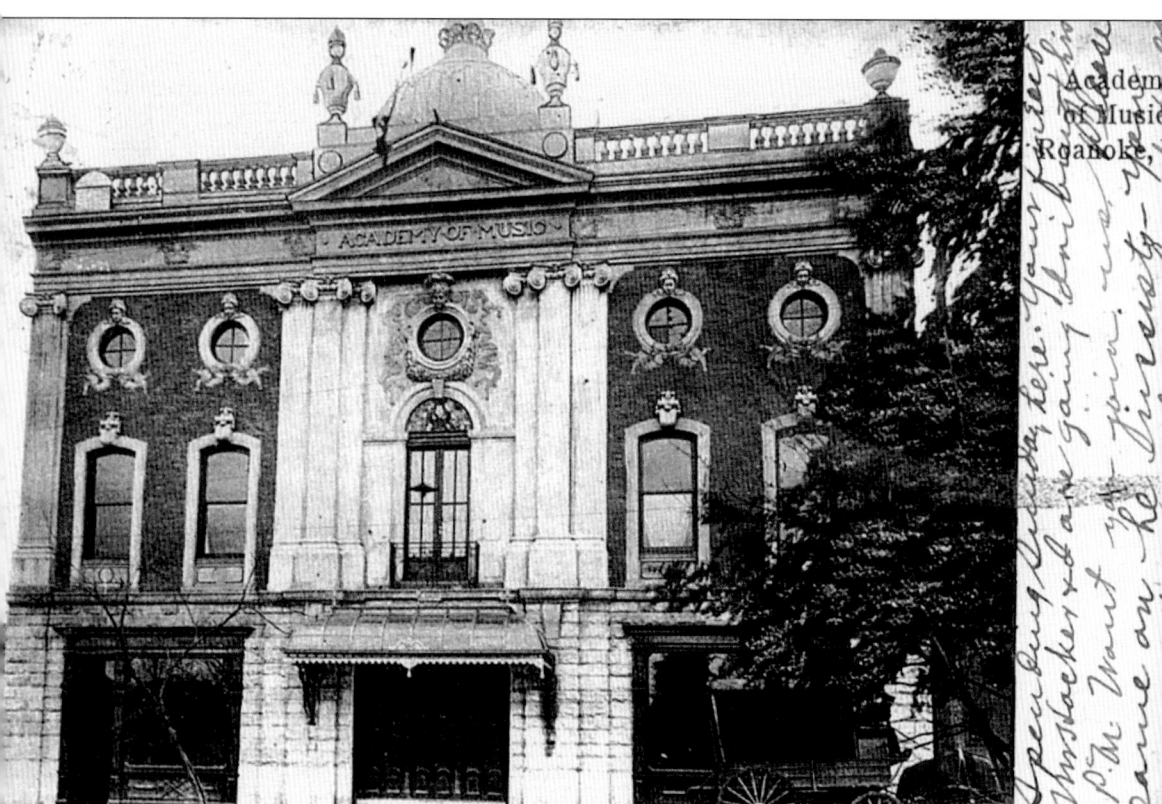

ACADEMY OF MUSIC, 1907. The Academy of Music was one of the most ornate structures in Roanoke. The building fronted Salem Avenue and opened on October 7, 1892. Falling into neglect, the grand structure was demolished in 1953 to the regret of many.

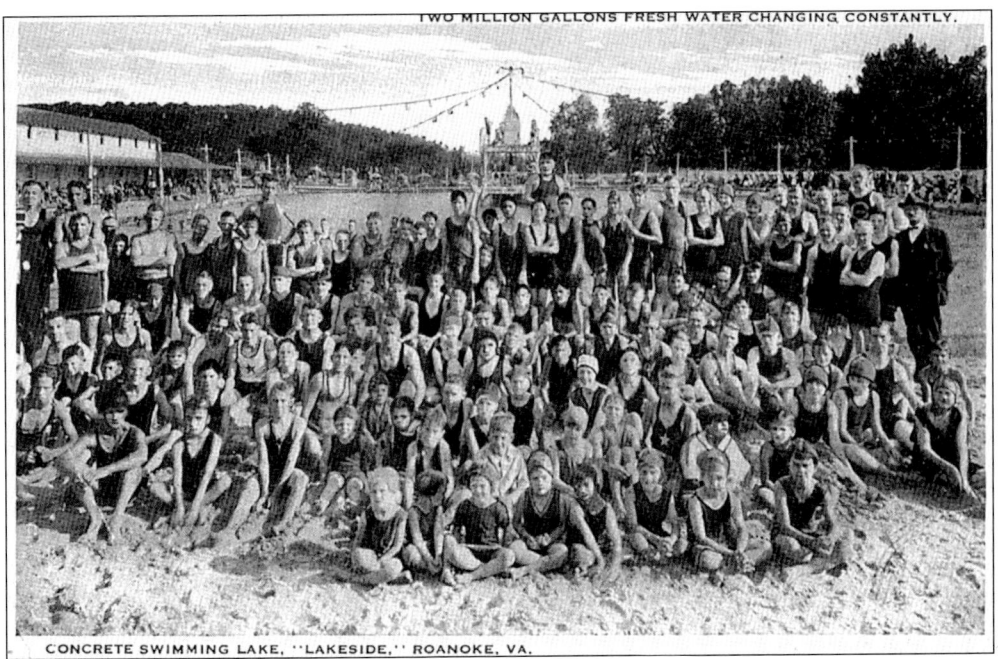

LAKESIDE, 1925. "Two million gallons, fresh water, changing constantly" was the message atop this card promoting the "concrete swimming lake" at Lakeside.

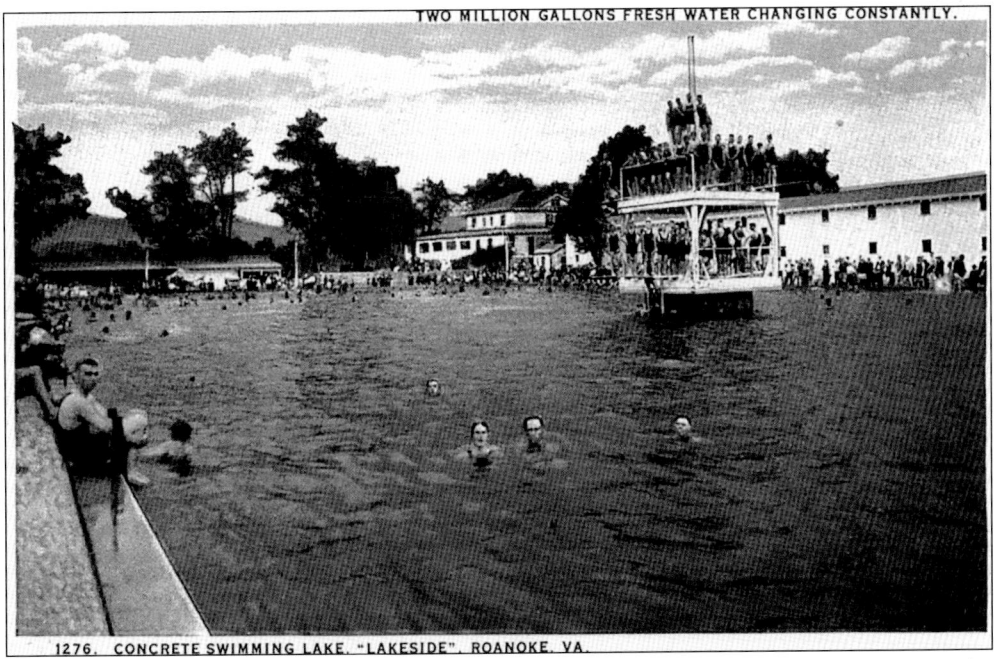

LAKESIDE, 1925. Lakeside's pool opened on July 10, 1920, to great success. For many it was the first opportunity to swim in a pool. Notice the diving platform in the middle.

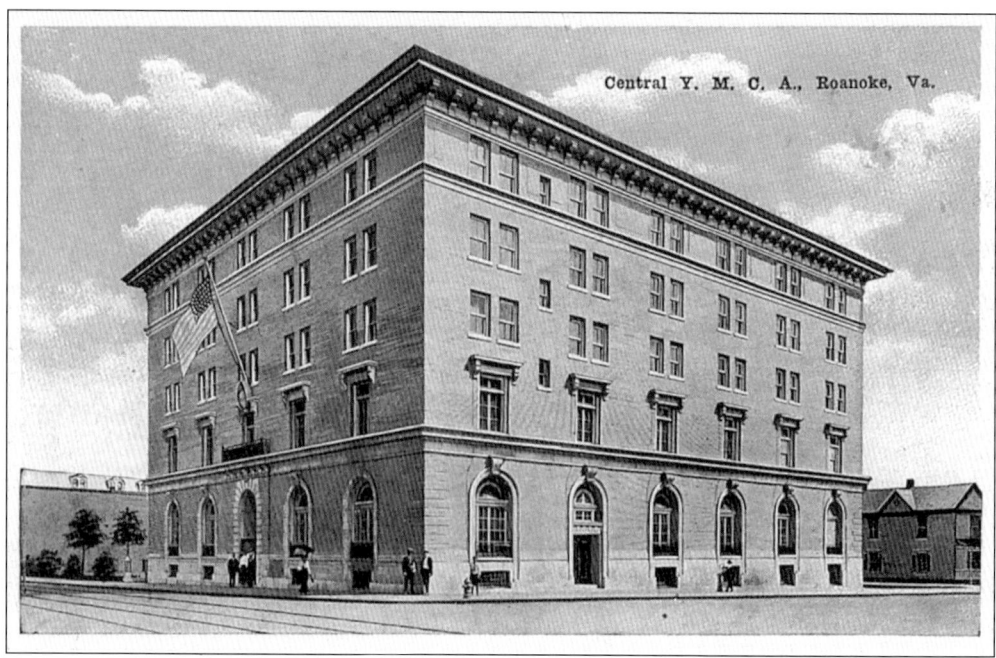

CENTRAL YMCA, 1920. The YMCA changed locations frequently during its infancy, but erected this building in 1914. The architect was H.M. Miller.

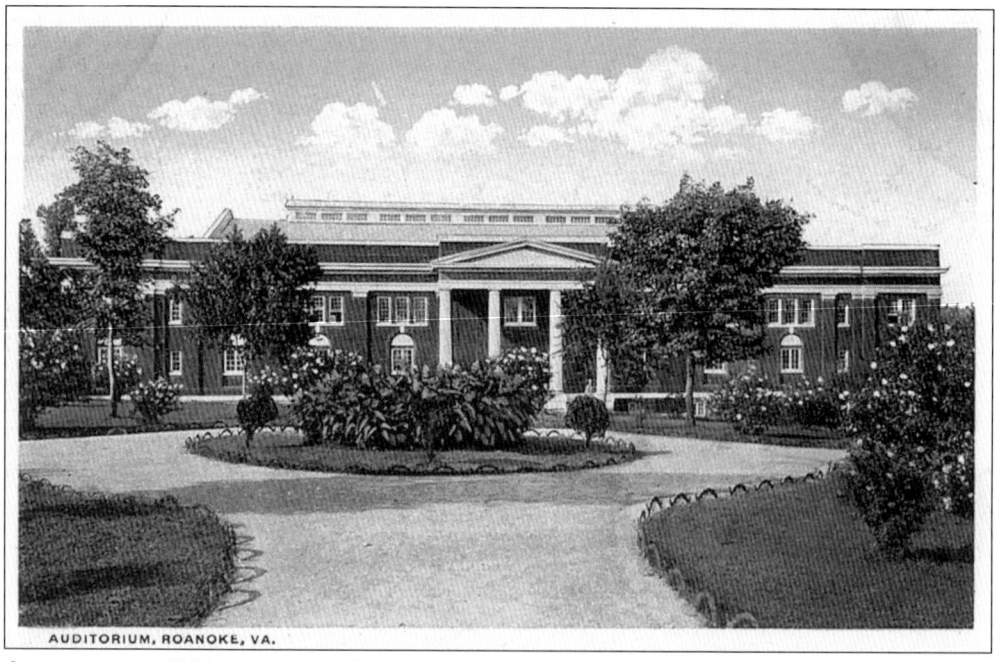

AUDITORIUM, 1921. Business and civic leaders citing the need for a large public space built the auditorium in 1916. While it no longer stands, the auditorium was in close proximity to the Hotel Roanoke and passenger station.

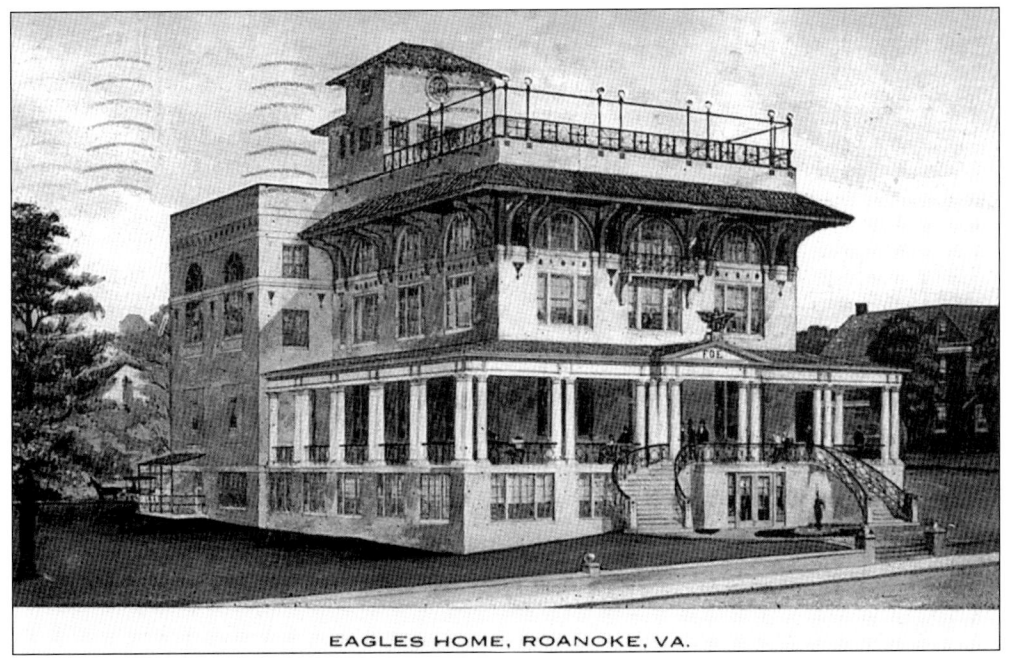

EAGLES HOME, 1917. The Fraternal Order of Eagles needed a home, so in 1913 they erected this structure which was later acquired by the National Business College in 1919. The home stood on Franklin Road near the Shenandoah Club.

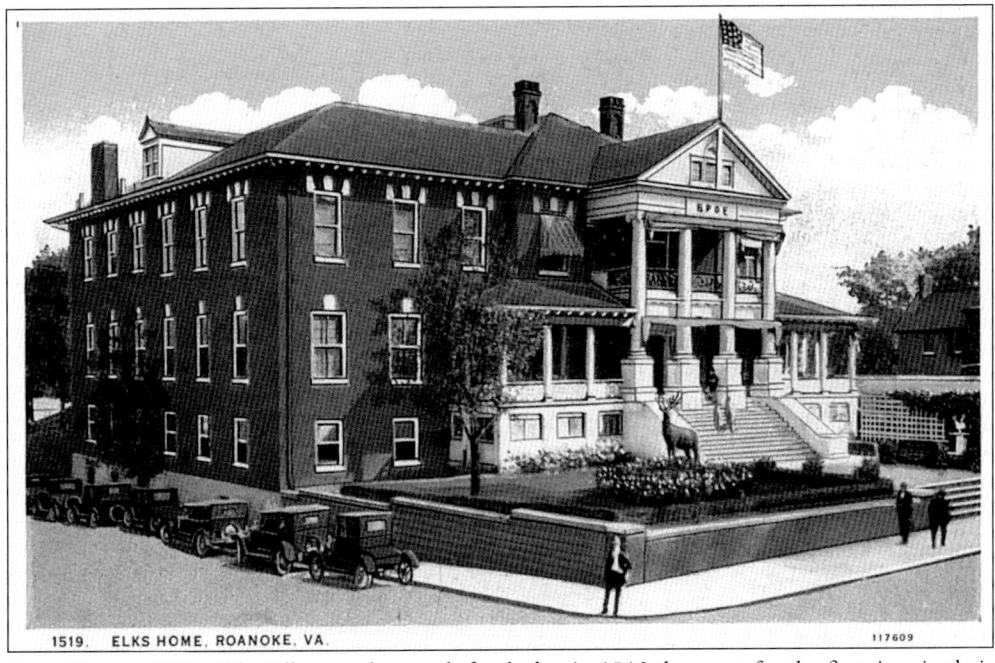

ELKS HOME, 1920. The Elks raised enough funds that in 1913 they met for the first time in their new home located at the corner of Jefferson and Franklin (formerly Tazewell).

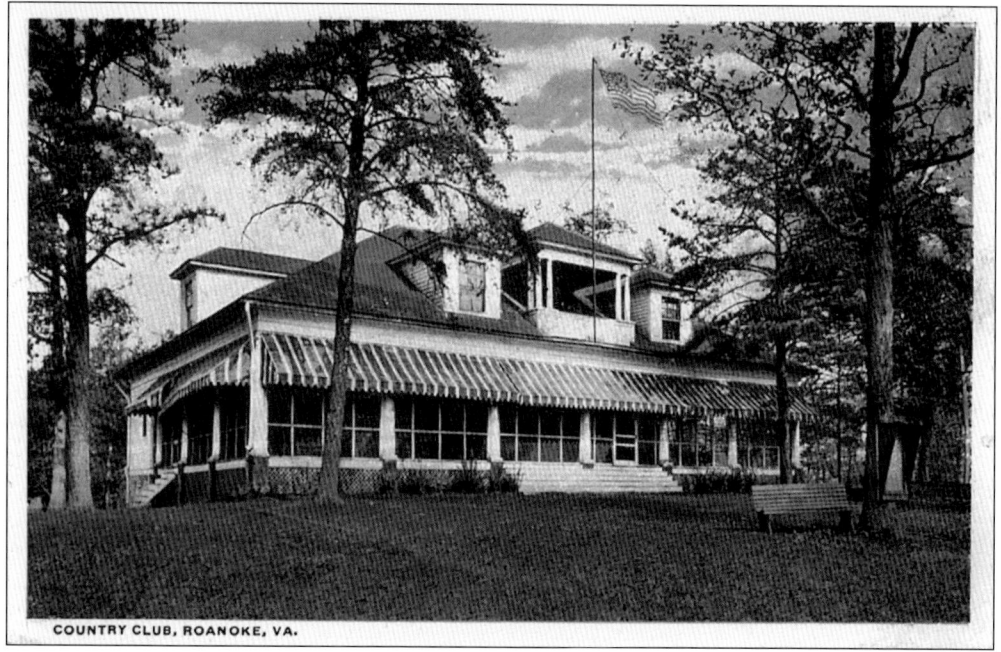

COUNTRY CLUB, 1919. Organized in 1899, the Roanoke Country Club built this frame home in 1908 as a club house after moving from South Roanoke to farmland west of the city that was purchased from Dr. Moomaw.

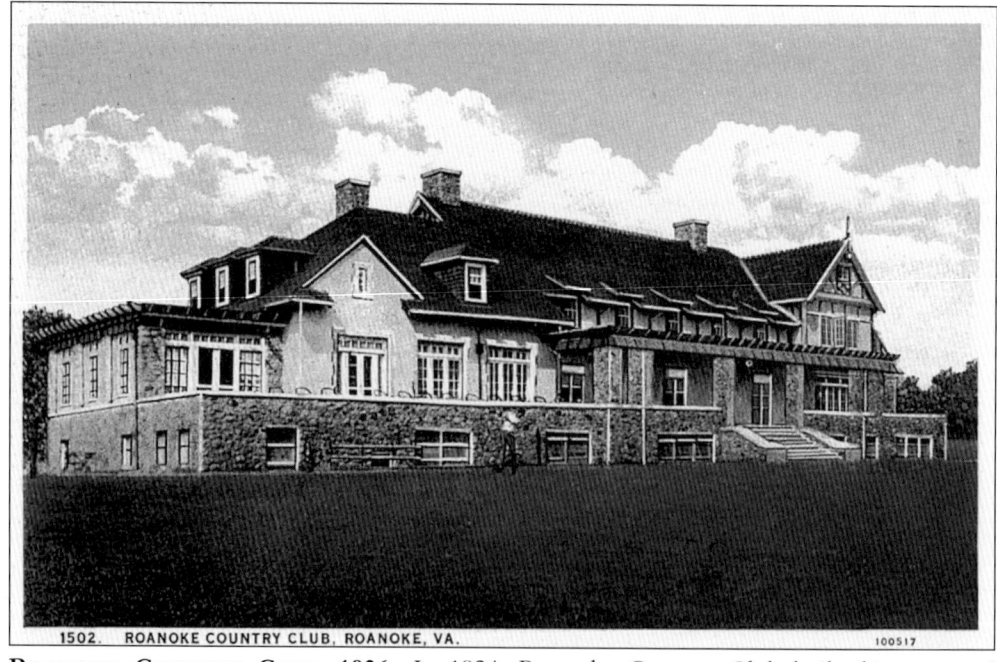

ROANOKE COUNTRY CLUB, 1926. In 1924, Roanoke Country Club built this new and expanded club house in response to its growing membership.

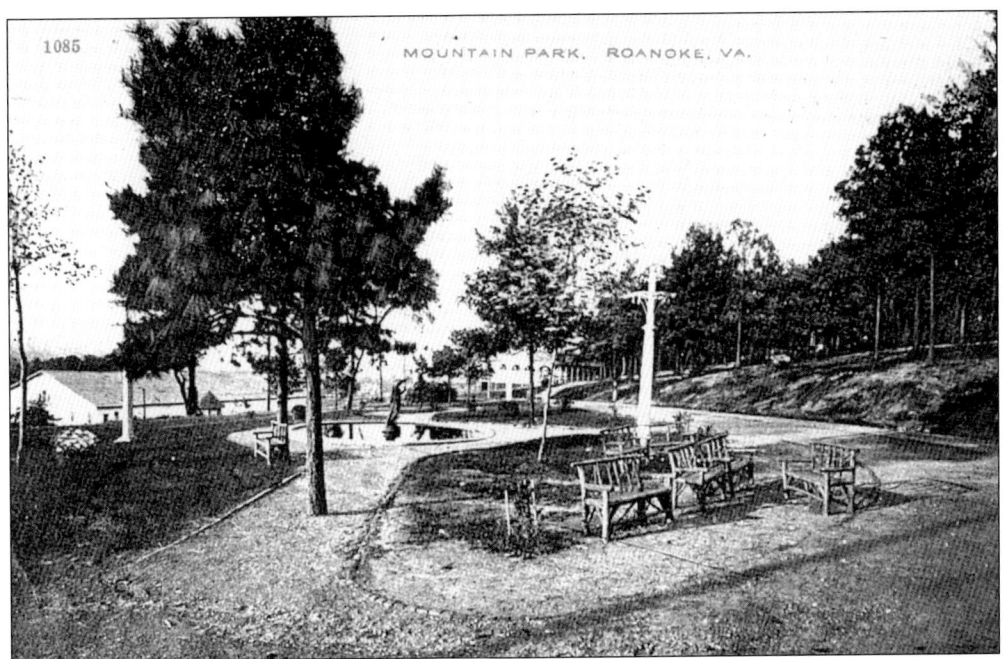

MOUNTAIN PARK, 1914. Mountain Park, located in the Crystal Spring area at the foot of Mill Mountain, was Roanoke's premier park, offering a variety of amenities and attractions. Notice here the pond and fountain.

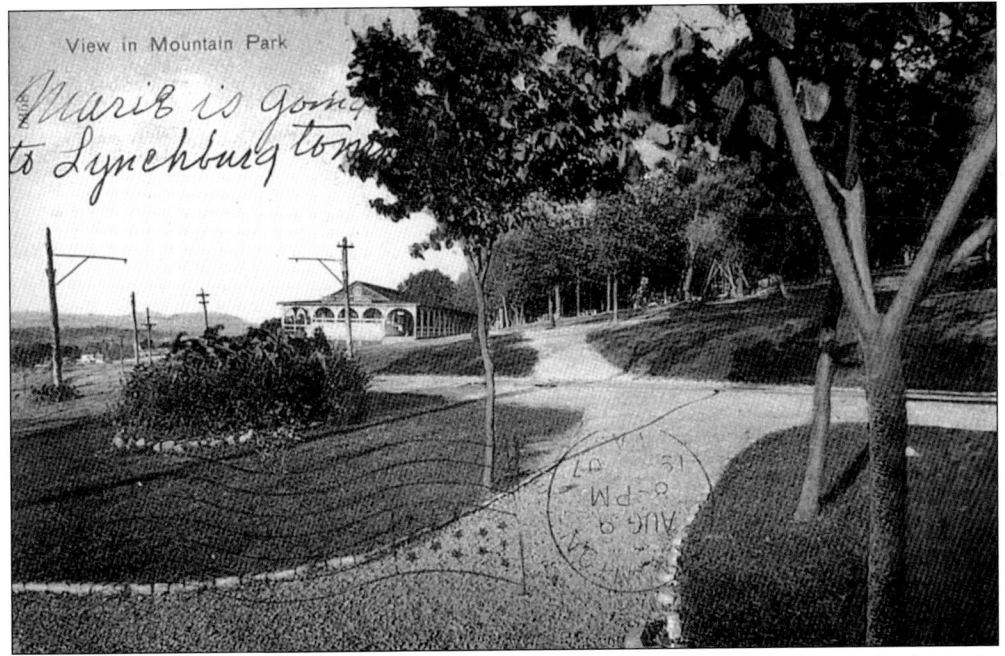

VIEW OF MOUNTAIN PARK, 1907. Another postcard view of Mountain Park shows its meandering paths, gardens, and expansive lawn.

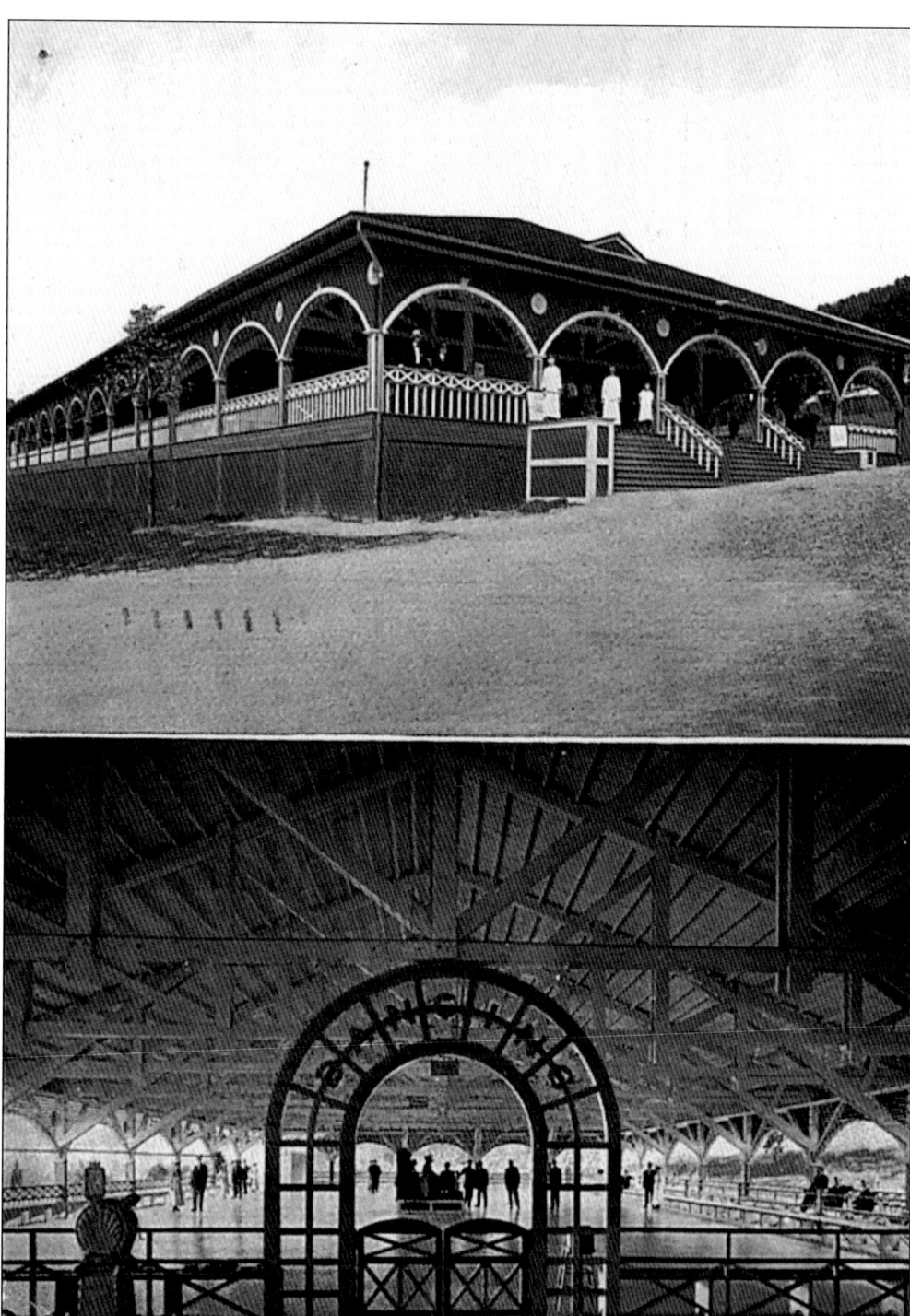

DANCING PAVILION, MOUNTAIN PARK, 1912. To add to Mountain Park's popularity, a dancing pavilion was created. Lighted at night, the pavilion had a center bandstand, bleachers for spectators, and a wide open dance floor.

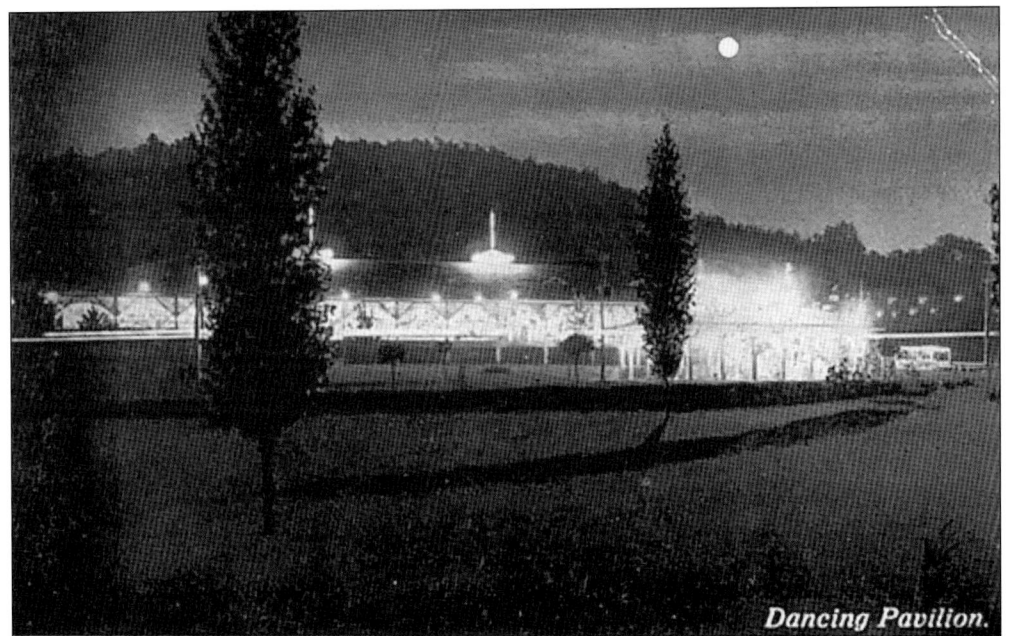

707. Scenes at Mountain Park by Night, Roanoke, Va.

Dancing Pavilion.

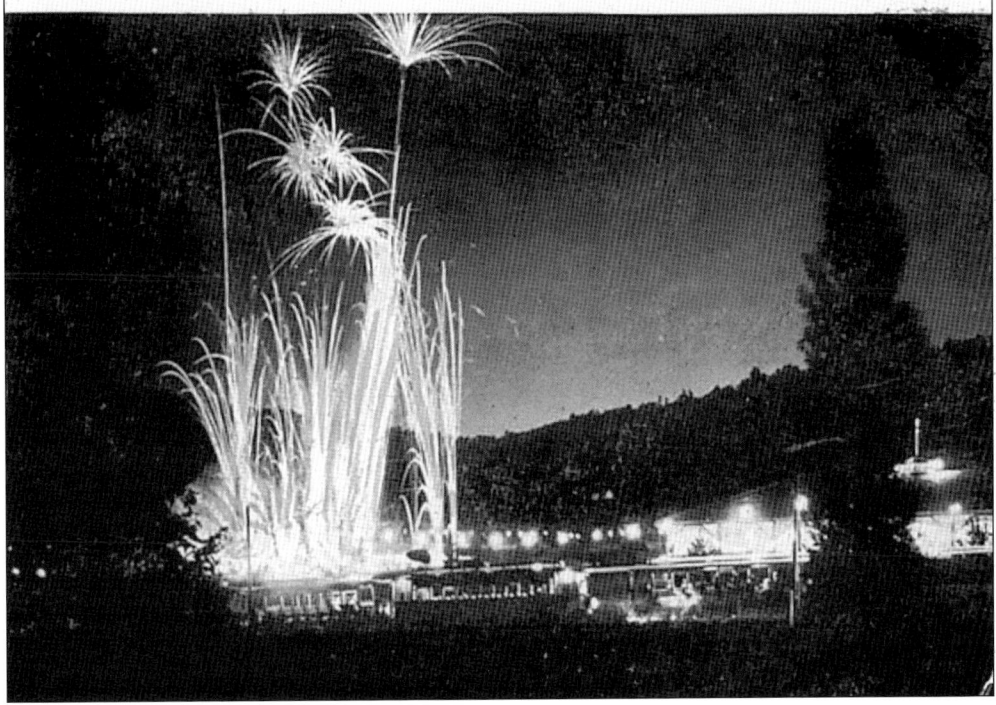

SCENES AT MOUNTAIN PARK BY NIGHT, 1912. Mountain Park was not only a center of daylight activities but festivities would often go into the night, as this card shows. The dancing pavilion is lit above and stands against the backdrop of fireworks below.

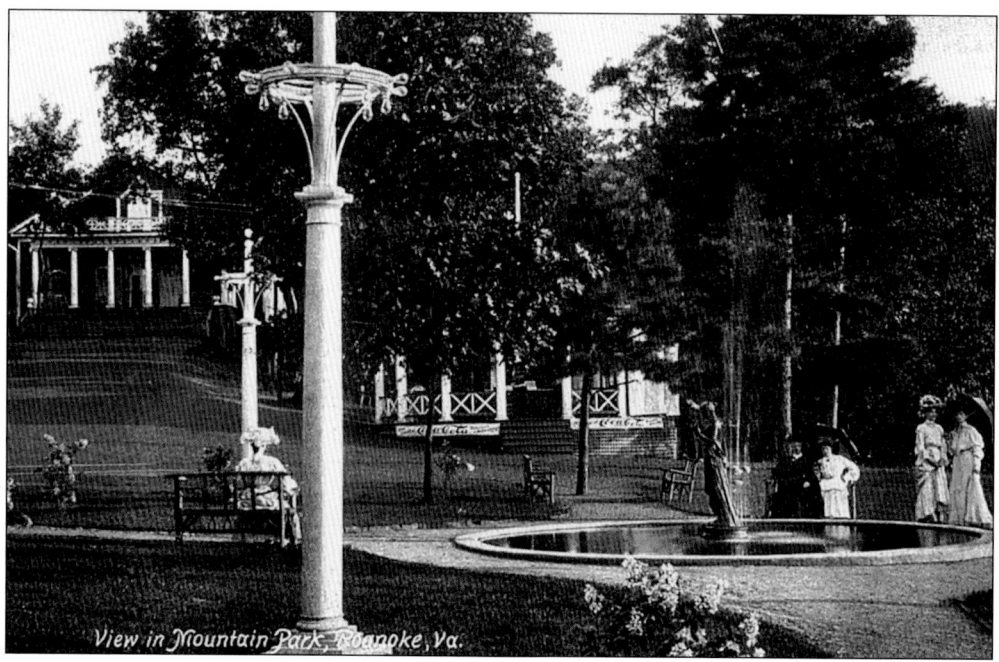

VIEW IN MOUNTAIN PARK, 1907. This view of Mountain Park shows, from left to right, the casino, an outside bandstand with banner ads for Coca-Cola, and the pond with fountain.

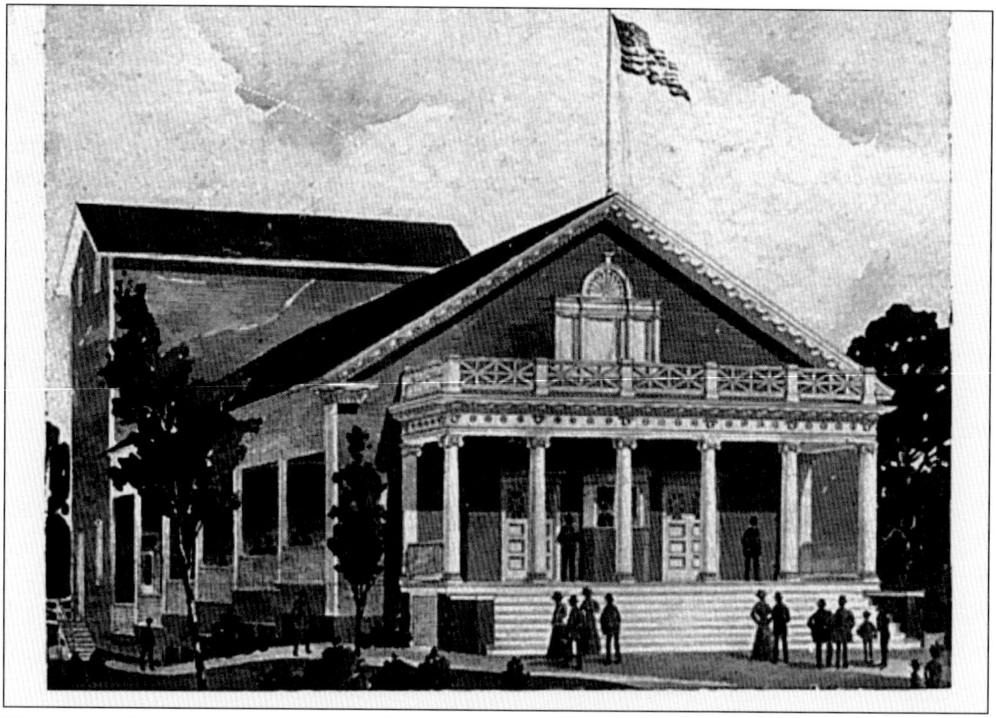

MOUNTAIN PARK CASINO, 1907. The Mountain Park Casino opened on June 15, 1903, with the play, "Too Much Married." Showing plays and movies, the casino only added to the popularity of Mountain Park. Films were changed every Monday and Friday.

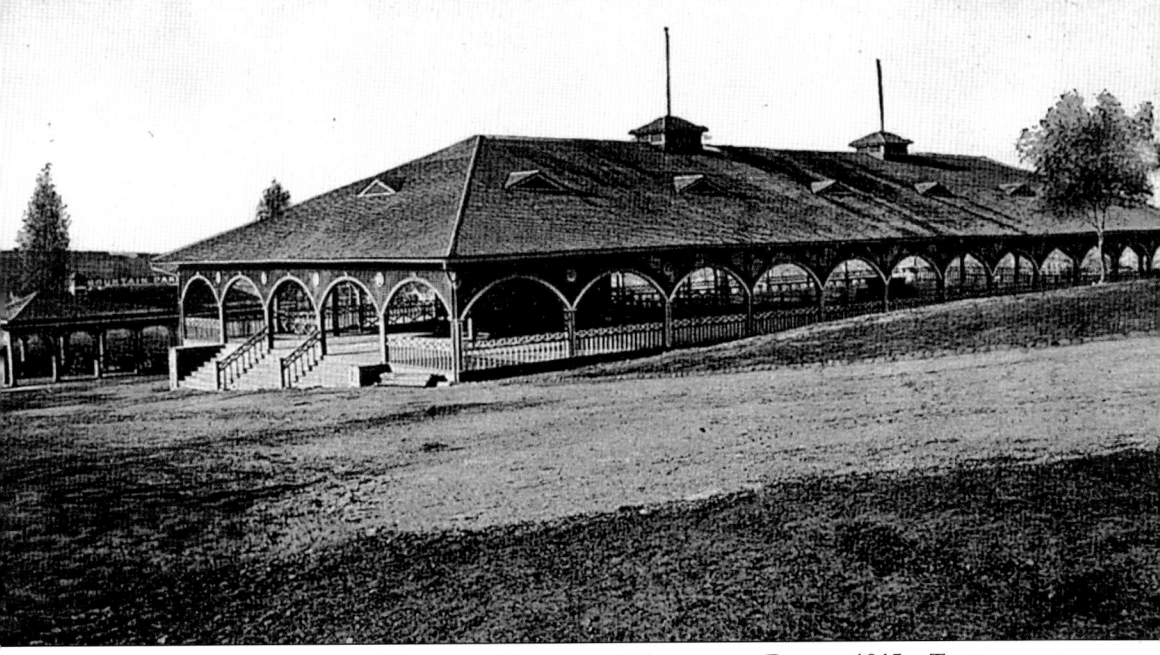

Dancing Pavilion & Trolley Station, Roanoke, Va.

DANCING PAVILION AND TROLLEY STATION, MOUNTAIN PARK, 1915. To transport Roanokers to Mountain Park, a trolley station was built almost adjacent to the dancing pavilion. This card shows how large the pavilion was, especially compared to the trolley station at left. With the growth of South Roanoke, land was in demand for residences. Thus, Mountain Park opened for the last time in the summer of 1922. Land occupied by the park was purchased for $80,000, which was 13 times the amount the park developer paid for it in 1902. For 20 years, Mountain Park entertained Roanoke, and, today, the land is covered with homes and streets.

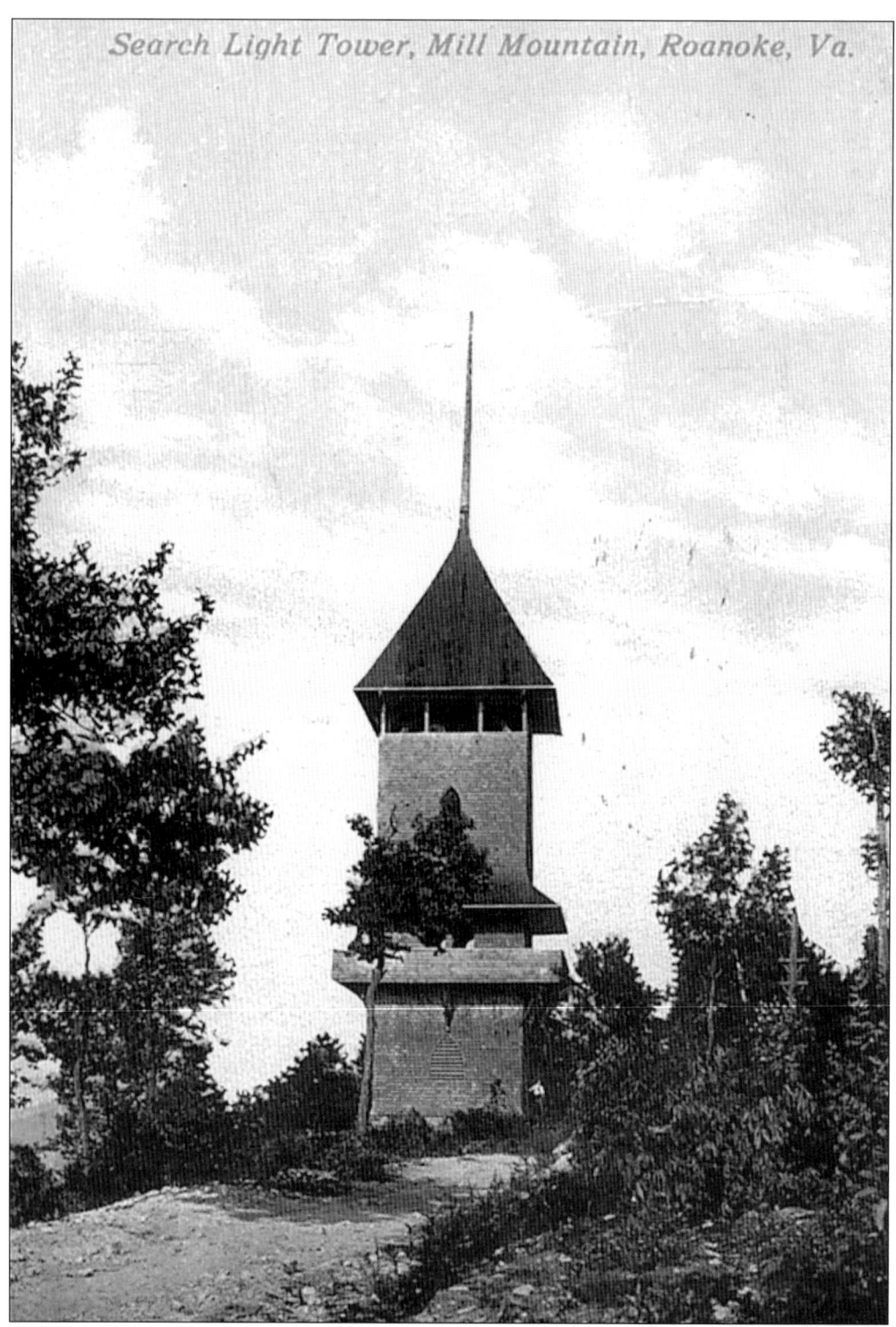

SEARCH LIGHT TOWER, MILL MOUNTAIN, 1913. The tower on this postcard was destroyed in a windstorm in 1914. A new tower was soon erected, but it burned in 1936.

MILL MOUNTAIN INCLINE, 1915. The Mill Mountain Incline contributed much to the many attractions both at the top and bottom of Mill Mountain. As with Mountain Park, the incline no longer exists, but its path up the mountain can still be seen today.

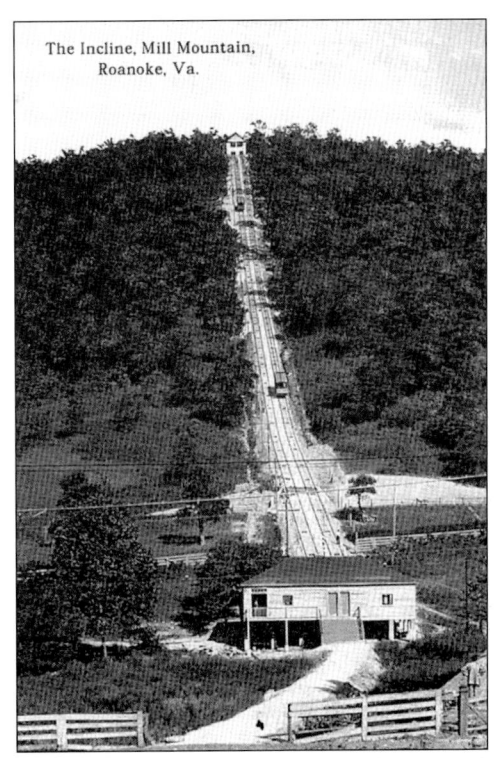

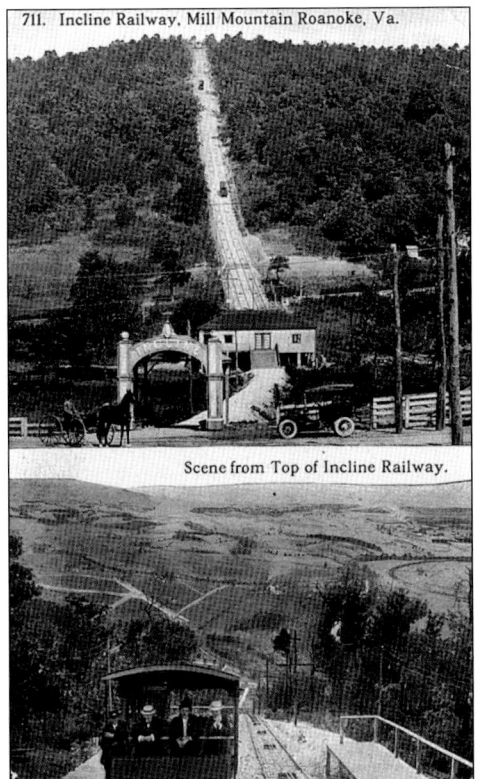

TWO VIEWS, INCLINE RAILWAY, 1912. This divided postcard shows the bottom and top views of the incline. Notice the sparsely developed Roanoke Valley from the top view. The cabled cars were powered by two large electric motors at the top of the mountain.

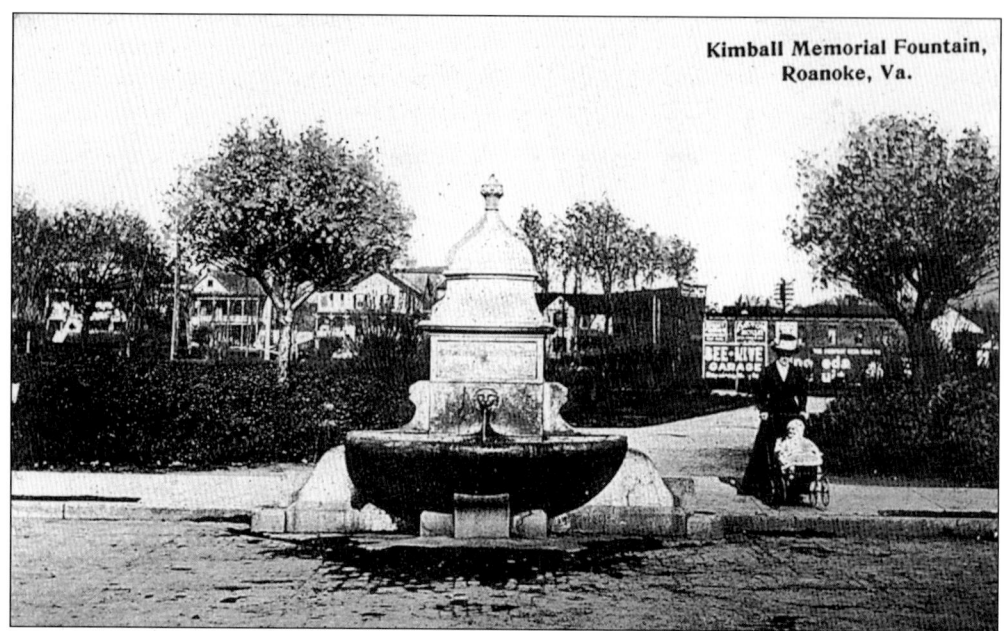

KIMBALL MEMORIAL FOUNTAIN, 1915. The Kimball Fountain, named in honor of Frederick J. Kimball, was dedicated in 1907. The fountain was in the park directly across from the Norfolk & Western Passenger Station.

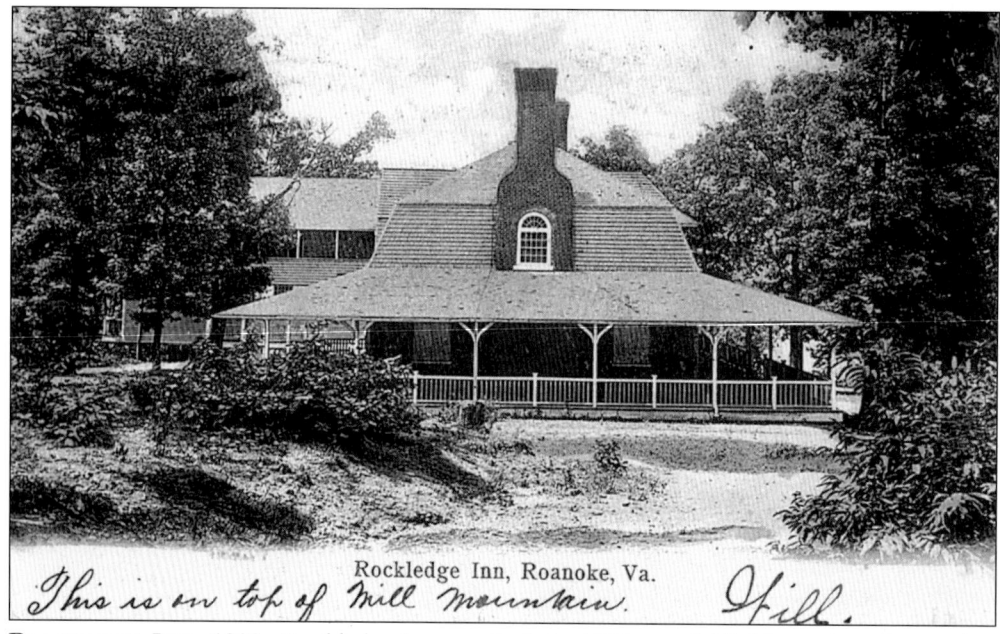

ROCKLEDGE INN, 1908. Rockledge Inn was built in 1892 atop Mill Mountain and served as one of Roanoke's better social spots. A nice evening out would have been to take the incline to the top, dine and dance at Rockledge, and take the incline back down. Rockledge Inn burned in the 1970s.

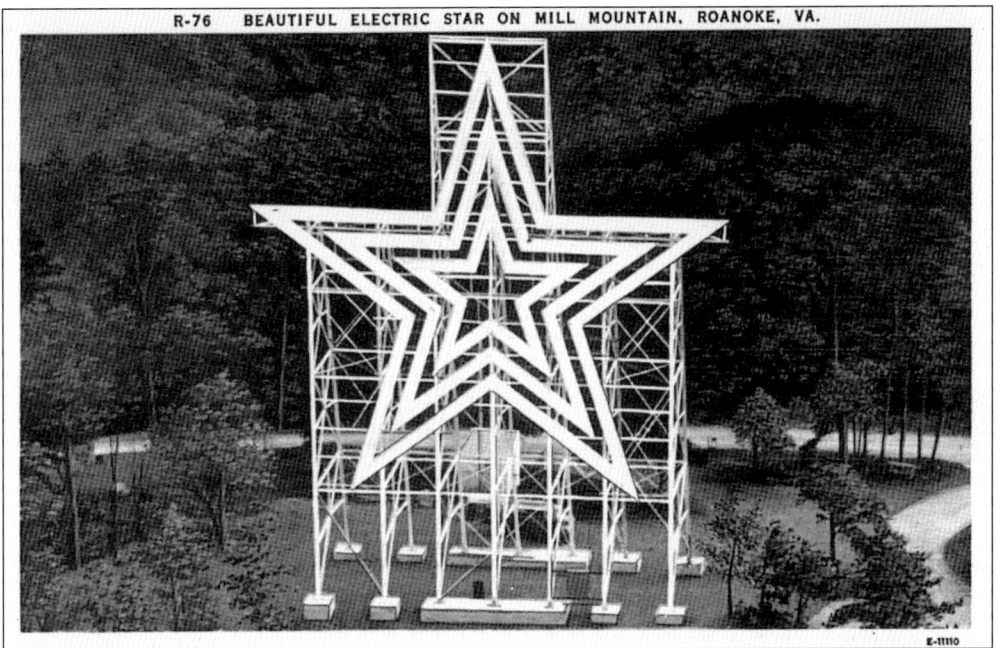

MILL MOUNTAIN STAR, 1954. The Mill Mountain Star was an idea developed by downtown merchants in 1949 as a way to attract shoppers for the holiday season. The star was so successful and endearing that it remains today.

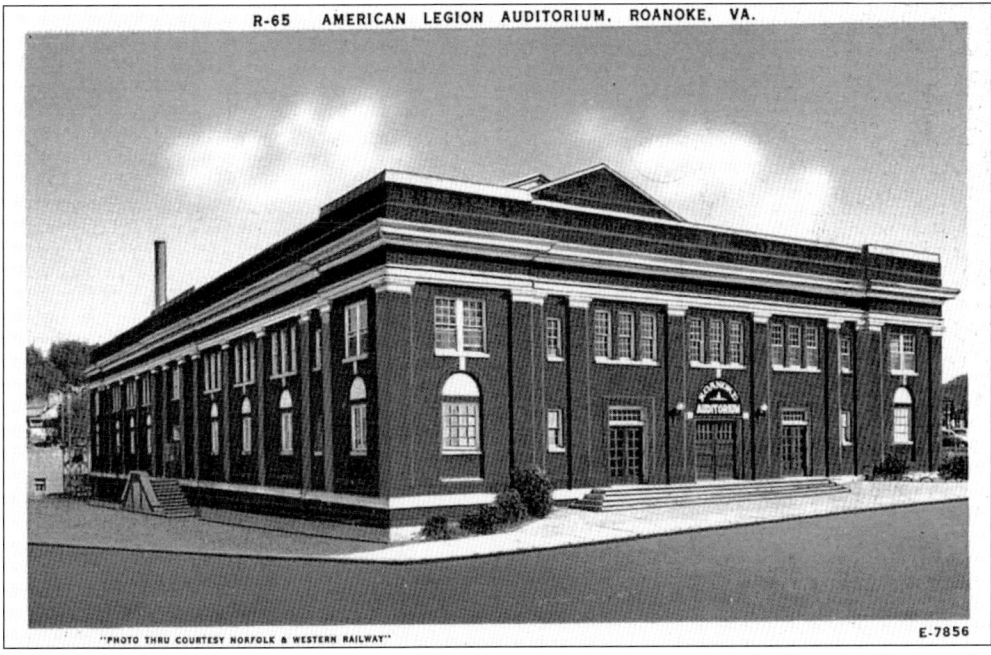

AMERICAN LEGION AUDITORIUM, 1950. The American Legion acquired to the former city auditorium building in 1947 and provided needed upgrades. Unfortunately, the building burned in 1957.

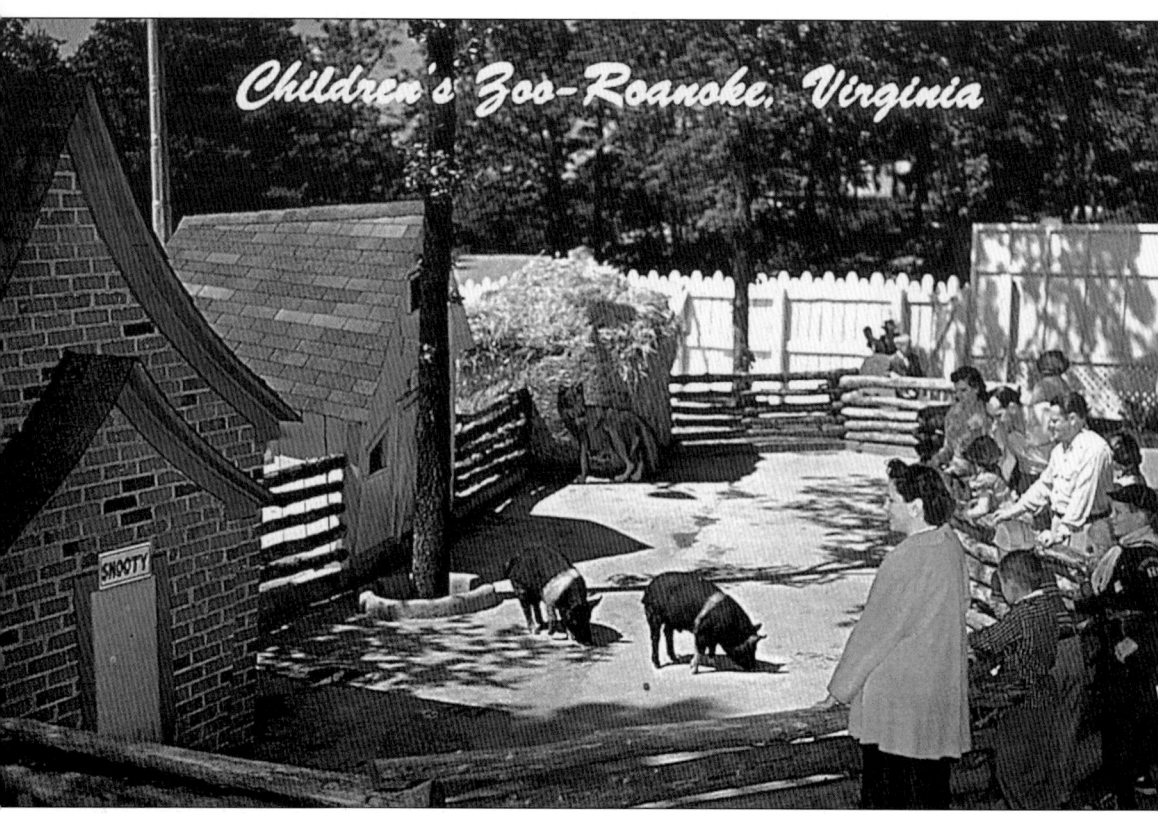

CHILDREN'S ZOO, MILL MOUNTAIN, 1960. The Mill Mountain Zoo opened in 1952 as a children's zoo with a Mother Goose theme. Here is the "Three Little Pigs."

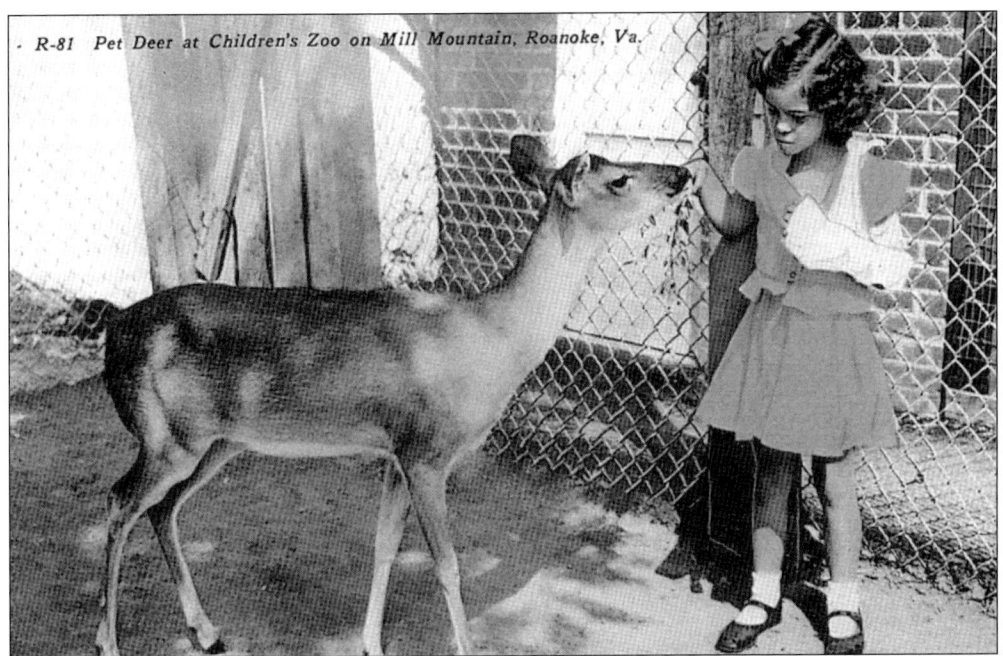

PETTING DEER AT CHILDREN'S ZOO, 1955. The Mill Mountain Zoo allowed city children the opportunity to get close to animals by offering a petting zoo.

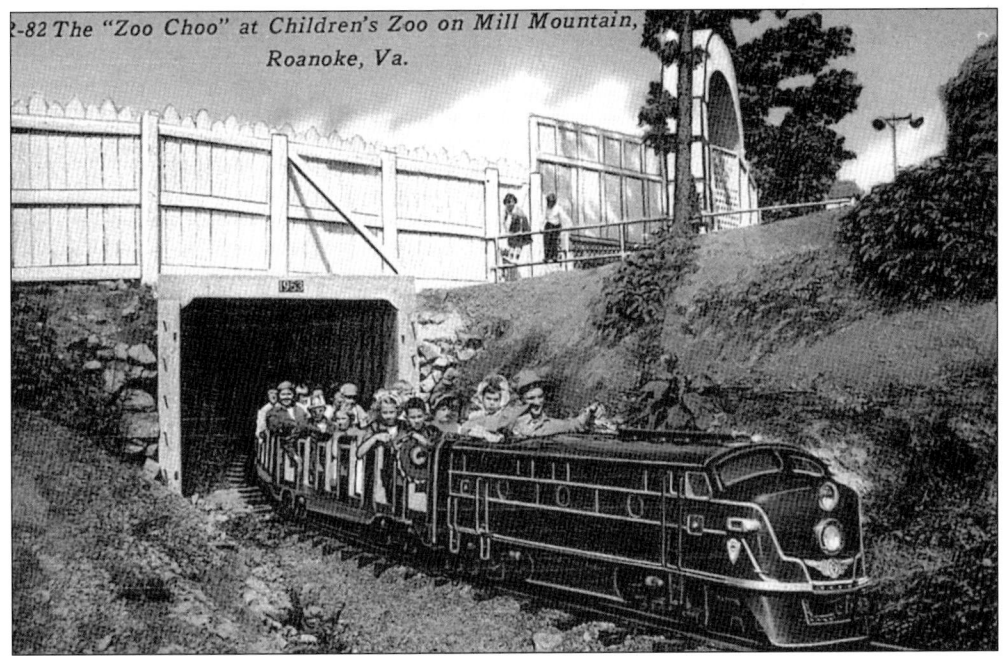

THE ZOO CHOO, 1955. The Zoo Choo was originally operated as a project of the Roanoke Jaycees and still runs today. The card boasts that the train can hold 36 passengers and goes through a 100-foot long tunnel.

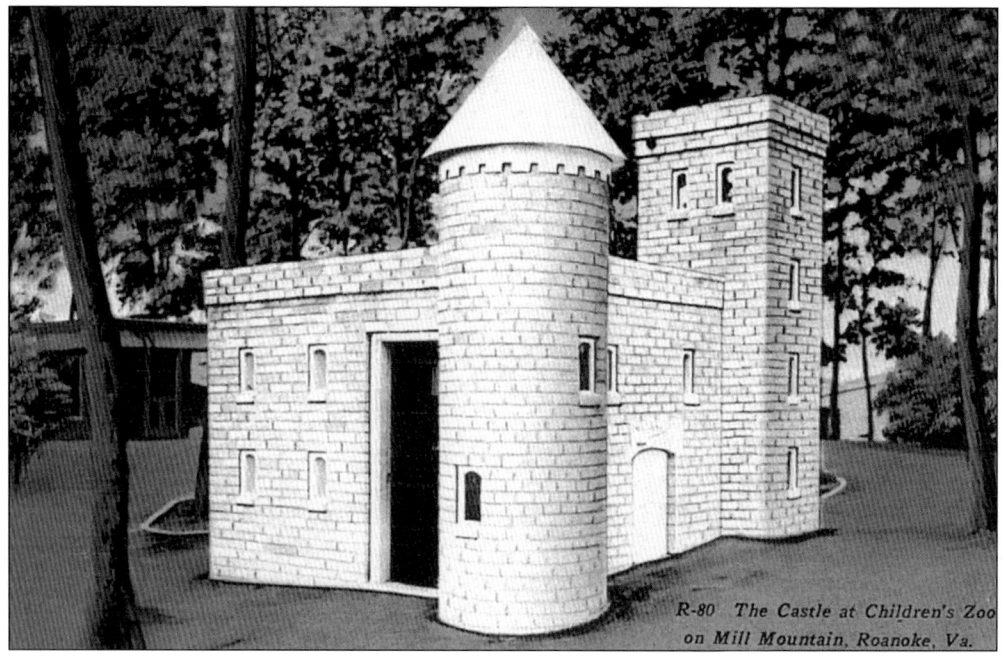

THE CASTLE AT THE CHILDREN'S ZOO, 1955. The castle inside the zoo exists no longer, but at one time contained parakeets, love birds, guinea pigs, hamsters, skunks, terrapins, and other small animals.

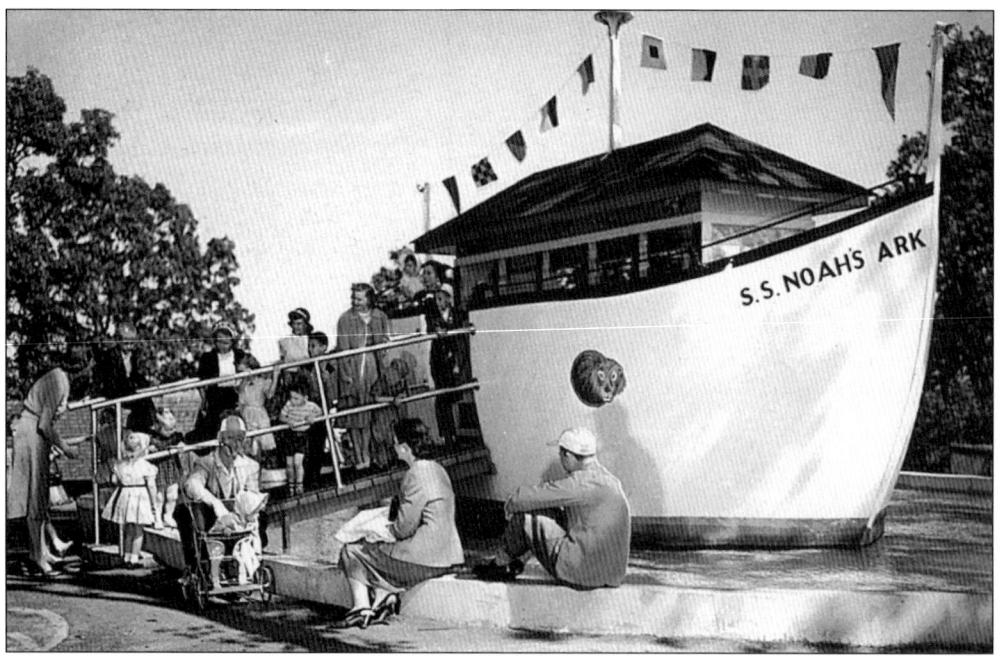

NOAH'S ARK, CHILDREN'S ZOO, 1960. The ark at one time contained several different kinds of birds. While the Mill Mountain Zoo has matured and expanded over five decades, it no longer uses the ark and other such displays.

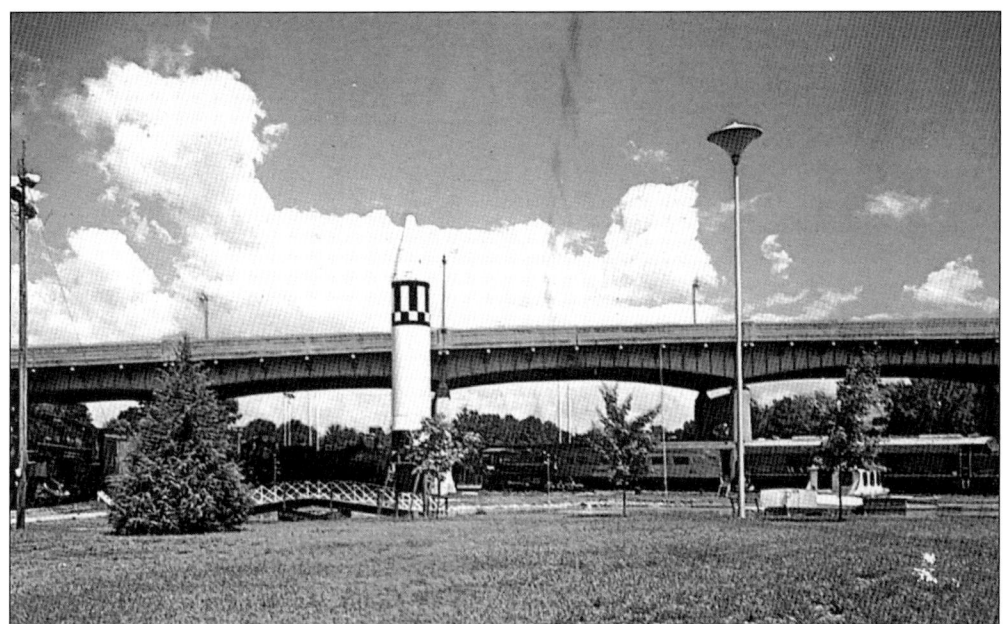

ROANOKE TRANSPORTATION MUSEUM, 1975. Before moving to its present location, Roanoke's Transportation Museum used to be located in Wasena Park beneath Wasena Bridge. Its most prominent display was a space rocket. The museum began in 1963 and is known today as the Virginia Museum of Transportation.

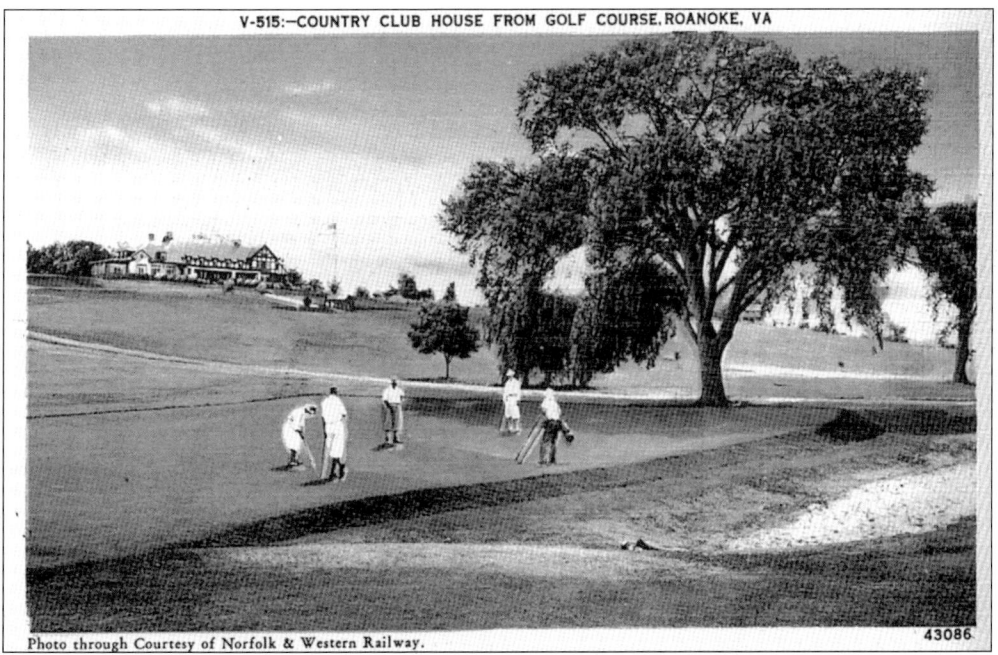

COUNTRY CLUB FROM GOLF COURSE, 1940. This postcard shows one of the holes at the Roanoke Country Club, Roanoke's oldest golf club.

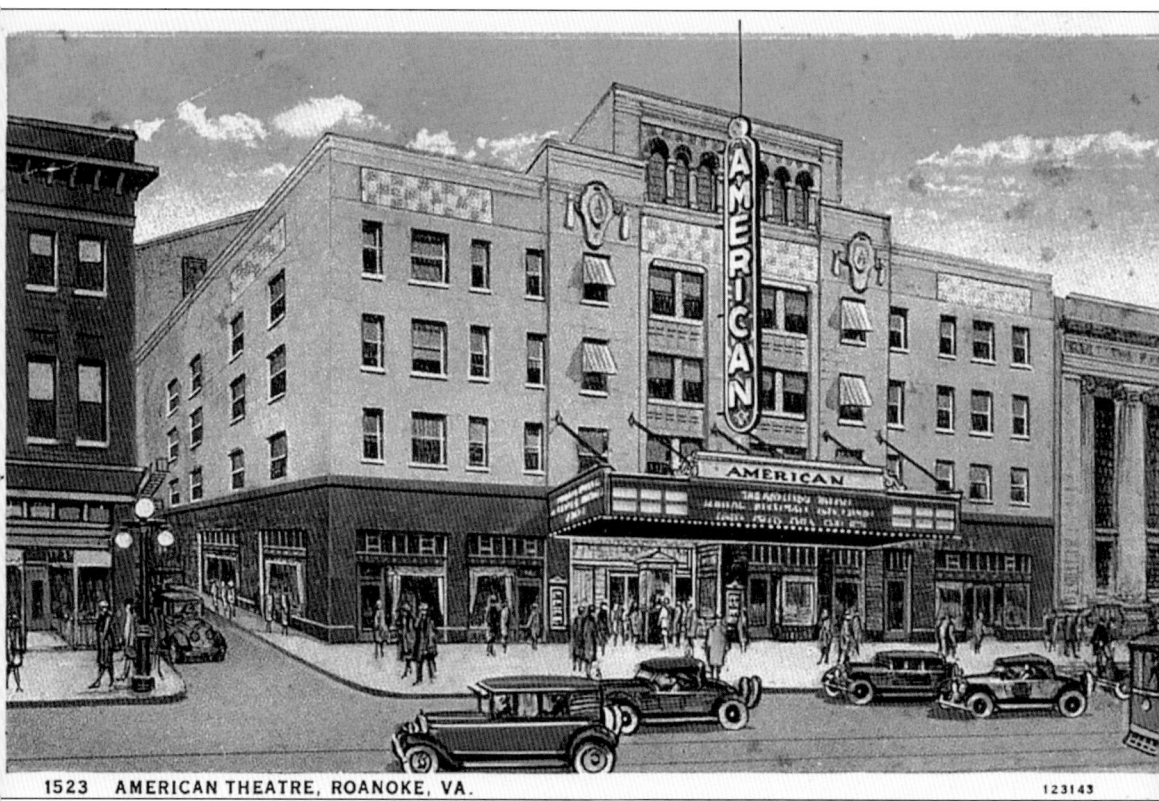

1523 AMERICAN THEATRE, ROANOKE, VA.

AMERICAN THEATER, 1934. The American Theater was Roanoke's finest movie house. It opened its doors on March 26, 1928, and closed on September 30, 1971. This movie "palace" with fish pond, grand foyer, mosaic tiles, wrought-iron chandeliers, and swag-draped balcony was razed in 1973.

Six
SCENERY AND TRAVEL

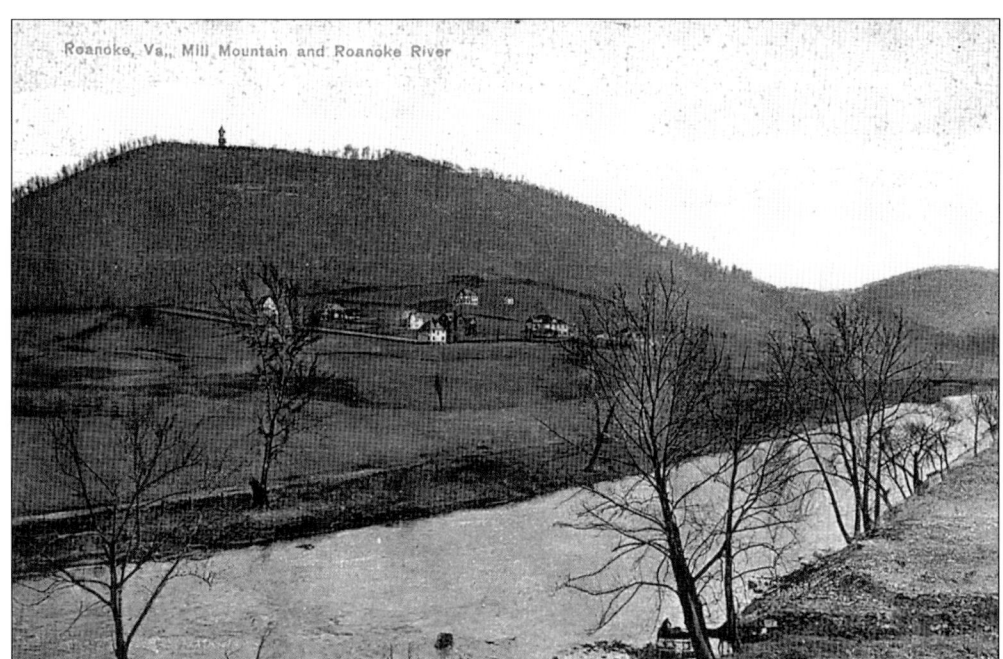

MILL MOUNTAIN AND ROANOKE RIVER, 1910. This pastoral scene of Mill Mountain shows the first few homes being built at its base. The river is flanked by farm land on both sides as Roanoke had only just begun to expand beyond its core commercial and residential areas.

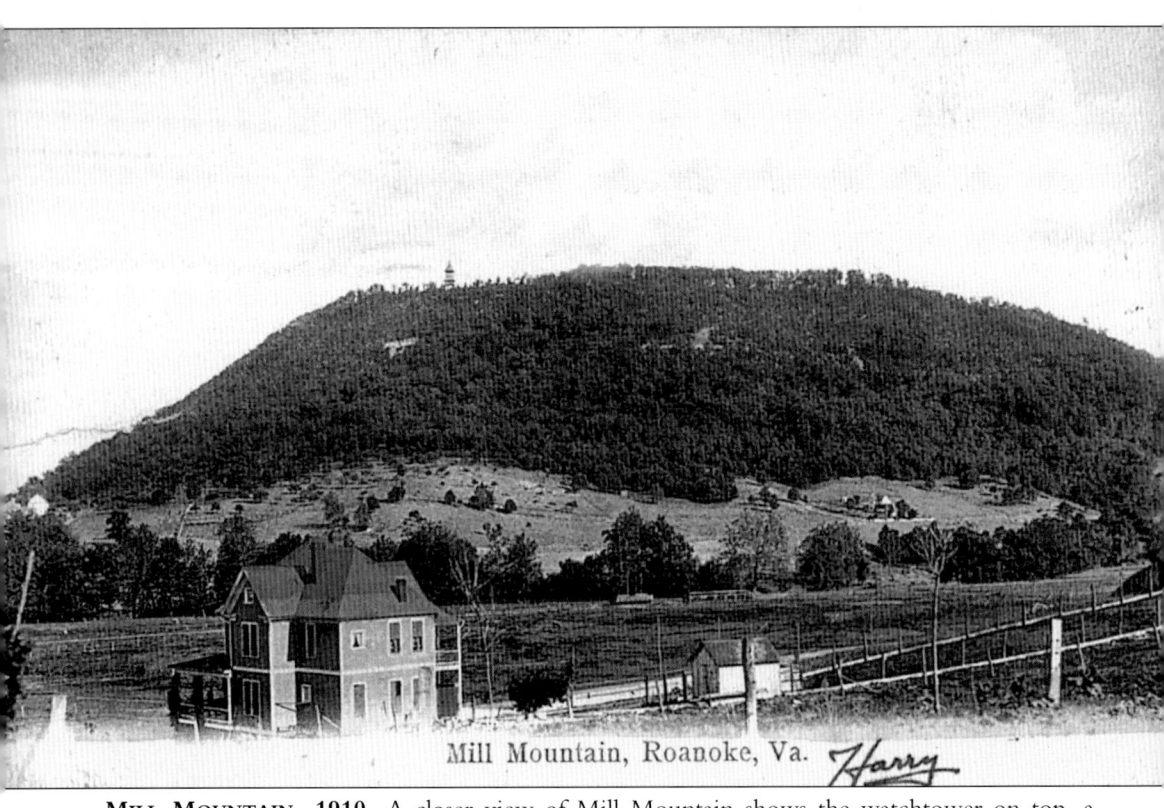

MILL MOUNTAIN, 1910. A closer view of Mill Mountain shows the watchtower on top, a "new" home, and farms.

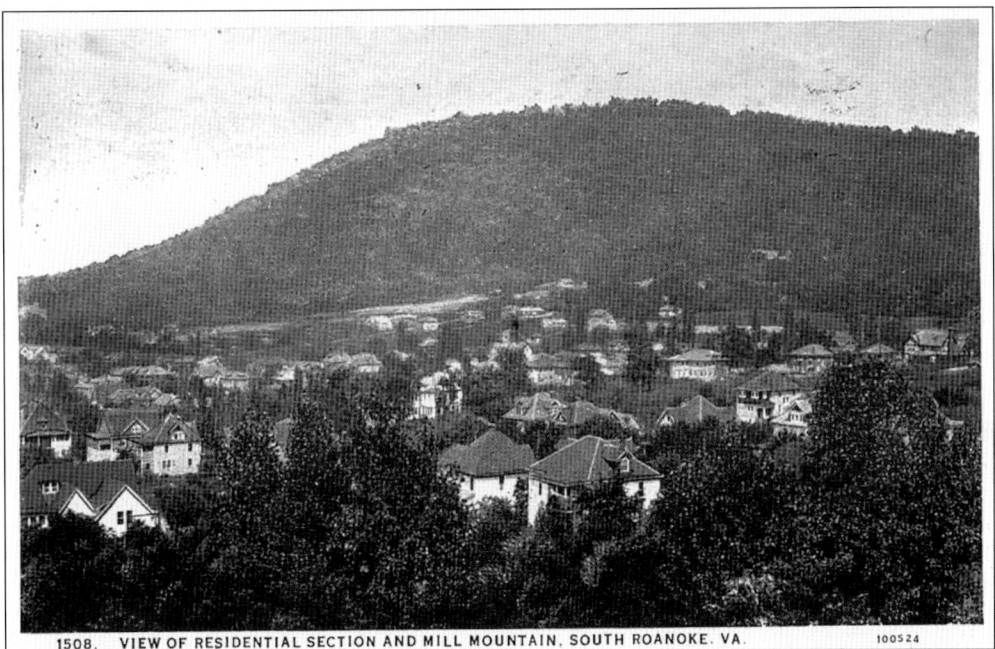

VIEW OF SOUTH ROANOKE, 1929. This card illustrates just how rapidly Roanoke was developing in the first two decades of the last century. This aerial view is of South Roanoke, which has gone from farmland to a residential area.

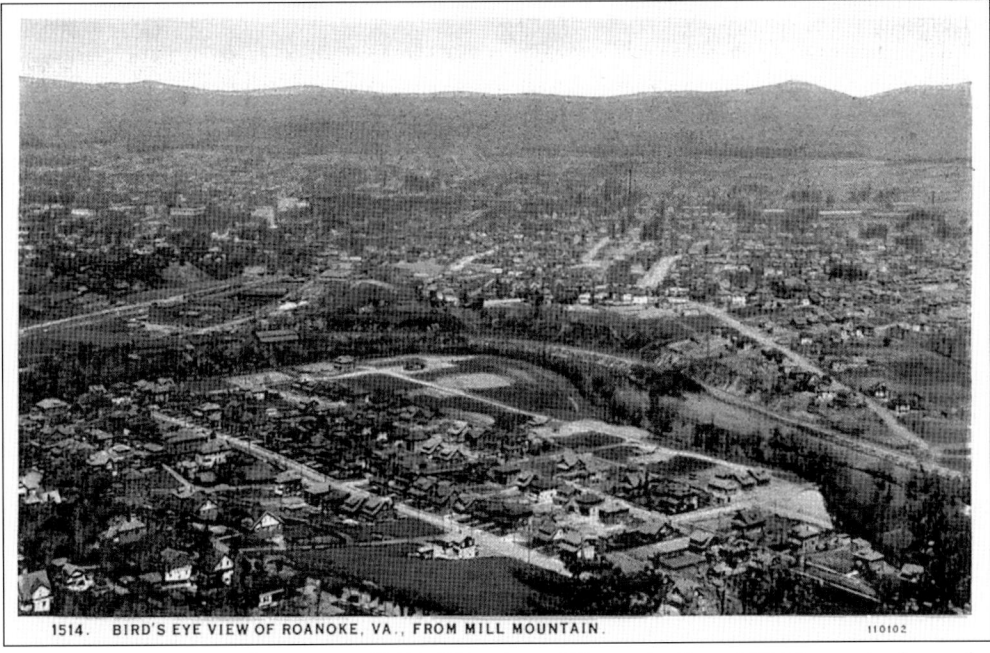

BIRD'S EYE VIEW OF ROANOKE, 1937. This view of Roanoke from Mill Mountain shows the emergence of business and housing. The Roanoke River, once flanked by farms, is now couched between neighborhoods and industries.

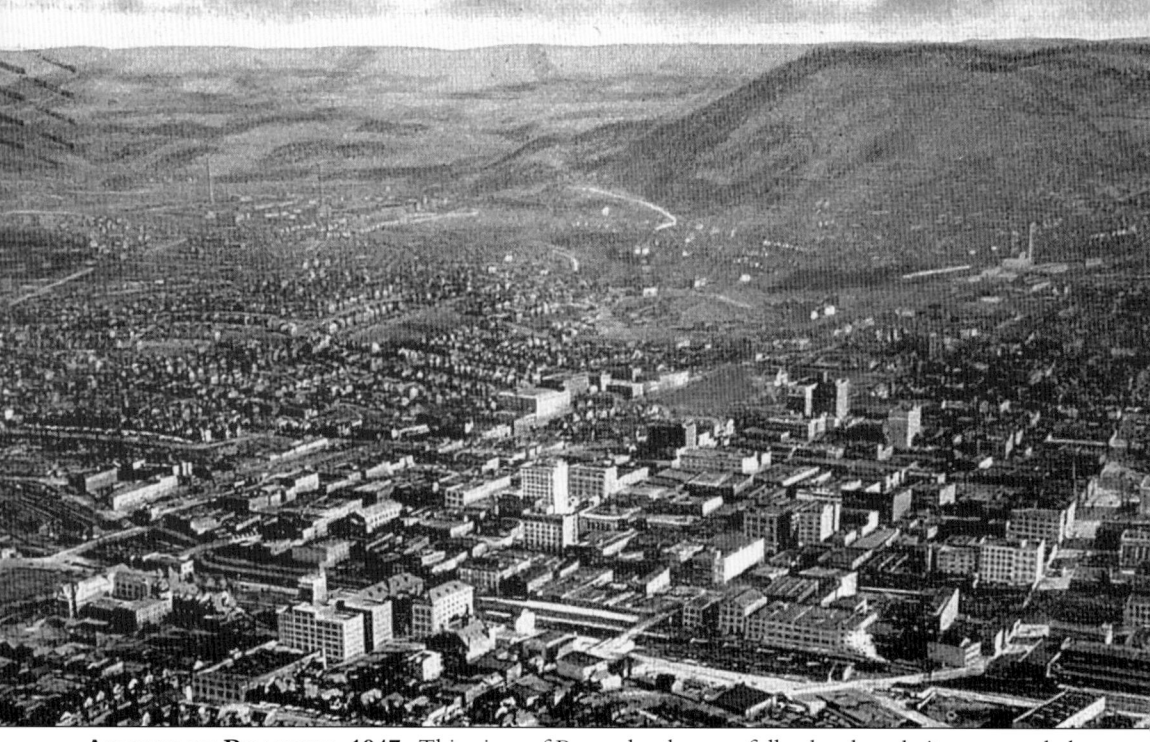

AIRVIEW OF ROANOKE, 1947. This view of Roanoke shows a fully-developed city, a crowded downtown skyline, and burgeoning residential sections.

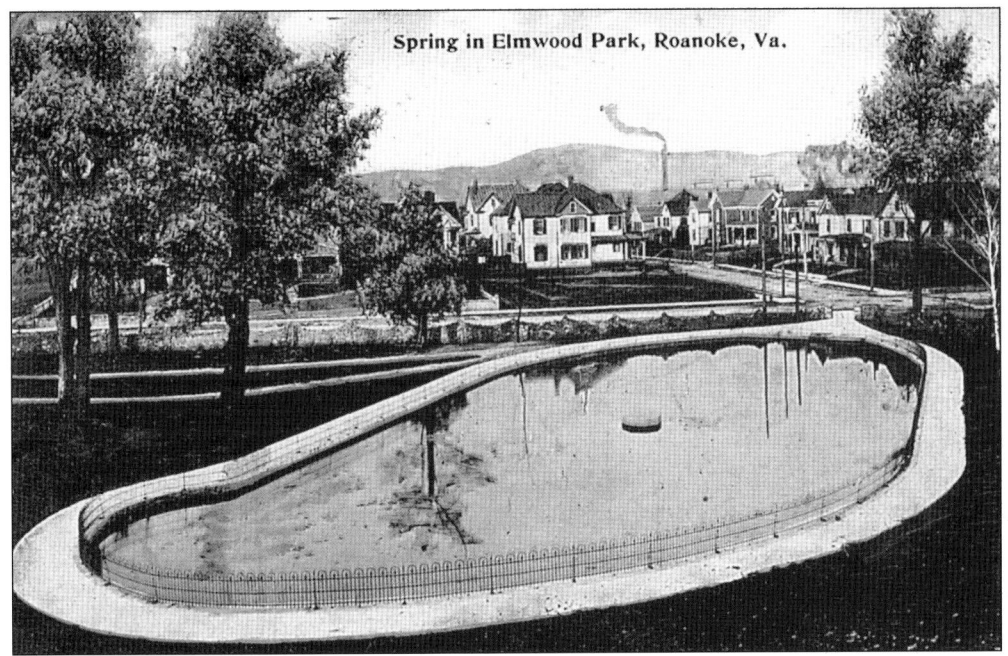

SPRING IN ELMWOOD PARK, 1913. Elmwood Park, Roanoke's oldest municipal park, once contained a spring-fed pond bordered by an intricate, wrought-iron fence.

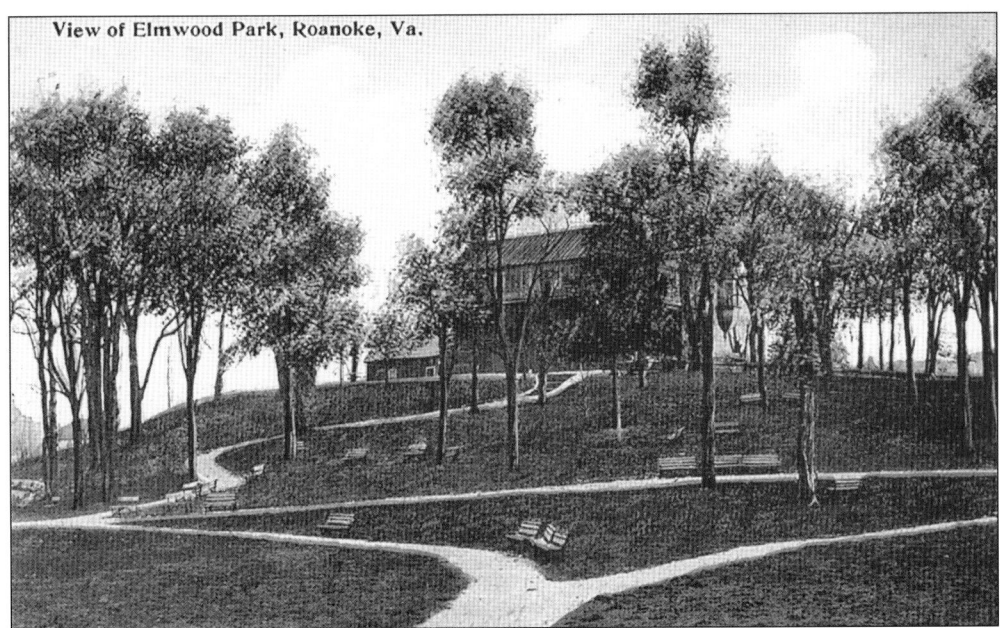

VIEW OF ELMWOOD PARK, 1913. This view of Elmwood Park shows the old Elmwood home for which the park was named.

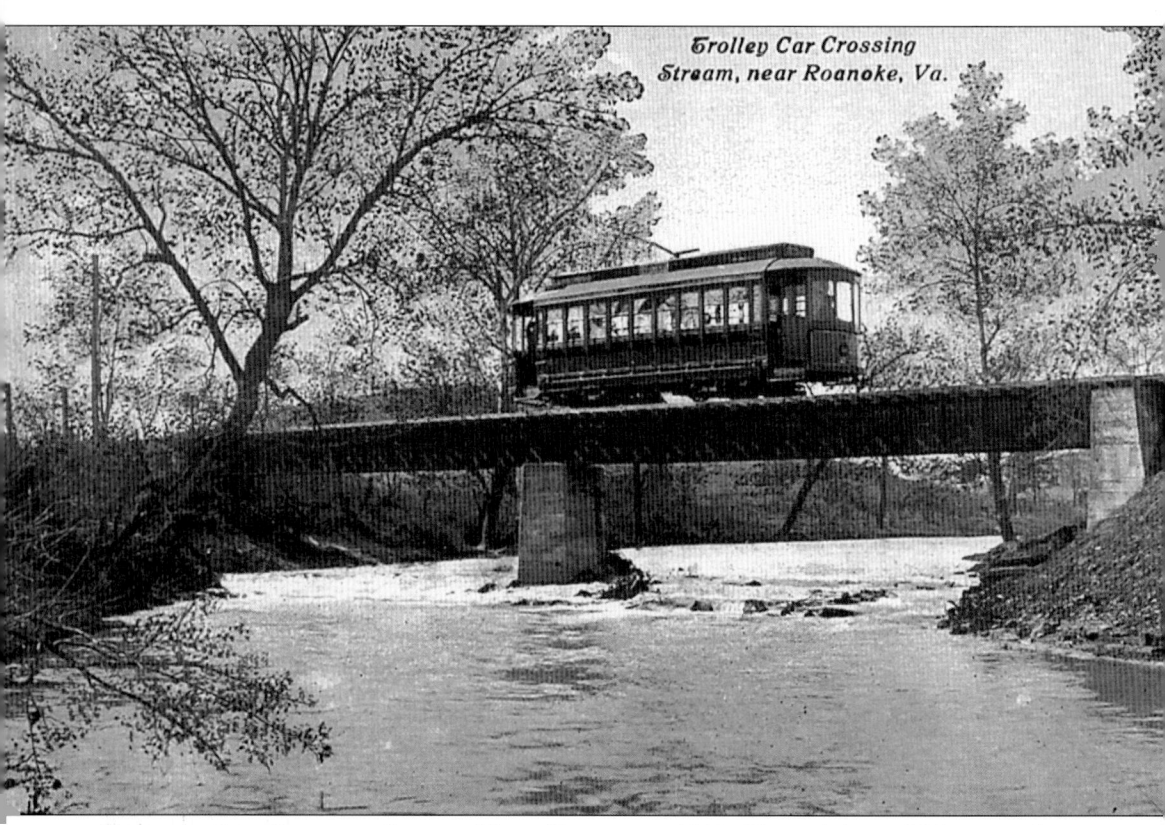

TROLLEY CAR CROSSING STREAM NEAR ROANOKE, 1912. The recipient of this postcard may have raised her eyebrow a bit. "Having a dandy time in Roanoke. Jamison and myself here together. You can guess the rest!"

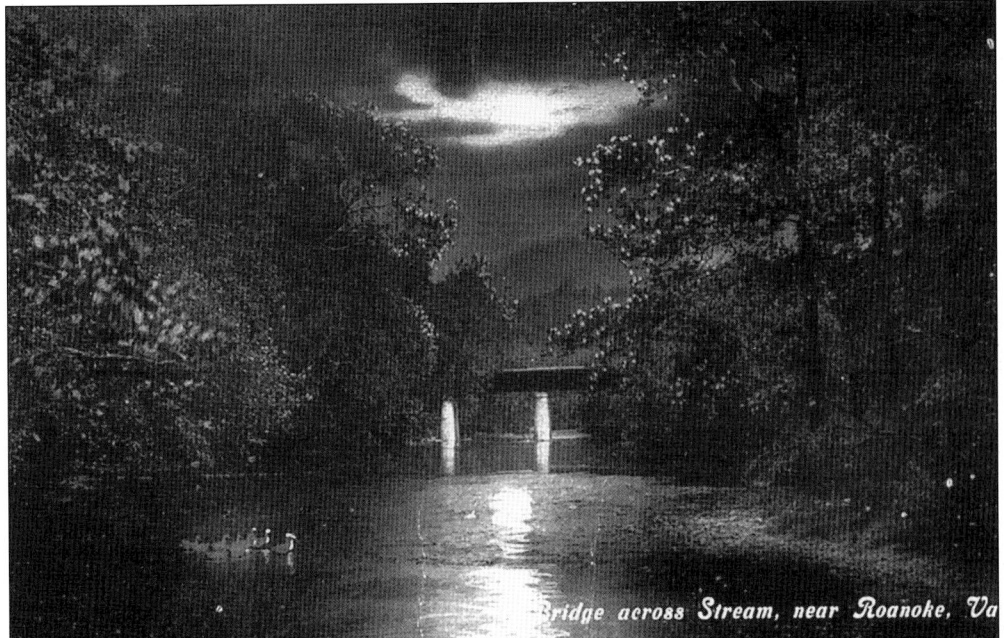

BRIDGE ACROSS STREAM NEAR ROANOKE, 1911. While the exact location depicted on this card in not known, the scene could be one of many in and around Roanoke with its river and many creeks and streams.

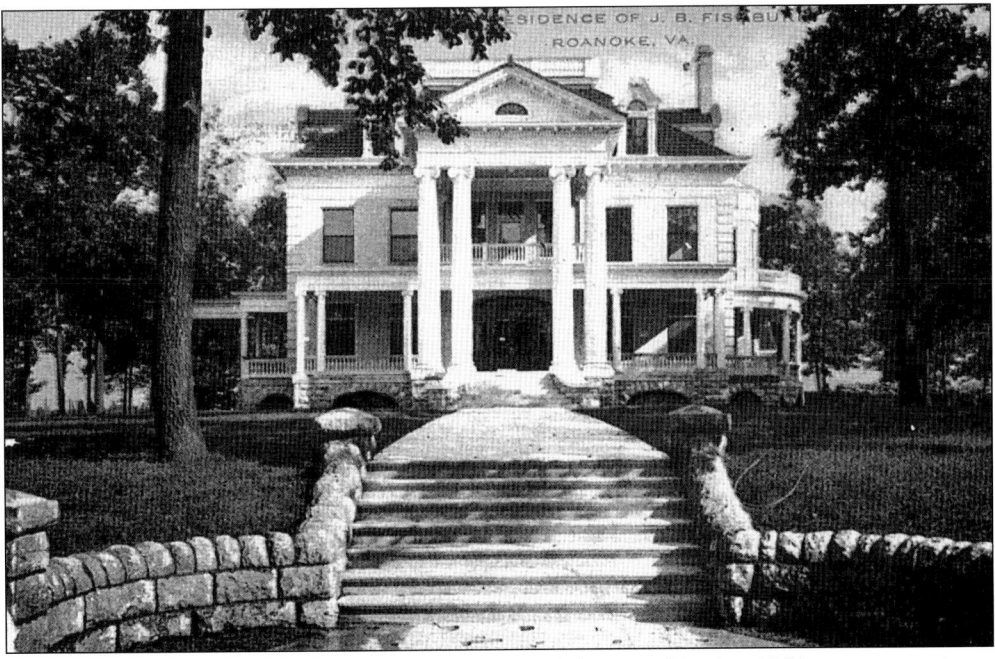

RESIDENCE OF J.B. FISHBURN, 1910. This grand home of Junius Fishburn, a prominent Roanoke citizen, bespeaks the wealth acquired by many of Roanoke's most industrious and creative businessmen. The home, known as "Mountain View," is now the property of the city and is operated as community center.

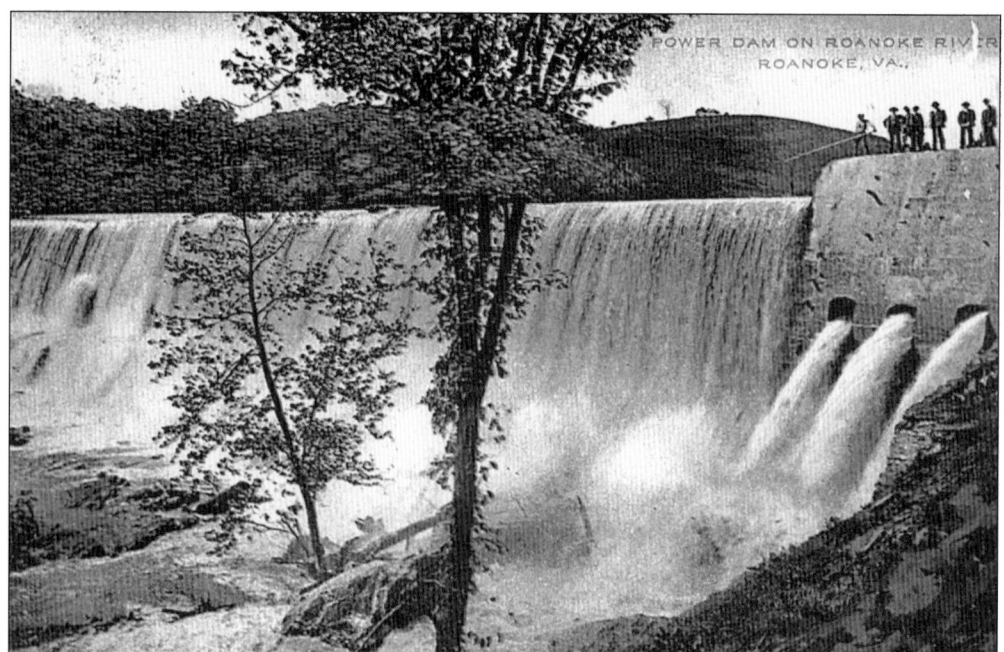

POWER DAM ON ROANOKE RIVER, 1911. This power dam was completed in 1906 and served to provide electricity to the citizens of Roanoke. Roanokers also found that the dam created a nice spot to boat and fish.

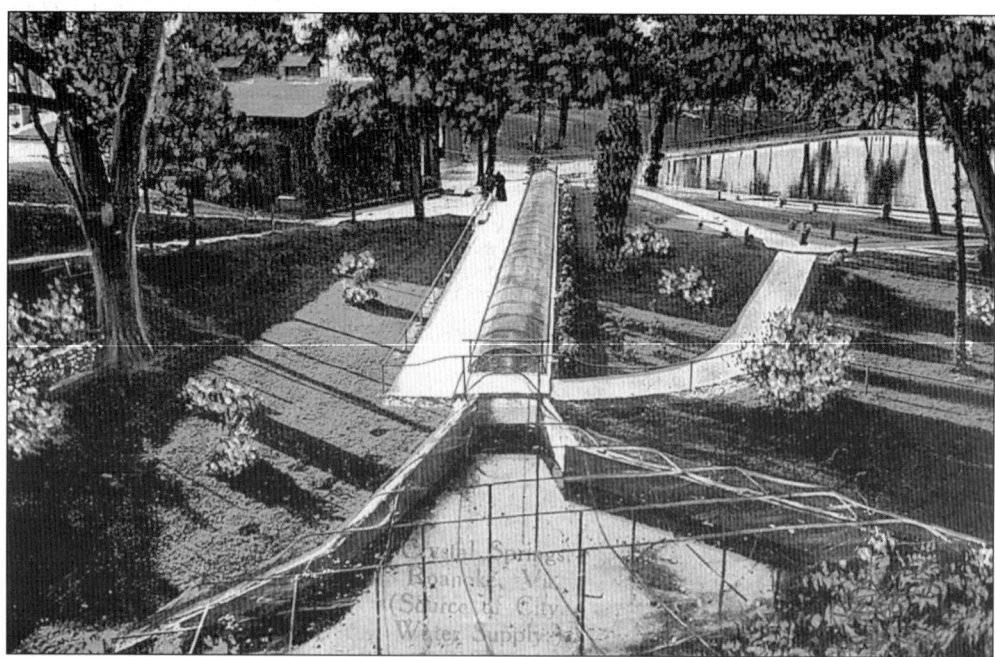

CRYSTAL SPRINGS, 1915. Although the Roanoke River flowed through the city, Roanoke's main water supply was Crystal Spring. The intricate channels and collecting pond also made for a nice park.

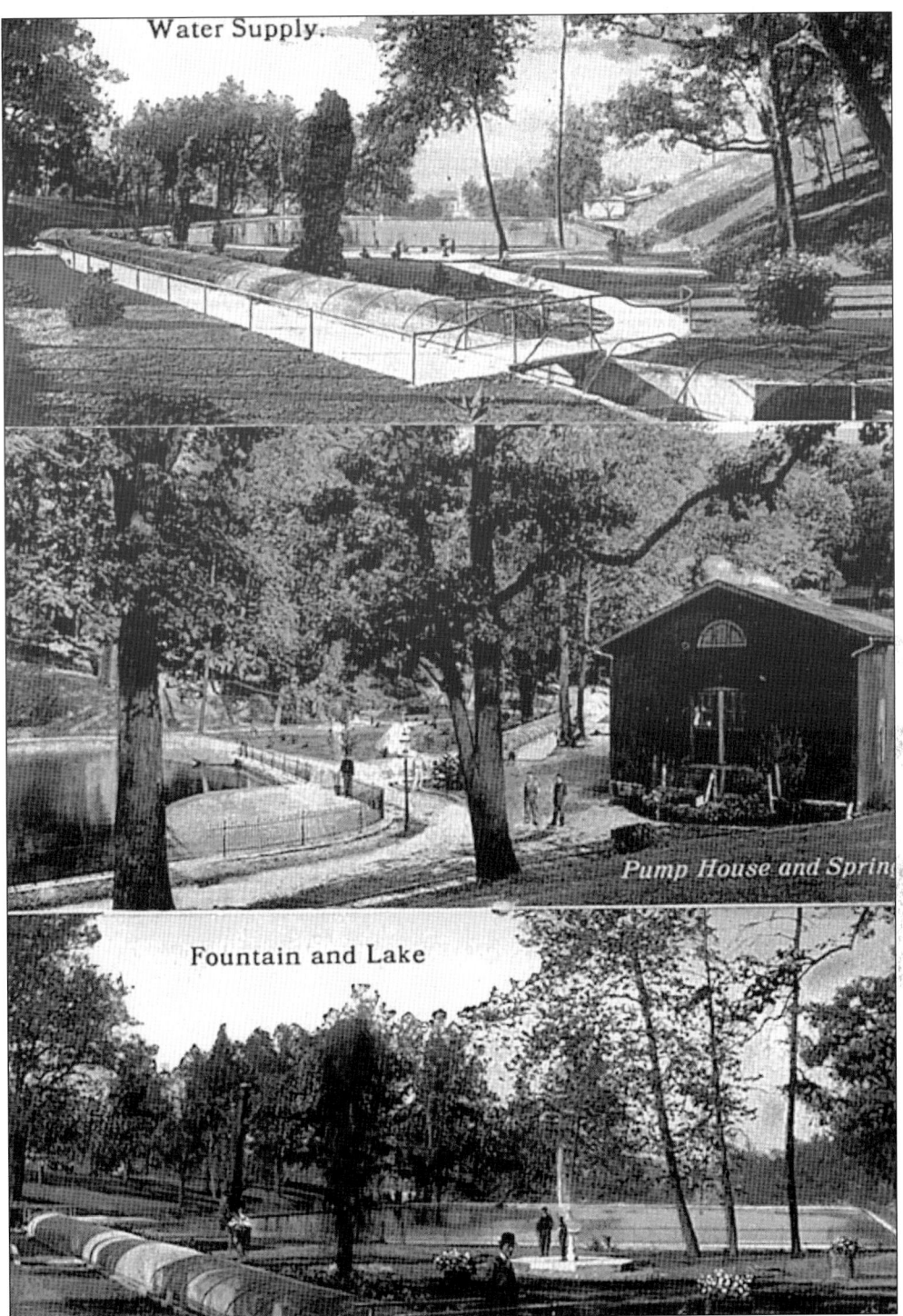

SCENES AT CRYSTAL SPRING, 1915. This three-view card shows (beginning at top) the Crystal Spring pond and channel, the pump house, and the fountain and lake. While the lake is no longer in existence, Crystal Spring remains a vital source of water for Roanoke City.

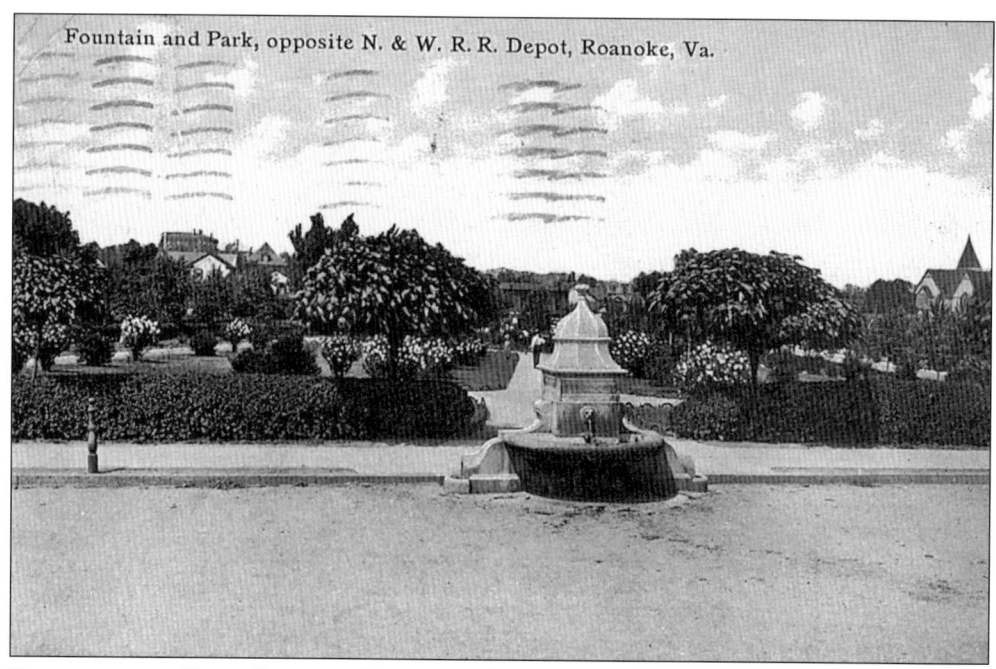

FOUNTAIN AND PARK OPPOSITE RAILROAD DEPOT, 1911. This shows the landscaped gardens across from the Norfolk & Western Depot, adjoining the entrance to the Hotel Roanoke. The fountain is the Kimball Memorial Fountain.

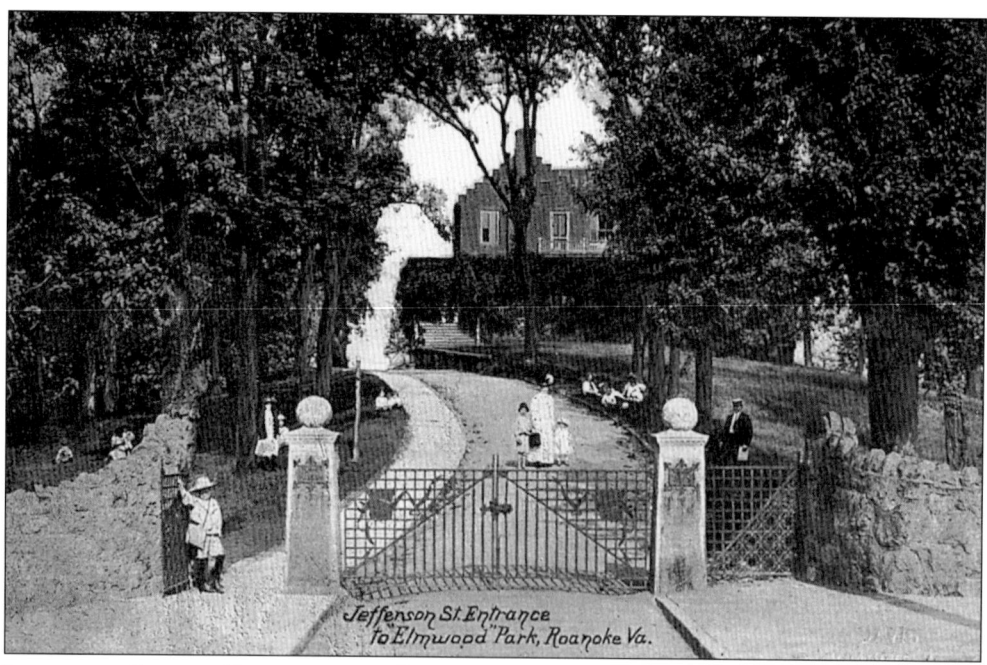

JEFFERSON STREET ENTRANCE TO ELMWOOD PARK, 1915. The gated entrance and drive leading to the Elmwood home provided an air of distinction to Roanoke's downtown park.

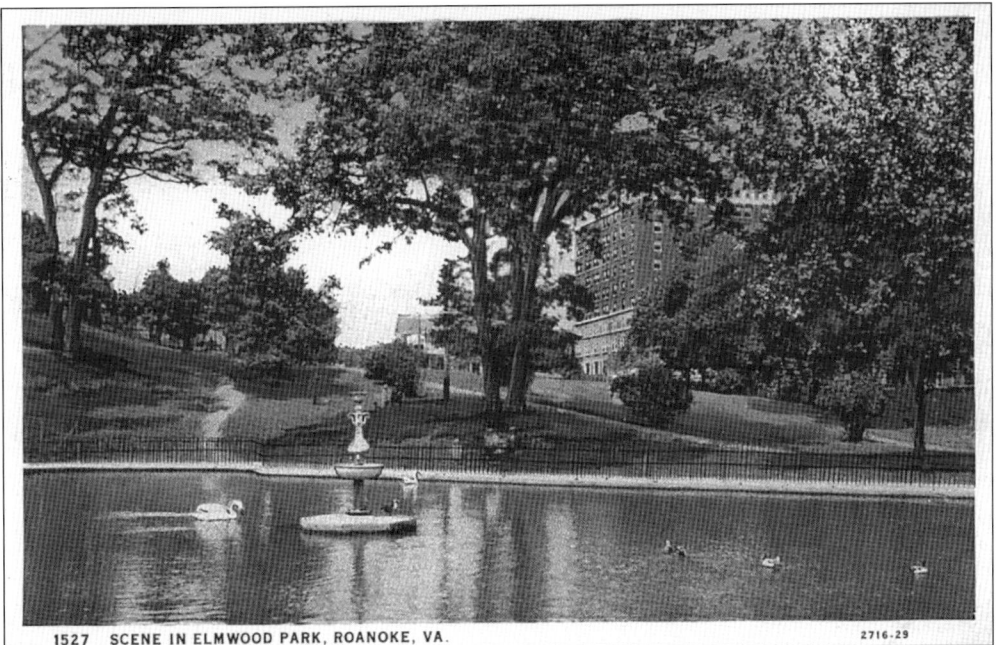

SCENE IN ELMWOOD PARK, 1925. This card shows the pond in Elmwood Park. The Patrick Henry Hotel is in the background. The pond was drained to make room for the construction of the city's main library.

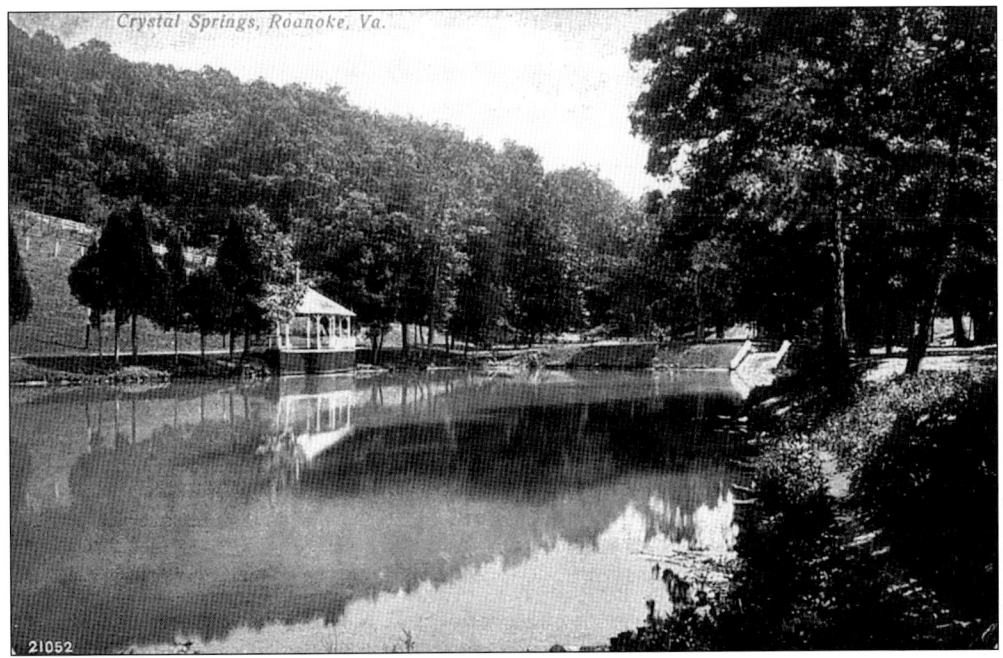

CRYSTAL SPRING, 1910. This is another view showing Crystal Spring Lake and its surroundings, including a gazebo.

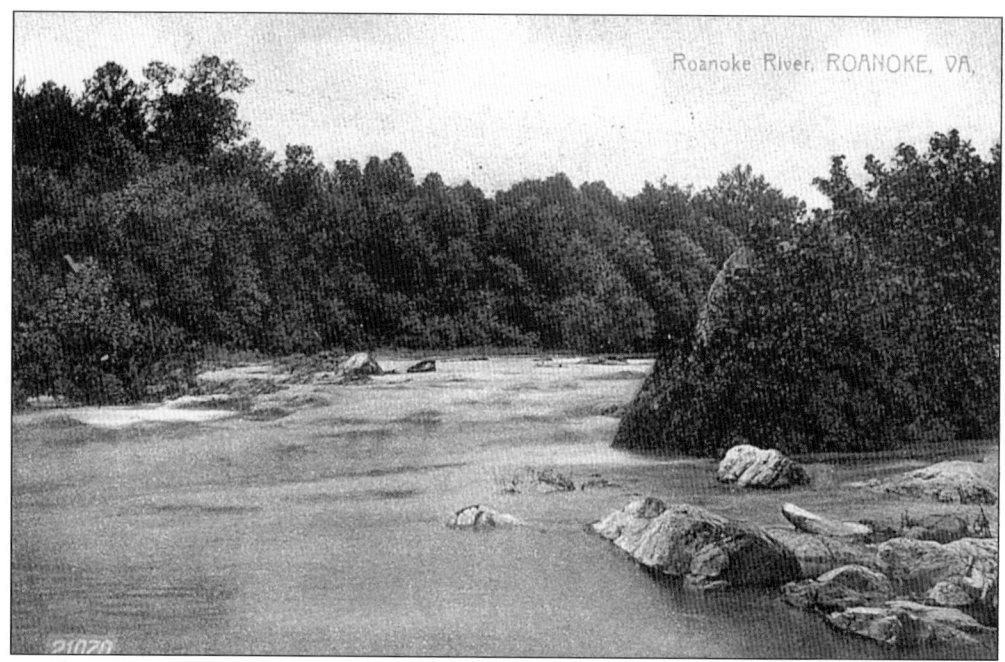

ROANOKE RIVER, 1908. The Roanoke River has provided many natural vistas for relaxing, fishing, and canoeing.

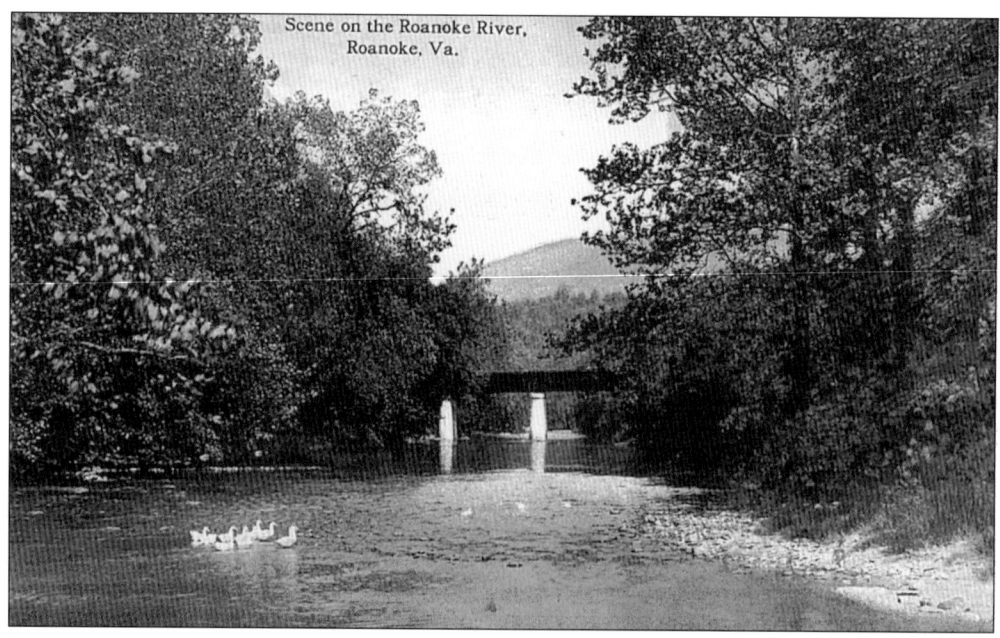

SCENE OF THE ROANOKE RIVER, 1910. A bridge spans the river while ducks below enjoy a swim.

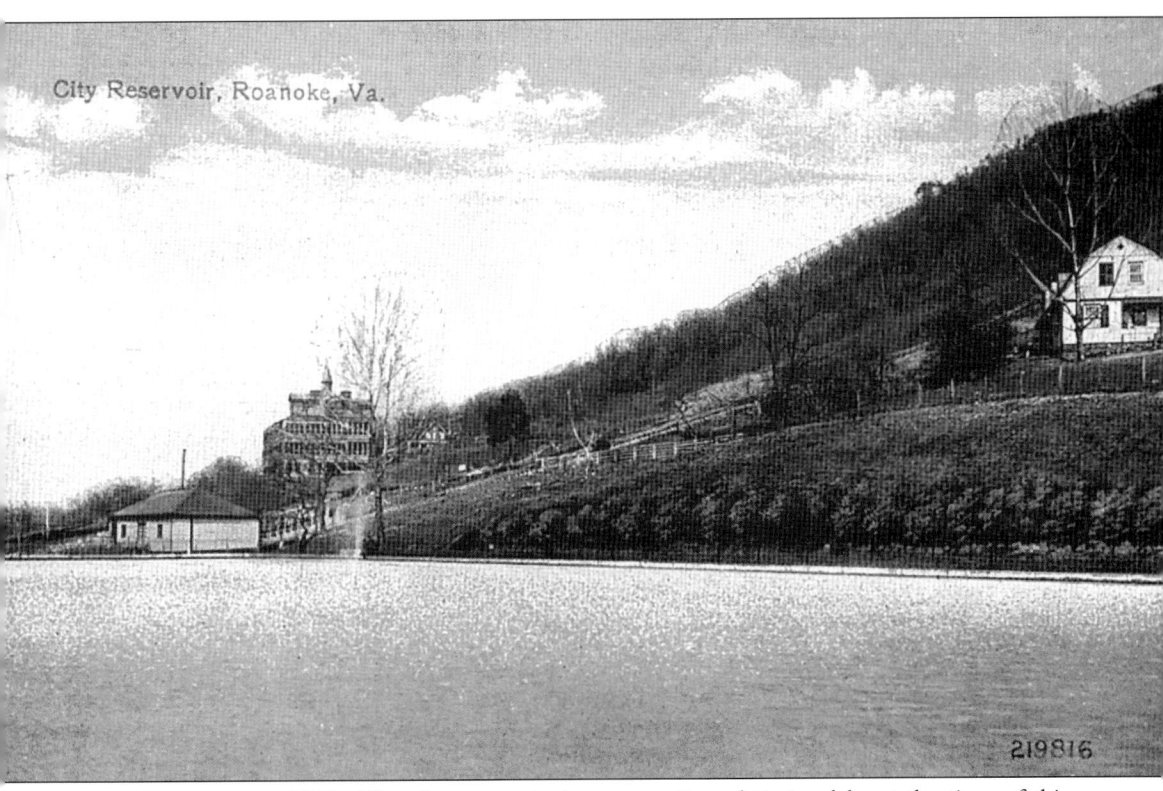

CITY RESERVOIR, 1908. The city reservoir, known as Crystal Spring lake at the time of this postcard, was at the base of Mill Mountain. In the background, the city hospital is visible.

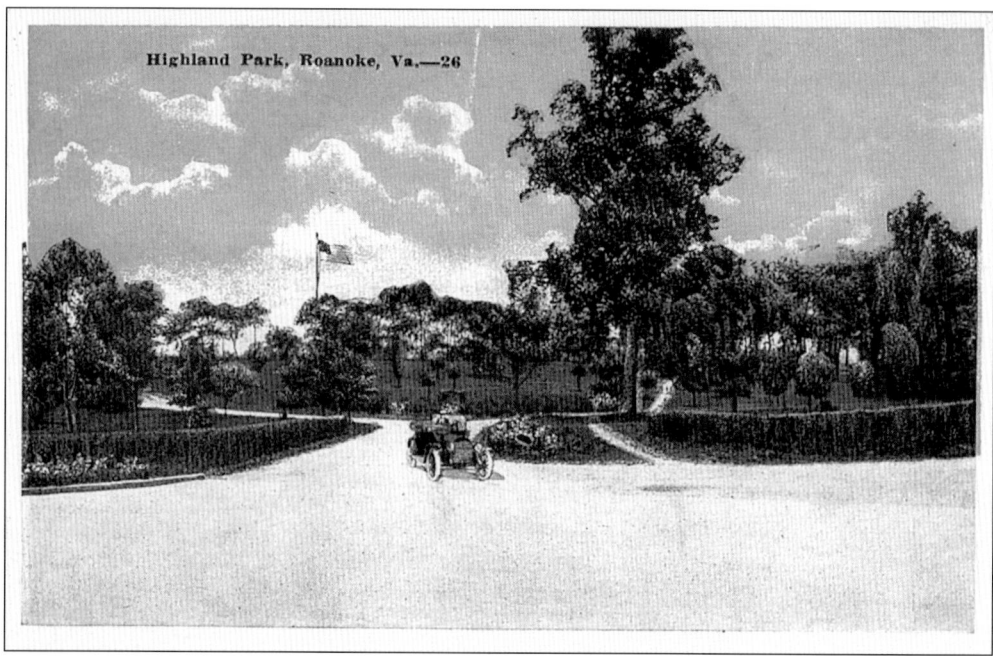

HIGHLAND PARK, 1914. Highland Park was one of Roanoke's first parks in a residential section. The land on which the park is located was originally the Gish farm. The city acquired the property in 1901 for $10,000.

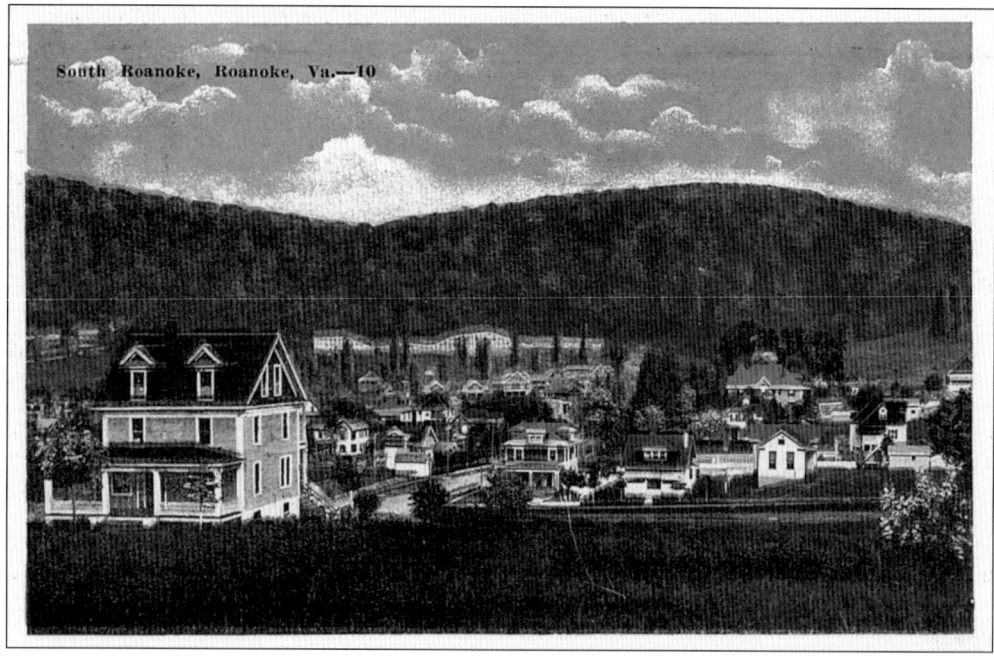

SOUTH ROANOKE, 1927. Shown here are some of the early homes in South Roanoke. The horizontal white structure in the background is the roller coaster located in Mountain Park.

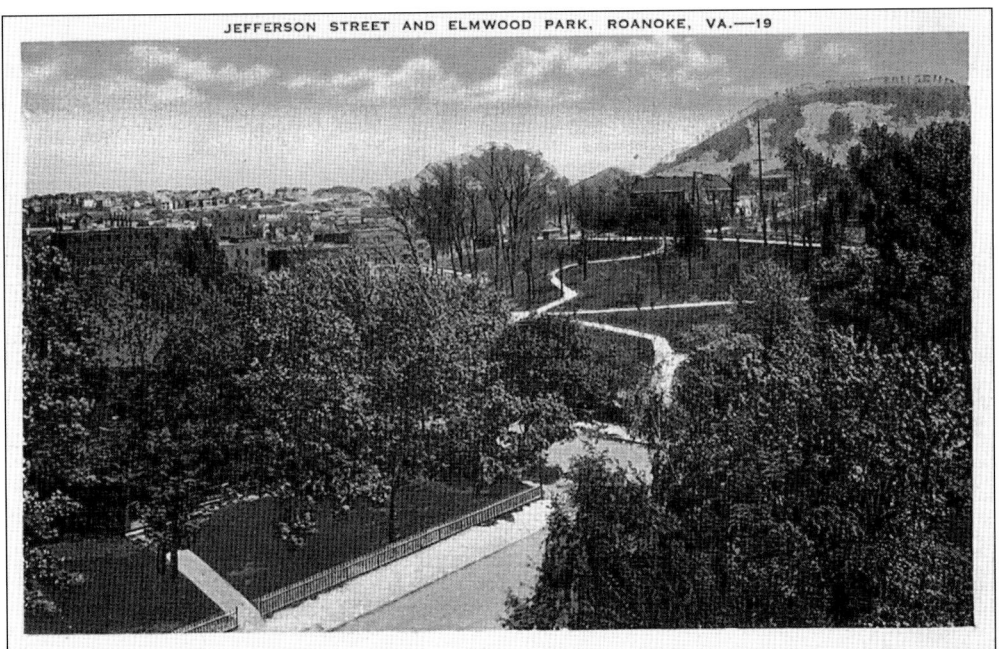

JEFFERSON STREET AND ELMWOOD PARK, 1943. This postcard provides a view from the top of the Patrick Henry Hotel showing most of Elmwood Park. Notice the park is in two sections and the Elmwood home sits on a knoll in the background.

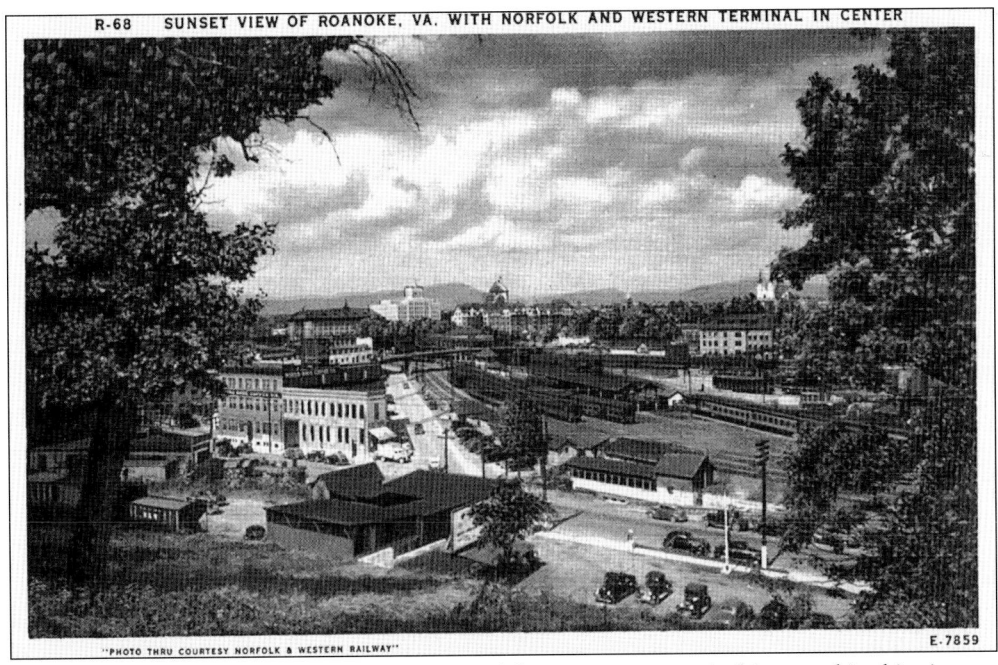

SUNSET VIEW OF ROANOKE, 1945. The Norfolk & Western terminal is central in this picture of Roanoke at dusk.

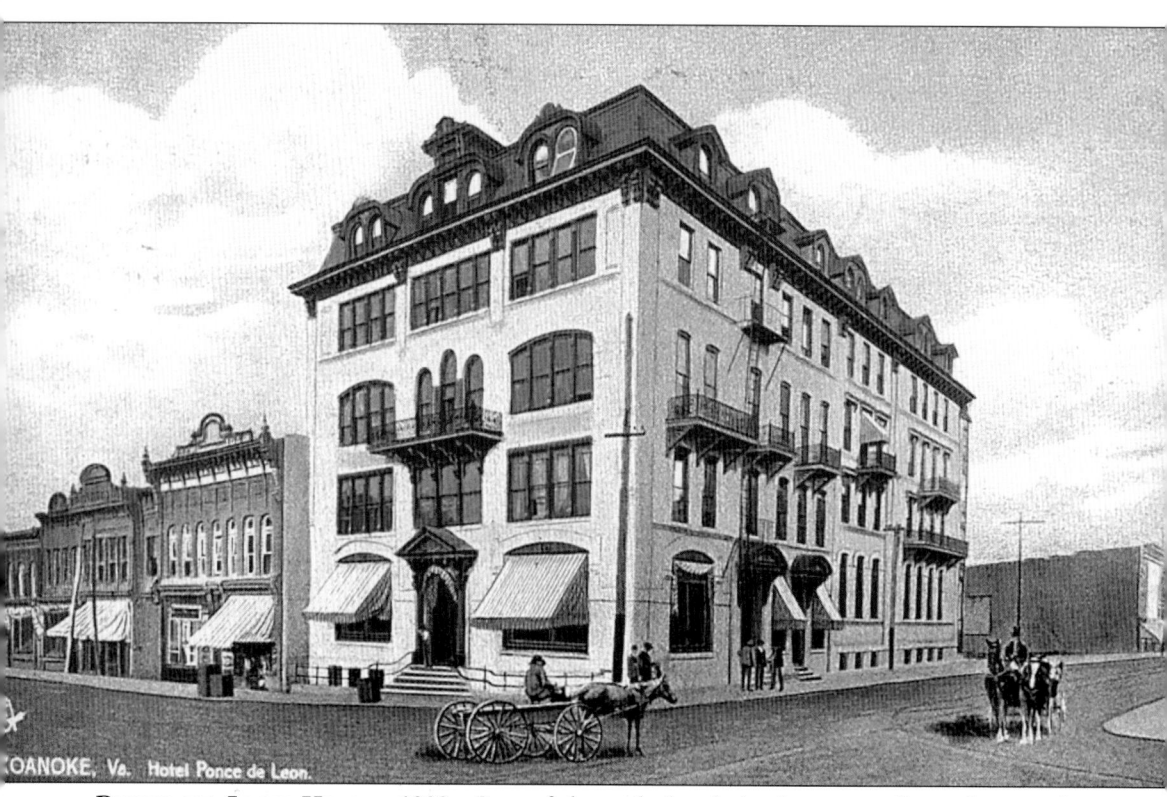

PONCE DE LEON HOTEL, 1908. One of the early hotels in downtown Roanoke was the Ponce de Leon. Graced with wrought-iron balconies and large dormer windows, the Ponce de Leon opened on Thanksgiving Day in 1890 and was, at that time, the tallest building in the city—6 stories with 120 rooms.

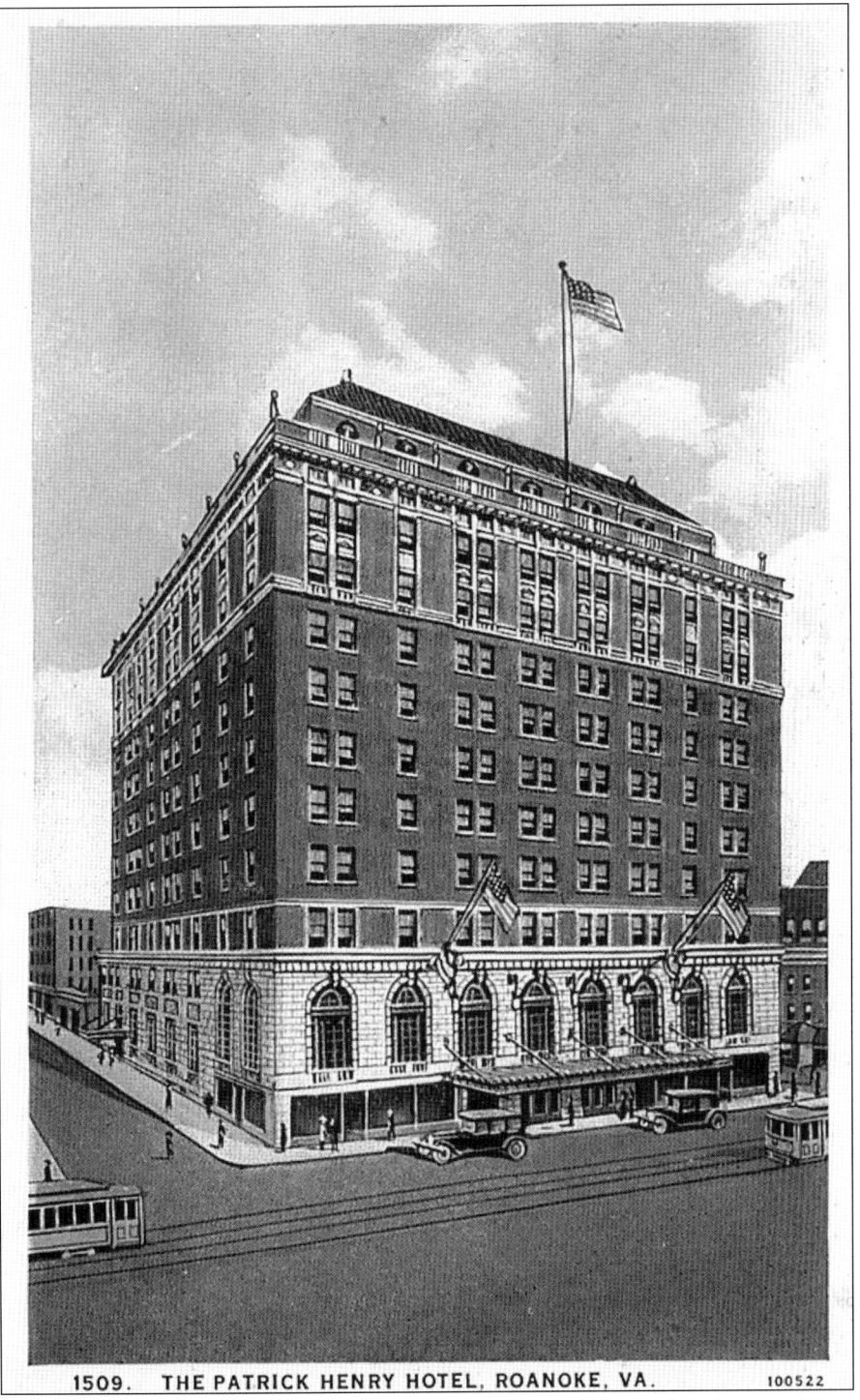

THE PATRICK HENRY HOTEL, 1930. The Patrick Henry Hotel opened its doors on November 10, 1925, with a grand reception for 500 invited guests. The hotel had been financed through a "community subscription" program led by Col. James Woods.

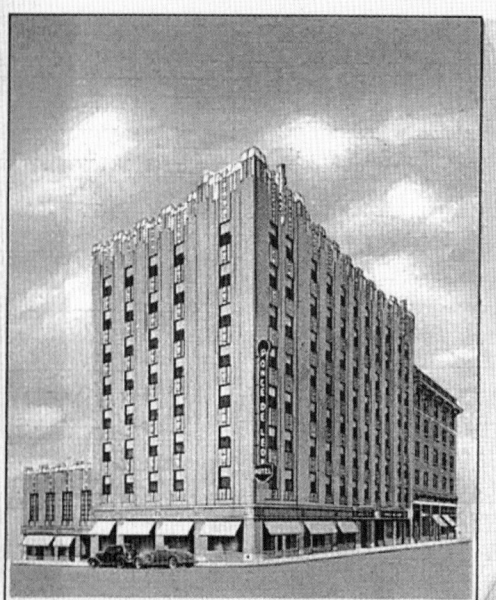
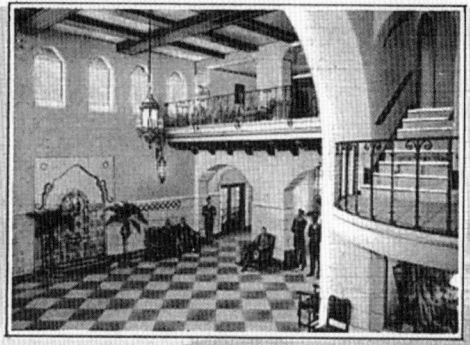
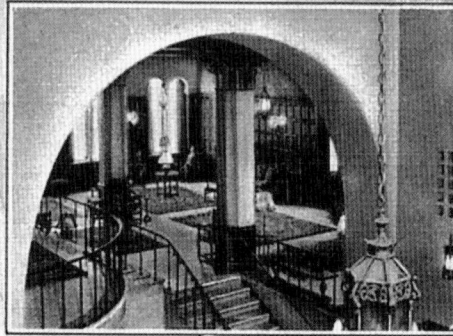

PONCE DE LEON HOTEL, 1936. One of numerous cards published for the Ponce de Leon Hotel during its years of operation, this one boasted "within easy walking distance of business and shopping district and of theaters" and "200 beautiful outside rooms each with individual bath, circulating ice water, and electric fan."

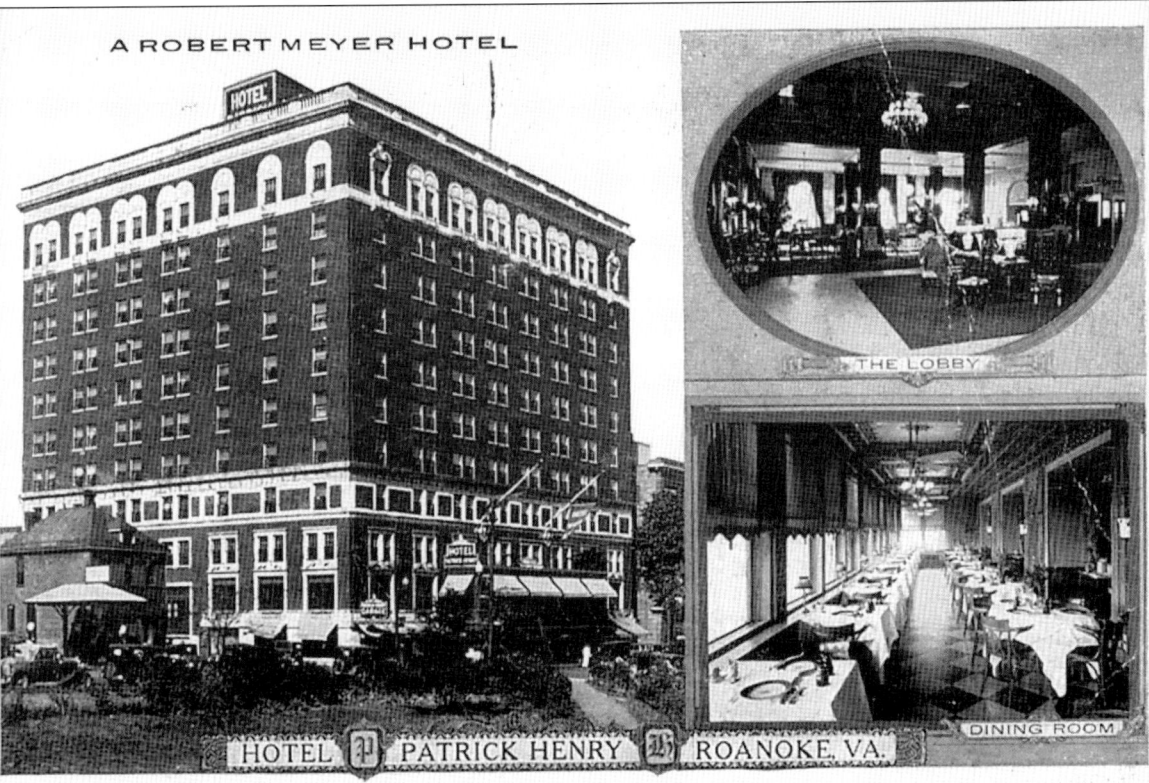

THE PATRICK HENRY HOTEL, 1925. This postcard of the Patrick Henry Hotel, managed by Fay Thomas, promoted its initial offerings to prospective visitors. The card read, "400 rooms with bath, ceiling fan, circulating ice water, and garage direct entrance to lobby."

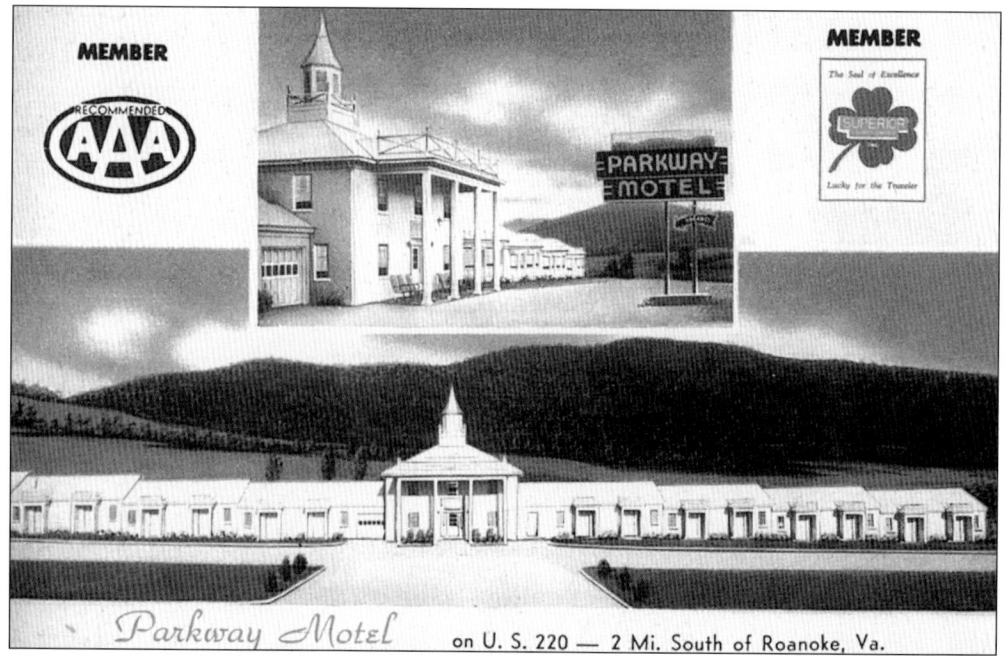

Parkway Motel, 1955. Before the interstate highway system there were numerous motels located on the main highways leading into Roanoke. The Parkway Motel, now demolished, sat on Route 220 and had 20 rooms and air foam mattresses!

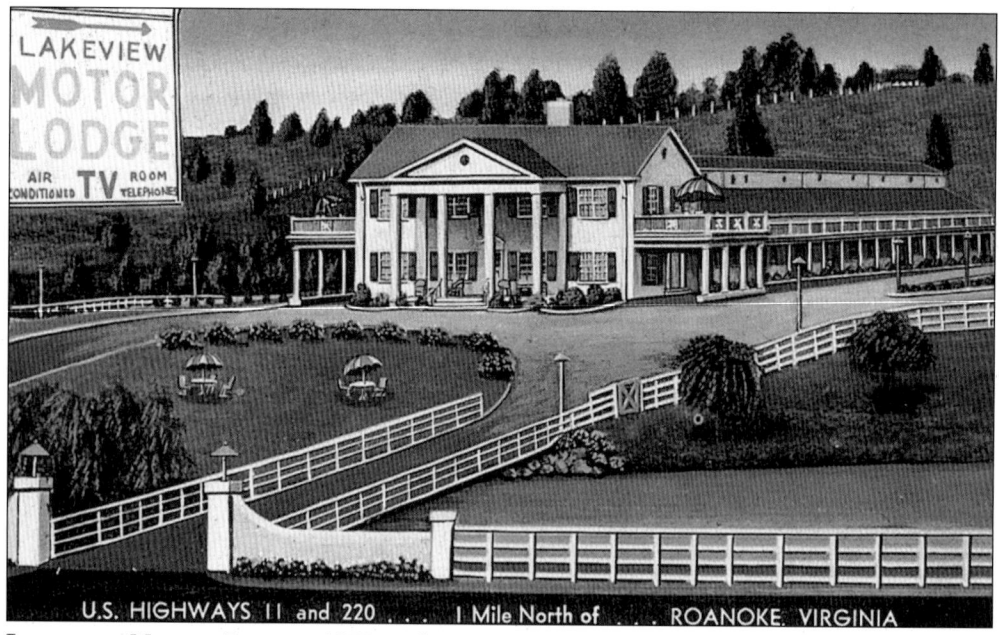

Lakeview Motor Lodge, 1958. Lakeview Motor Lodge on Route 11, now Williamson Road, had air-conditioned rooms with individual telephones. The pond and bridged entrance remain, but the main building of Lakeview was razed.

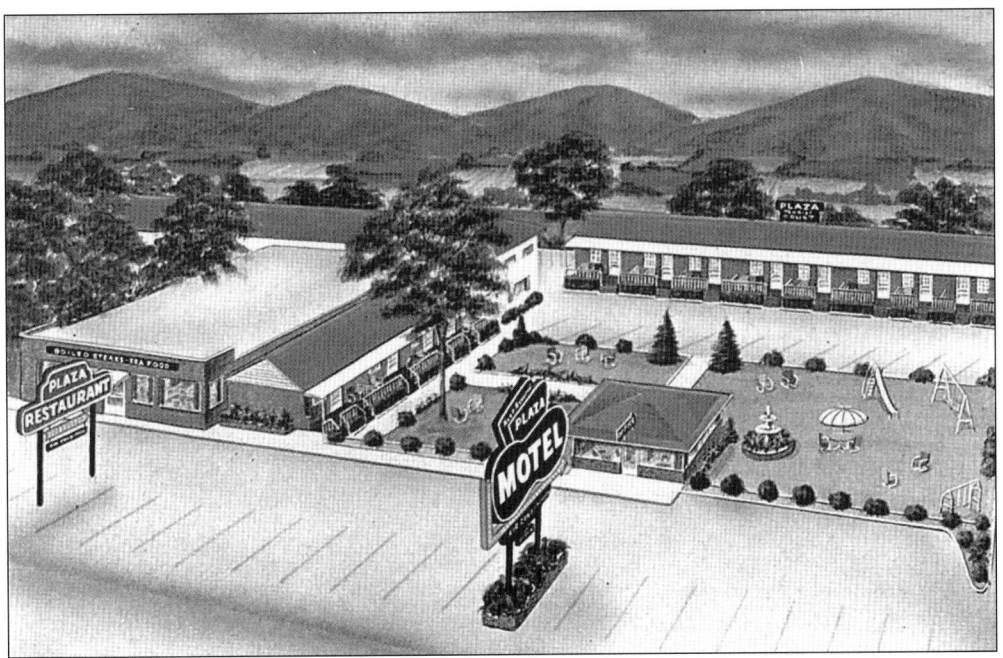

PLAZA MOTEL, 1960. Like many small motels, the Plaza sought to offer amenities for middle-income families. A playground, lawn, adjacent restaurant, and modest rates were its main attractions.

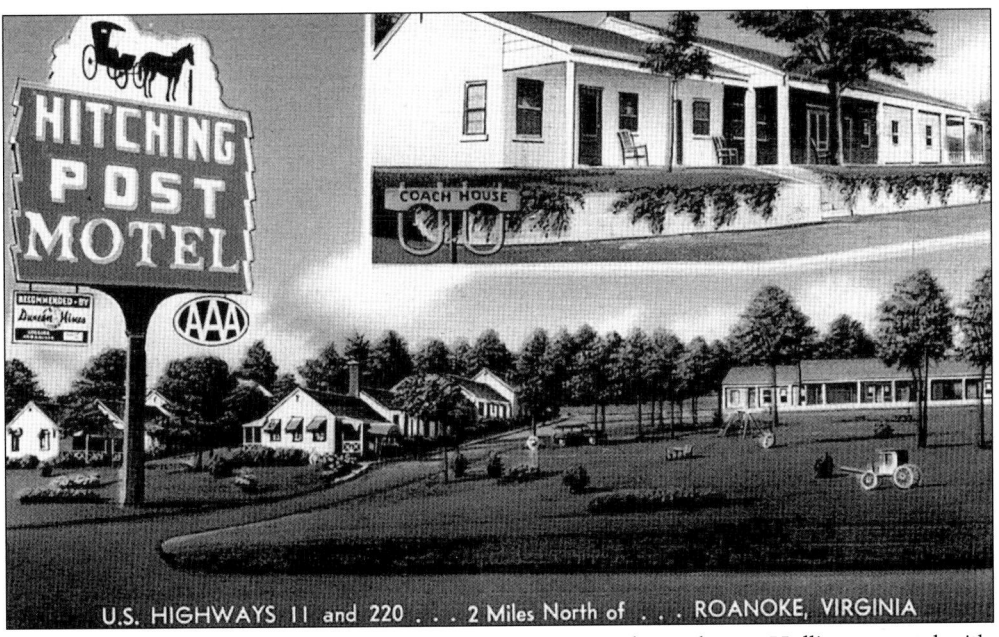

HITCHING POST MOTEL, 1958. The Hitching Post was located near Hollins on north side of the city. The Hitching Post, as its name suggests, sought to provide a woodsy setting for its guests.

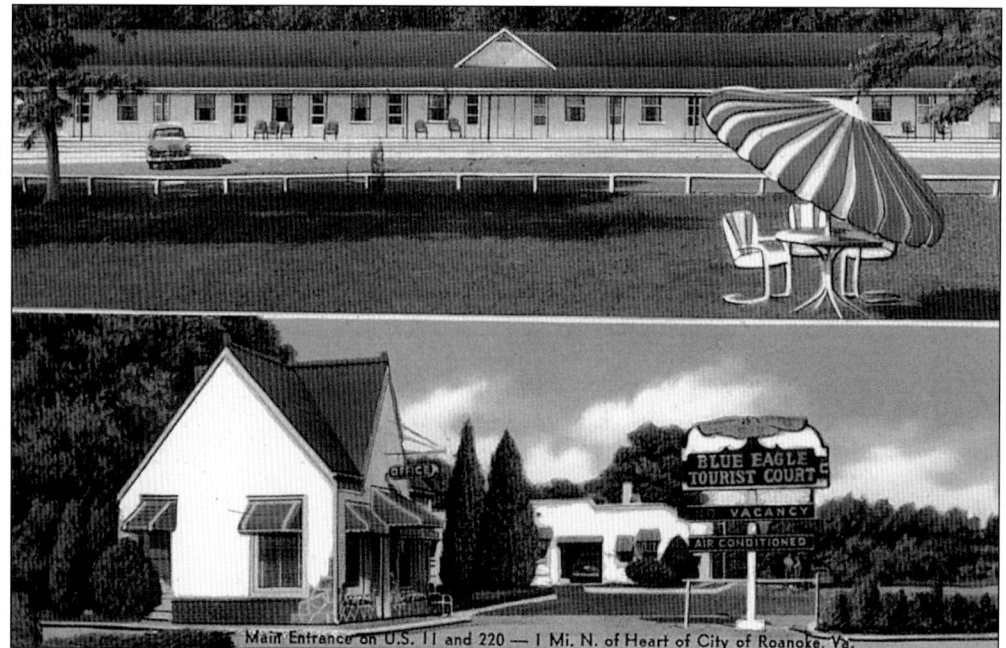

BLUE EAGLE TOURIST COURT, 1968. The Blue Eagle was one of the motels offering the unique services of individual garages for some guest rooms. It had 22 units and was one mile north on U.S. 11 from downtown Roanoke.

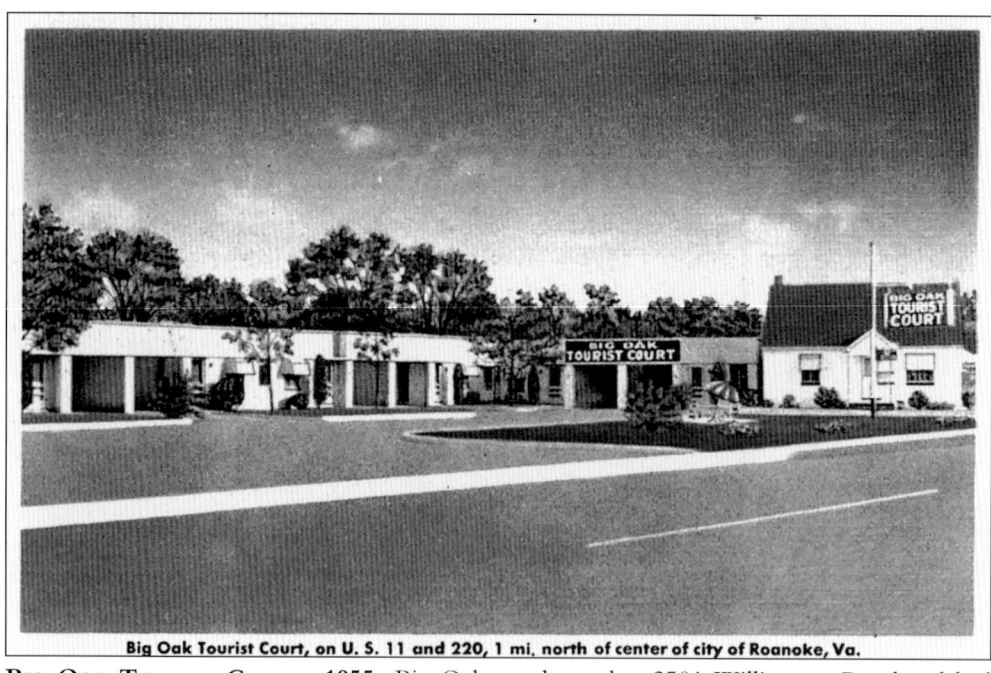

BIG OAK TOURIST COURT, 1955. Big Oak was located at 2501 Williamson Road and had "insulated cottages with tile baths."

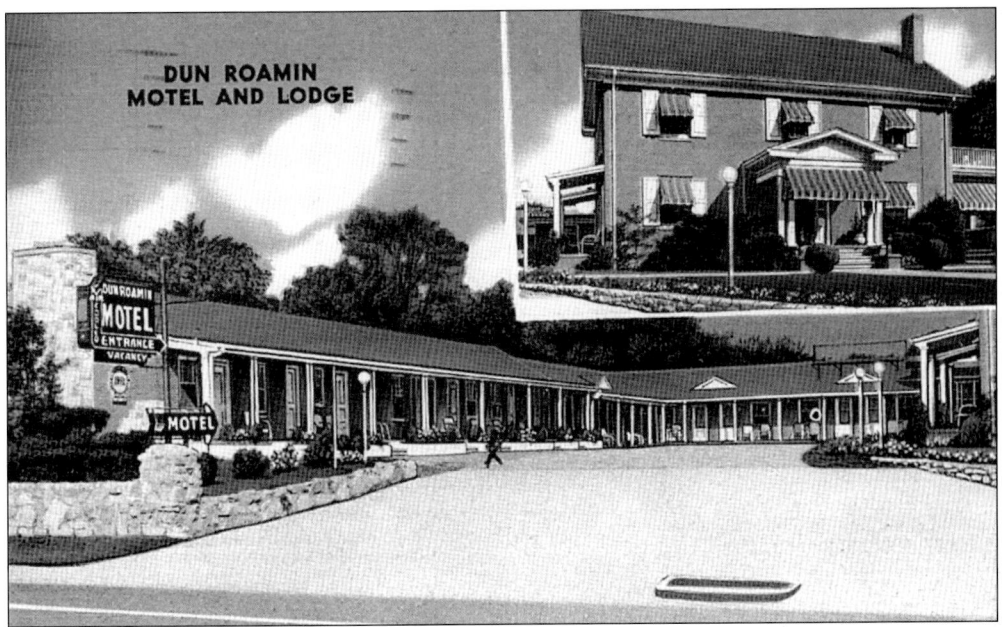

DUN ROAMIN MOTEL AND LODGE, 1959. The Dun Roamin Motel and Lodge's address was 1803 Williamson Road. Guests Herb and Erma used this card to update a friend about their travels. "Having a wonderful drive, and it sure was hot today (July 17), almost roasted. We're headed for Asheville, NC, tomorrow."

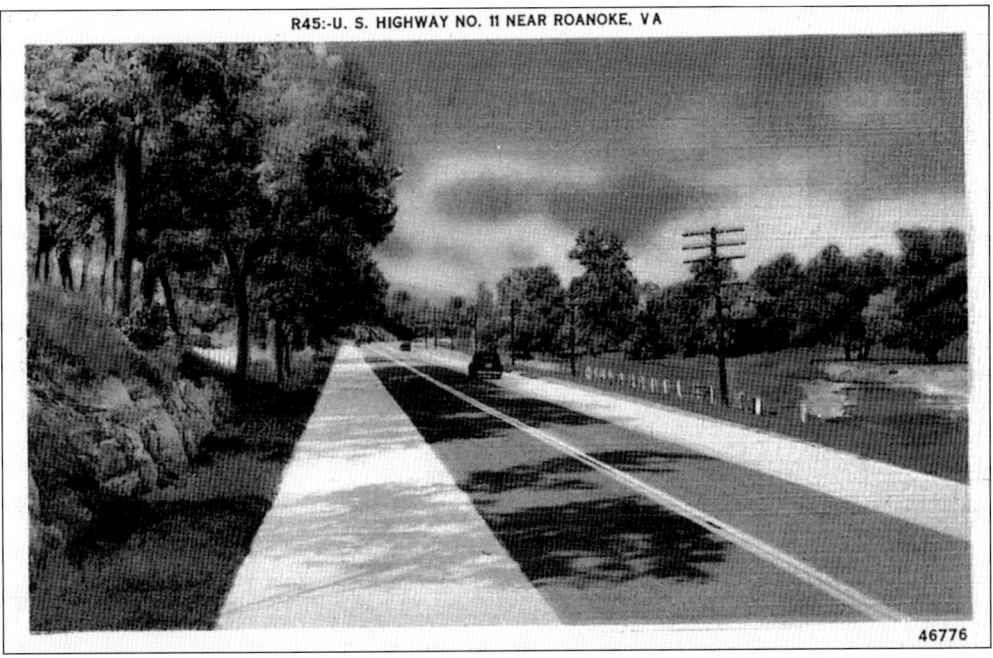

U.S. HIGHWAY 11, 1945. Although inconvenient by today's interstate standards, Route 11 was one of the most traveled and scenic highways in Western Virginia. This shows the northern approach of the highway to Roanoke.

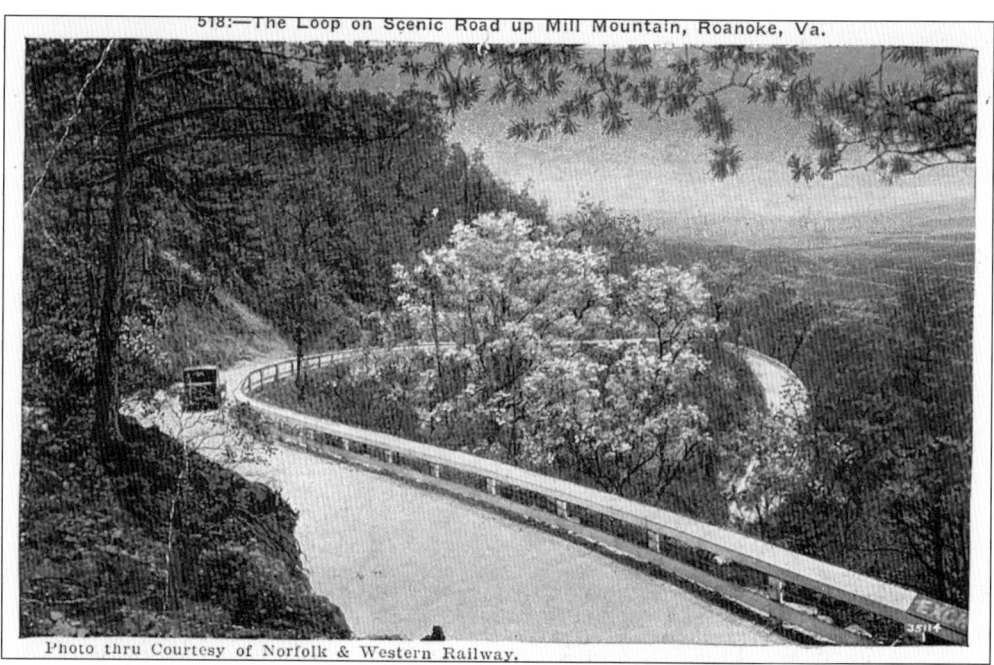

LOOP ON THE SCENIC ROAD UP MILL MOUNTAIN, 1931. The scenic loop up Mill Mountain provided a breath-taking view of the city. Mill Mountain stands 2,000 feet above sea level and is surrounded by the city.

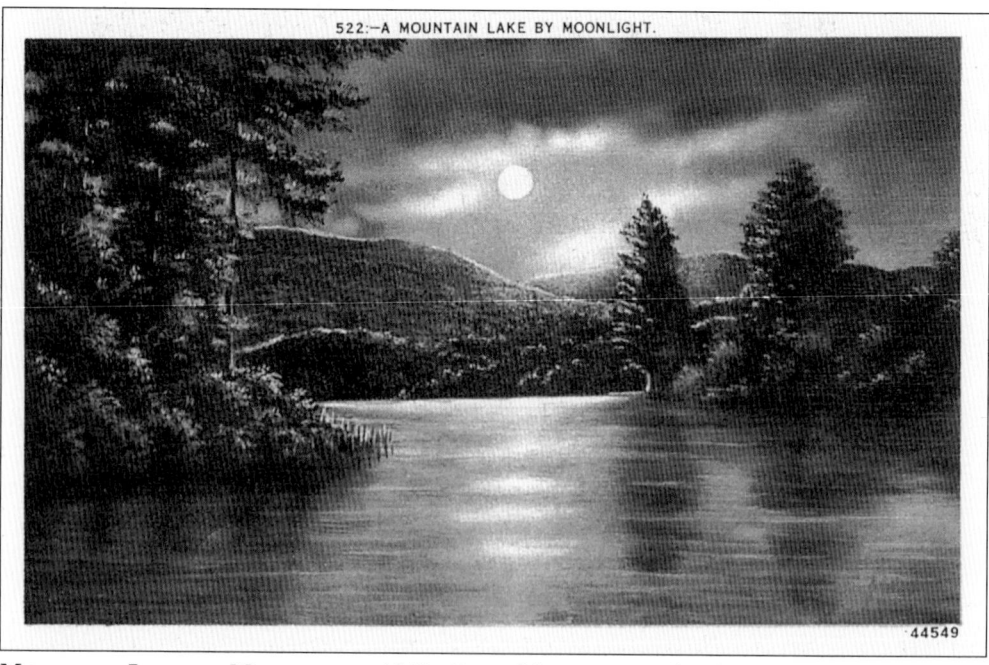

MOUNTAIN LAKE BY MOONLIGHT, 1940. One of the many weekend trips made by Roanokers was to Mountain Lake, as seen here in the glimmer of moonlight.

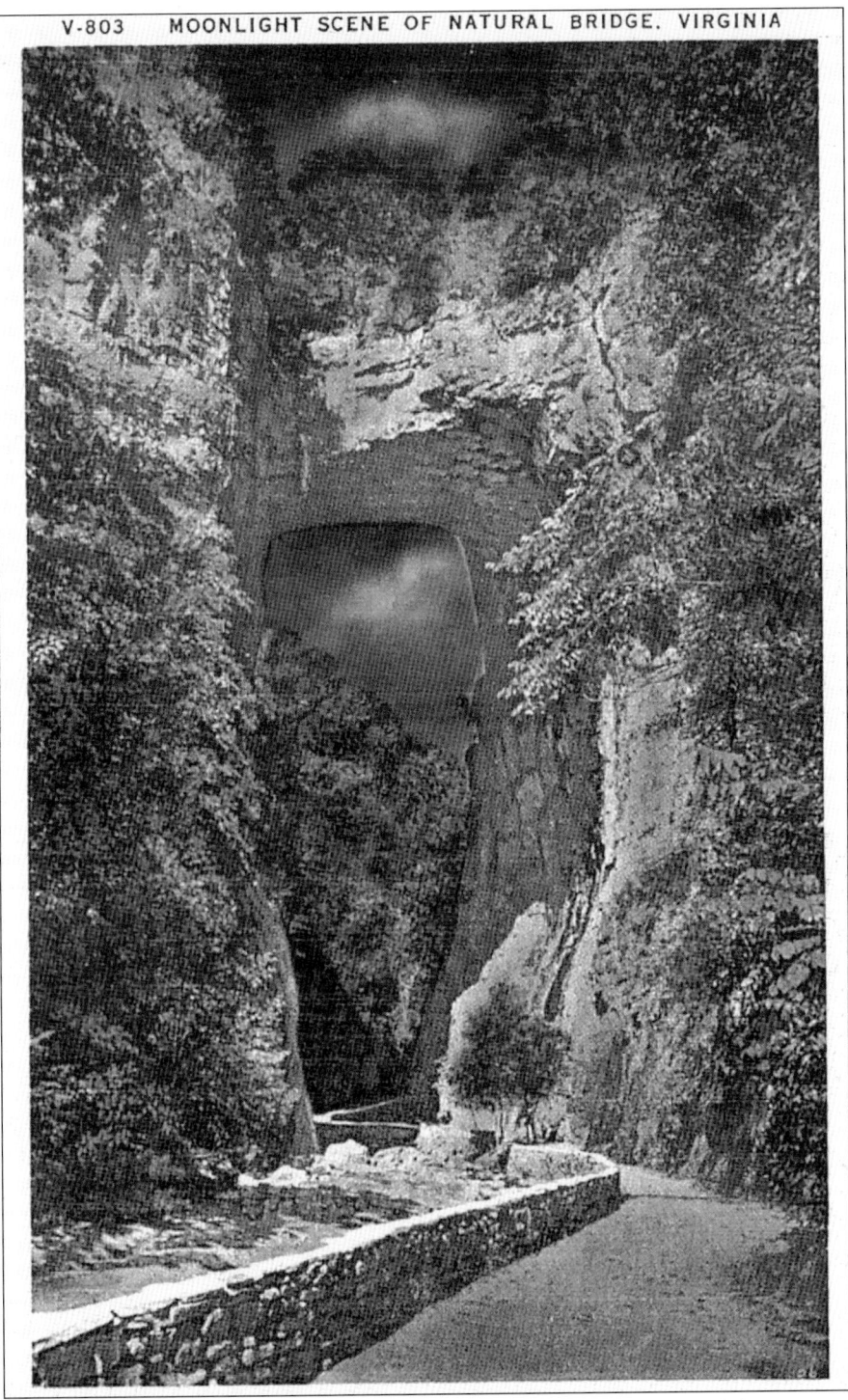

MOONLIGHT SCENE OF NATURAL BRIDGE, 1940. Natural Bridge, one of the seven natural wonders of the world, was surveyed by George Washington in 1750. A popular day excursion destination for Roanokers, the Bridge is 215 feet high with a span of 90 feet.

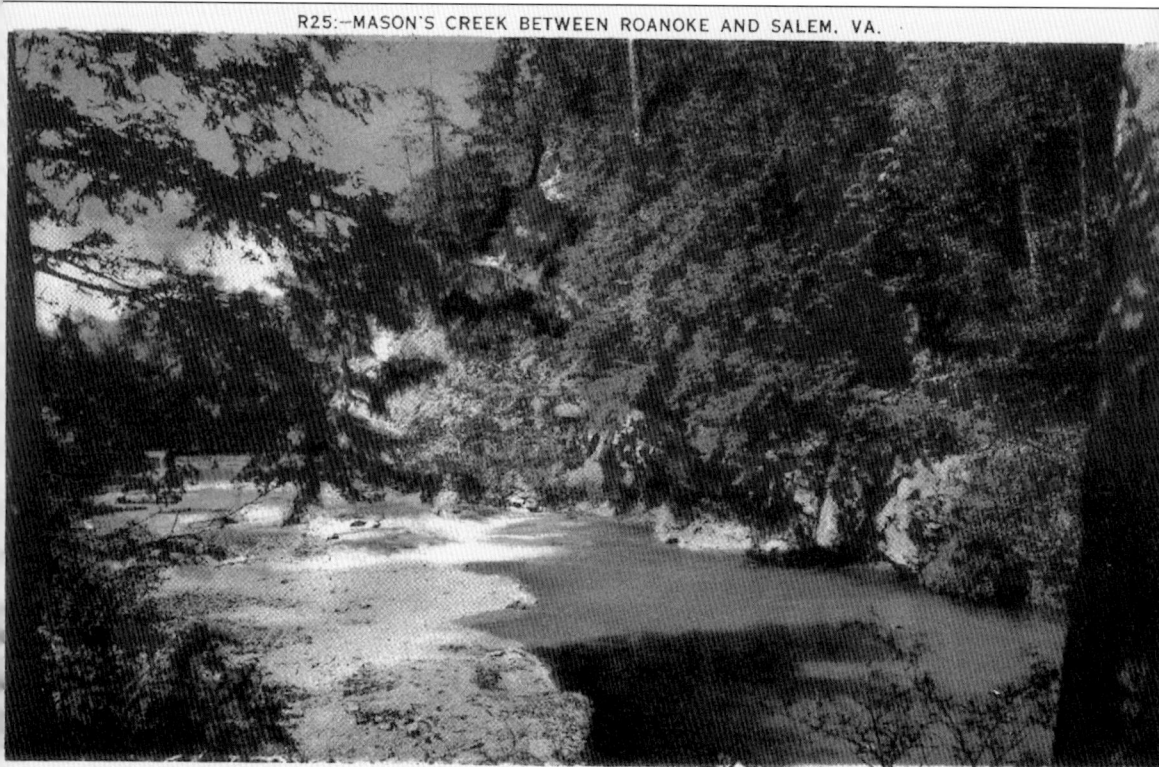

MASON'S CREEK BETWEEN ROANOKE AND SALEM, 1940. Mason's Creek is one of many streams and creeks in the Roanoke Valley flowing into the Roanoker River. It is believed to have derived its name from one of the early landowners along its banks.

Seven
HEALTHCARE

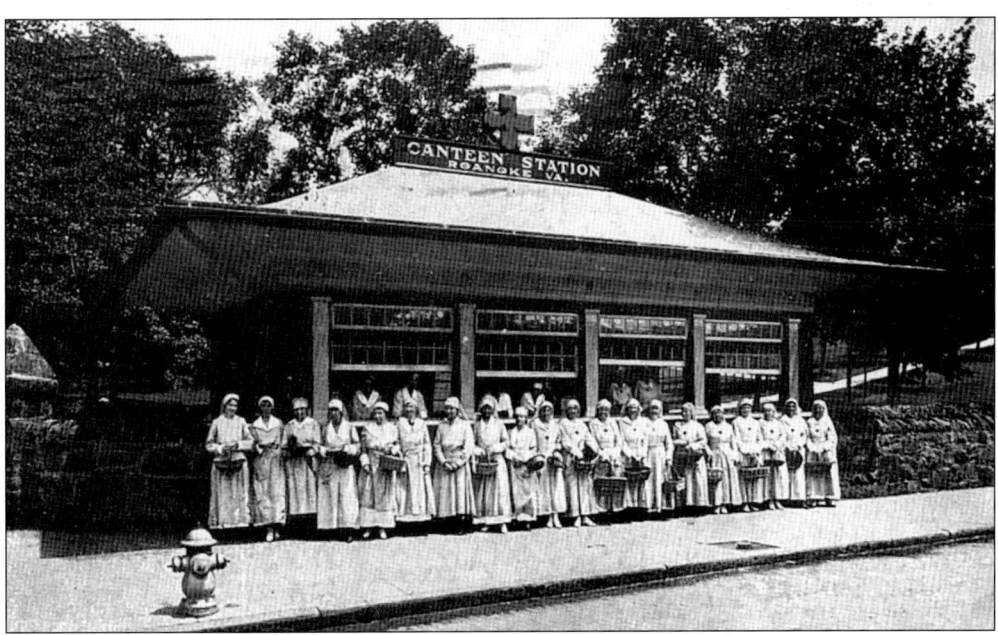

CANTEEN STATION, 1918. The Red Cross Canteen Station was located at the train depot. Here, young ladies dressed in white uniforms awaited young soldiers en route for duty in order to provide them hot coffee, sandwiches, and cigarettes.

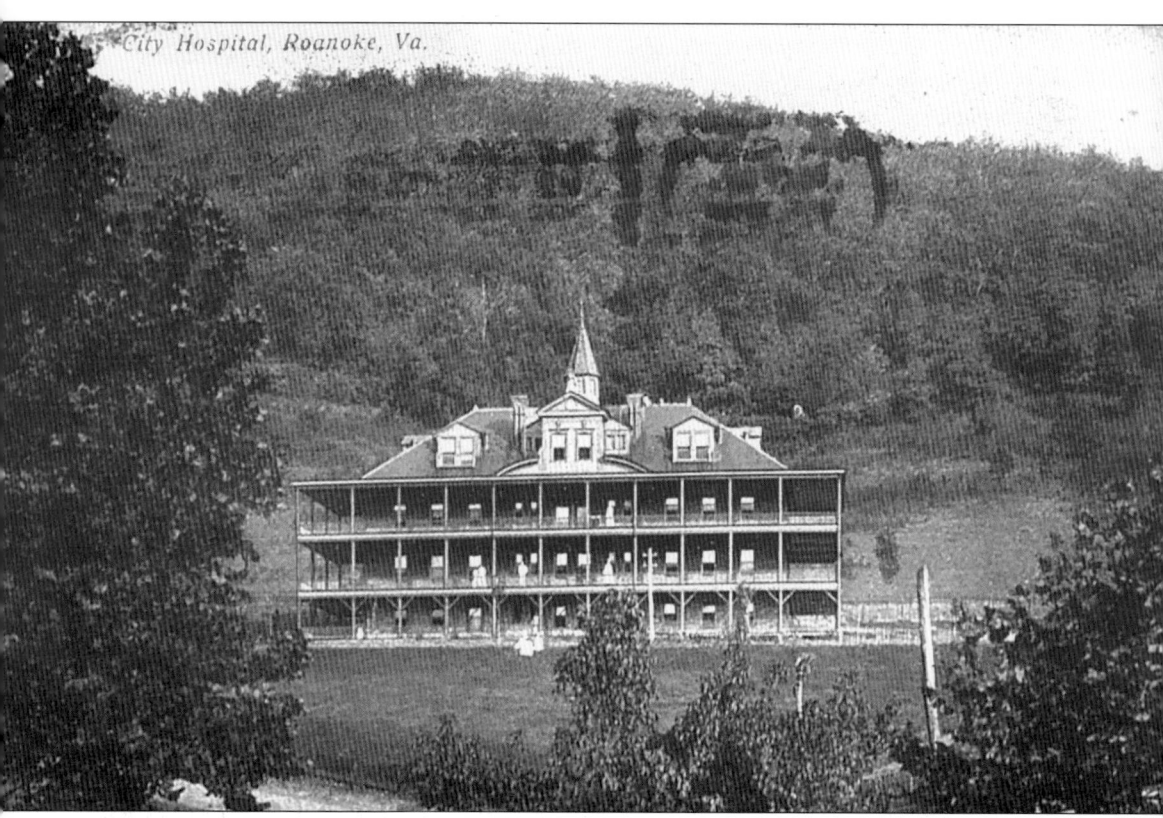

CITY HOSPITAL, 1909. The City Hospital stood at the base of Mill Mountain not far from the Mill Mountain Incline. The hospital opened in 1900 and the N&W Railway agreed to fund its operating expenses during the first year.

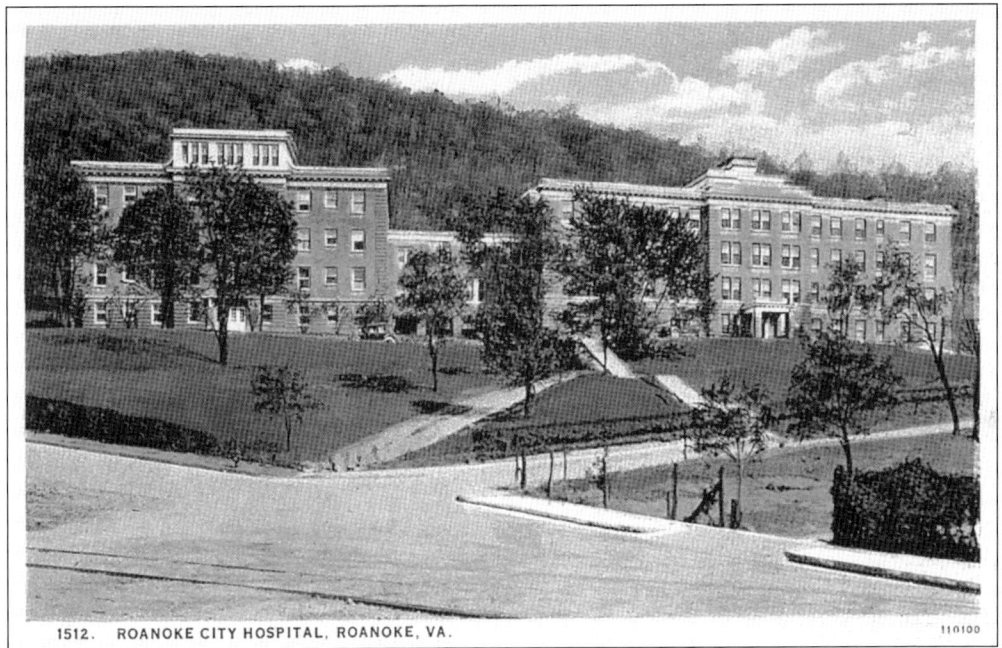

ROANOKE CITY HOSPITAL, 1930. The Roanoke City Hospital, forerunner of Roanoke Memorial, replaced the aging and underfunded City Hospital.

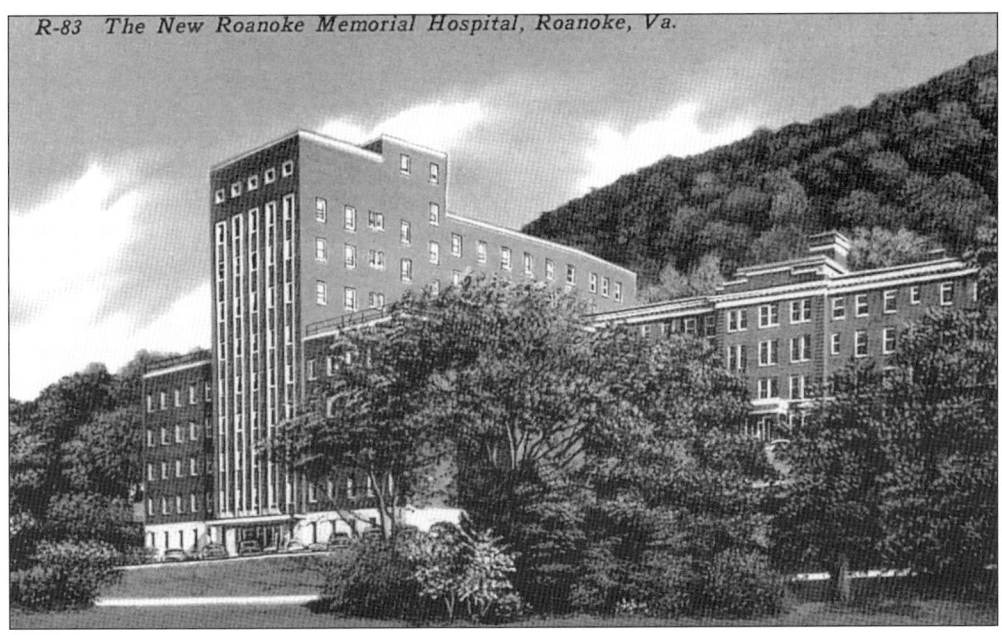

THE NEW ROANOKE MEMORIAL HOSPITAL, 1960. Roanoke Memorial Hospital quickly emerged as Roanoke's leading healthcare facility. When it opened it had 300 rooms with modern operating rooms and a laboratory. The construction cost for the hospital was $3 million.

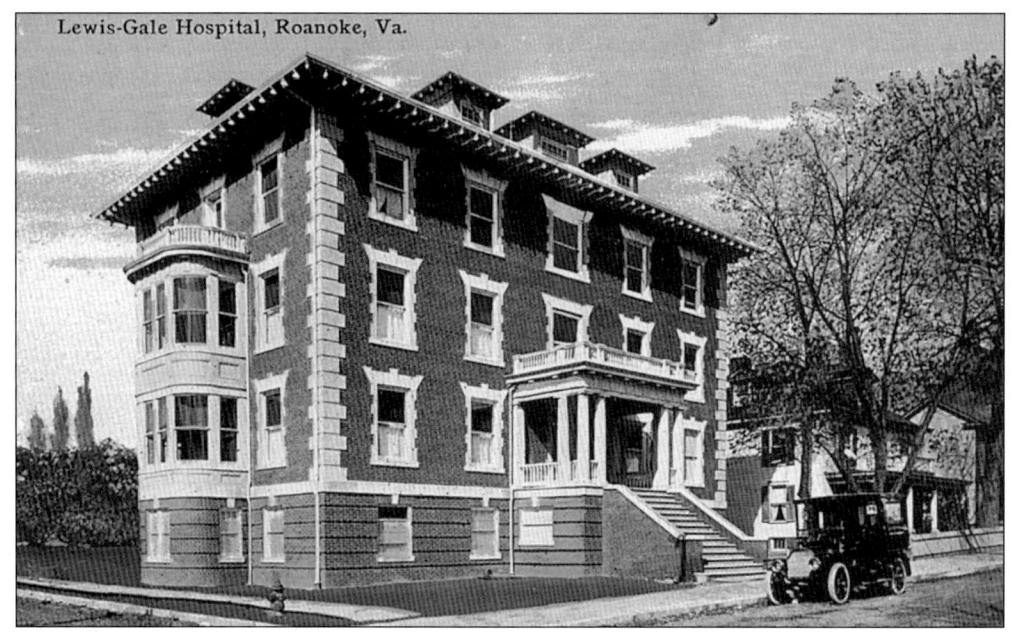

LEWIS-GALE HOSPITAL, 1918. Opened in 1910, the Lewis-Gale Hospital occupied the northwest corner at Third Street and Luck Avenue.

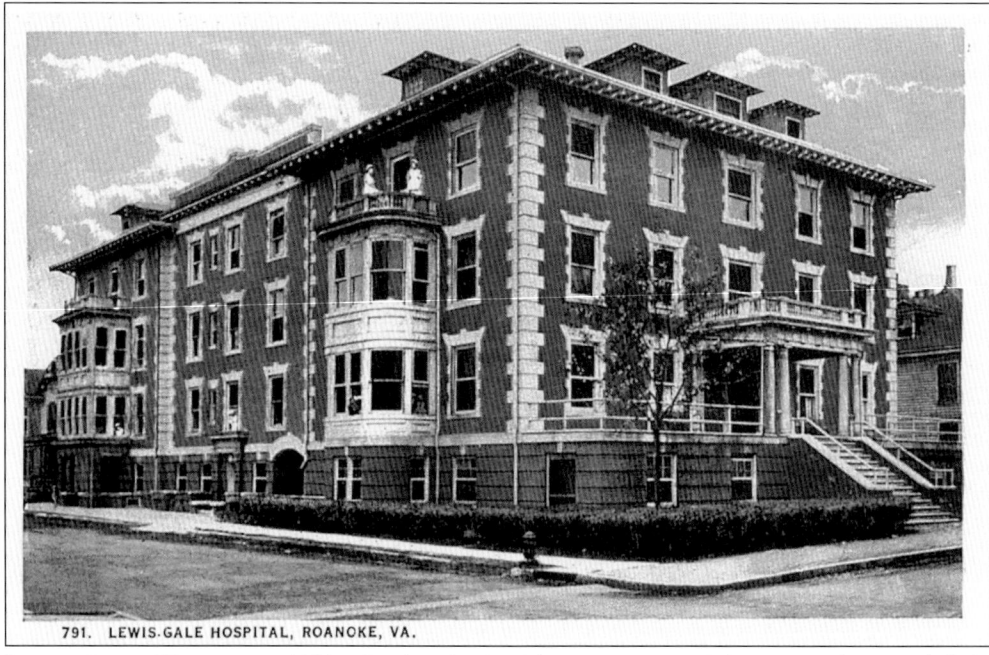

LEWIS-GALE HOSPITAL, 1929. During its initial years, Lewis-Gale Hospital expanded its capacity. Note the back addition to the hospital as compared to the postcard above.

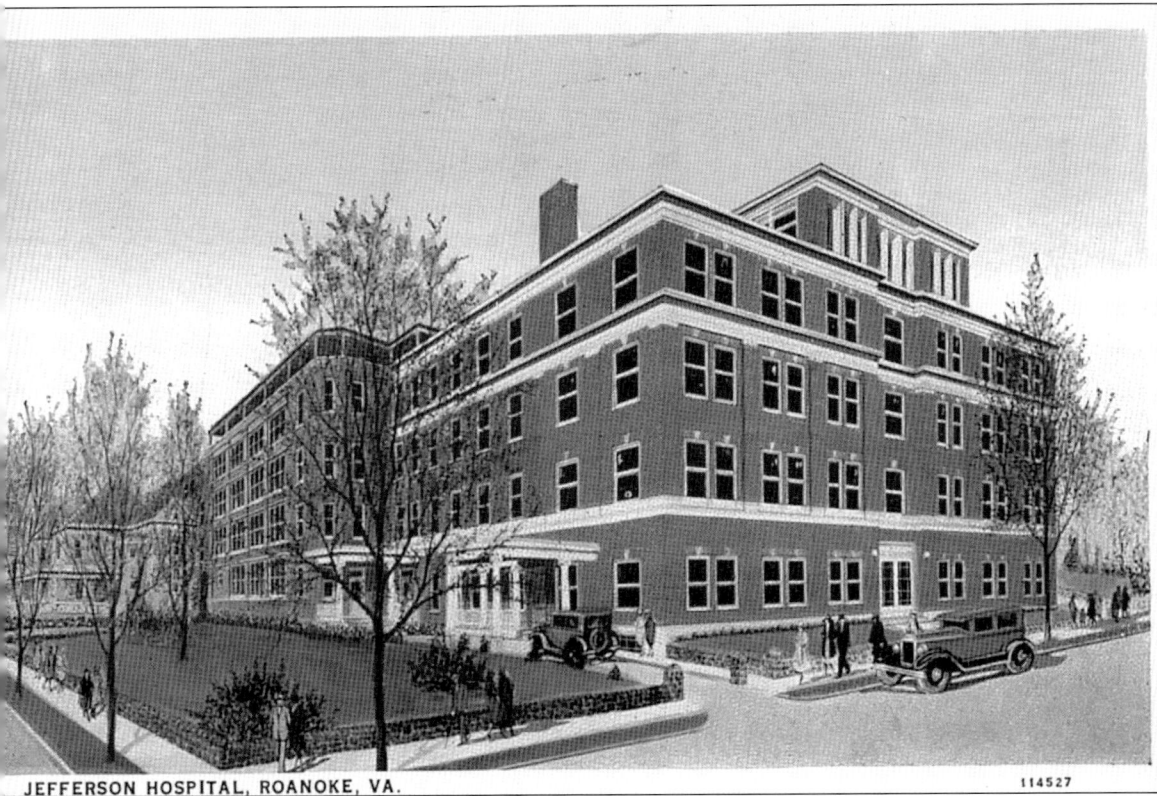

JEFFERSON HOSPITAL, ROANOKE, VA.

JEFFERSON HOSPITAL, 1930. An addition to the Jefferson Hospital in 1927 allowed for the care of 100 more patients. The "new" facility is shown here. The Jefferson Hospital was razed in the late 1960s.

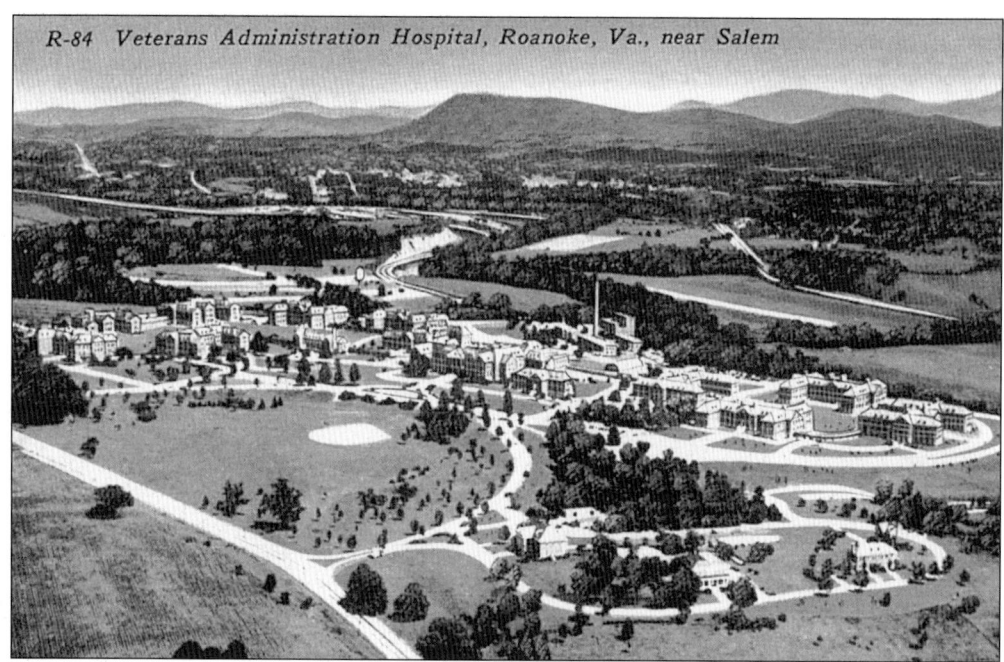

VETERANS ADMINISTRATION HOSPITAL, SALEM, 1945. The Veterans Administration Hospital complex was dedicated by President Franklin Roosevelt in 1934. The event was considered to be the single largest gathering in the history of the Roanoke Valley for that time.

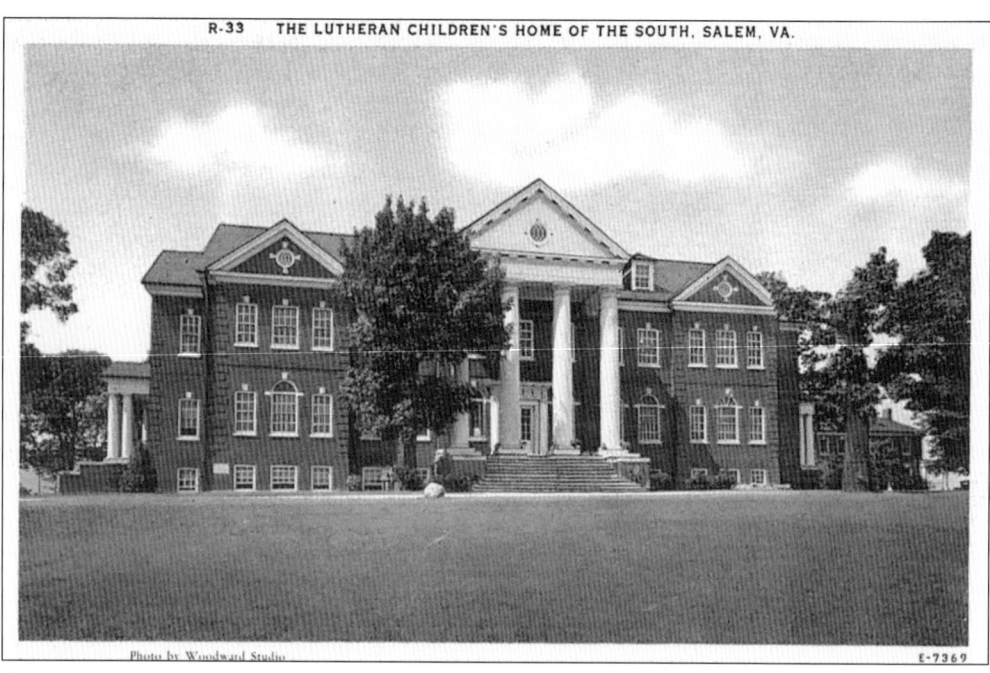

LUTHERAN CHILDREN'S HOME OF THE SOUTH, 1940. The Lutherans built an orphanage in Salem to care for and house children. Hundreds of children and families have benefited from their services.

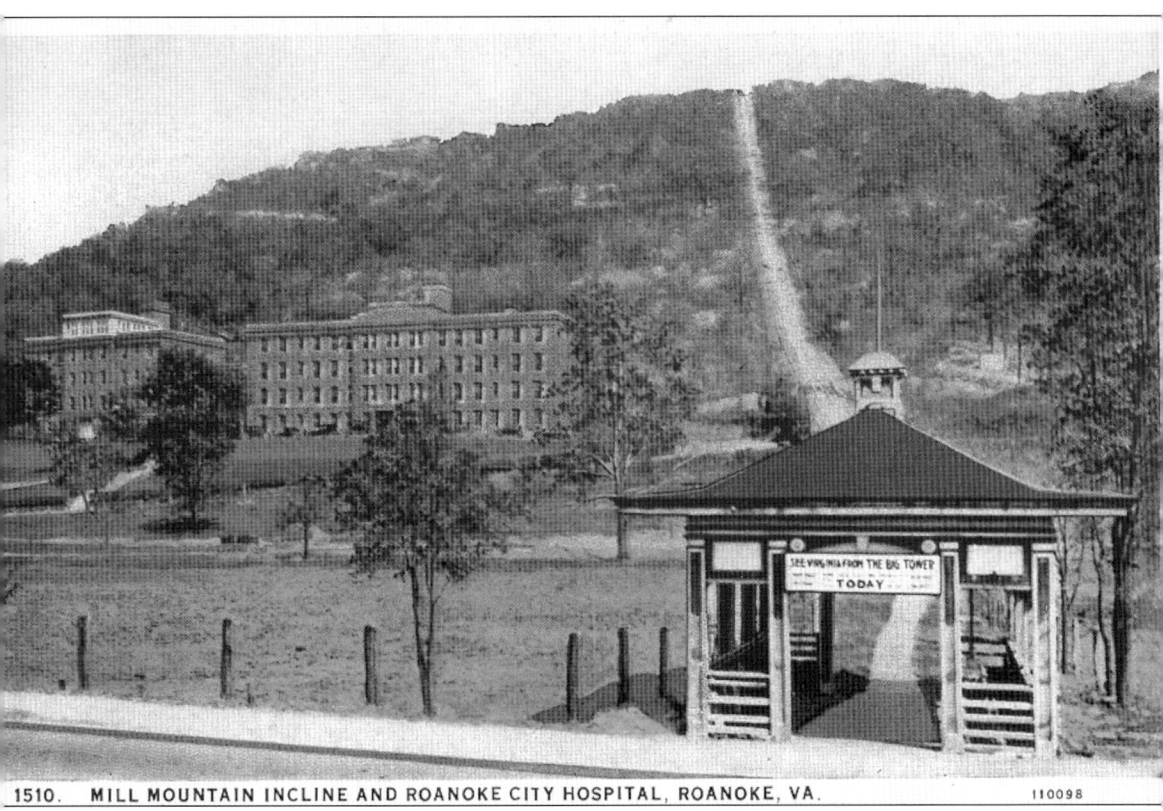

Mill Mountain Incline and Roanoke City Hospital, 1930. This card shows the proximity of the hospital and incline.

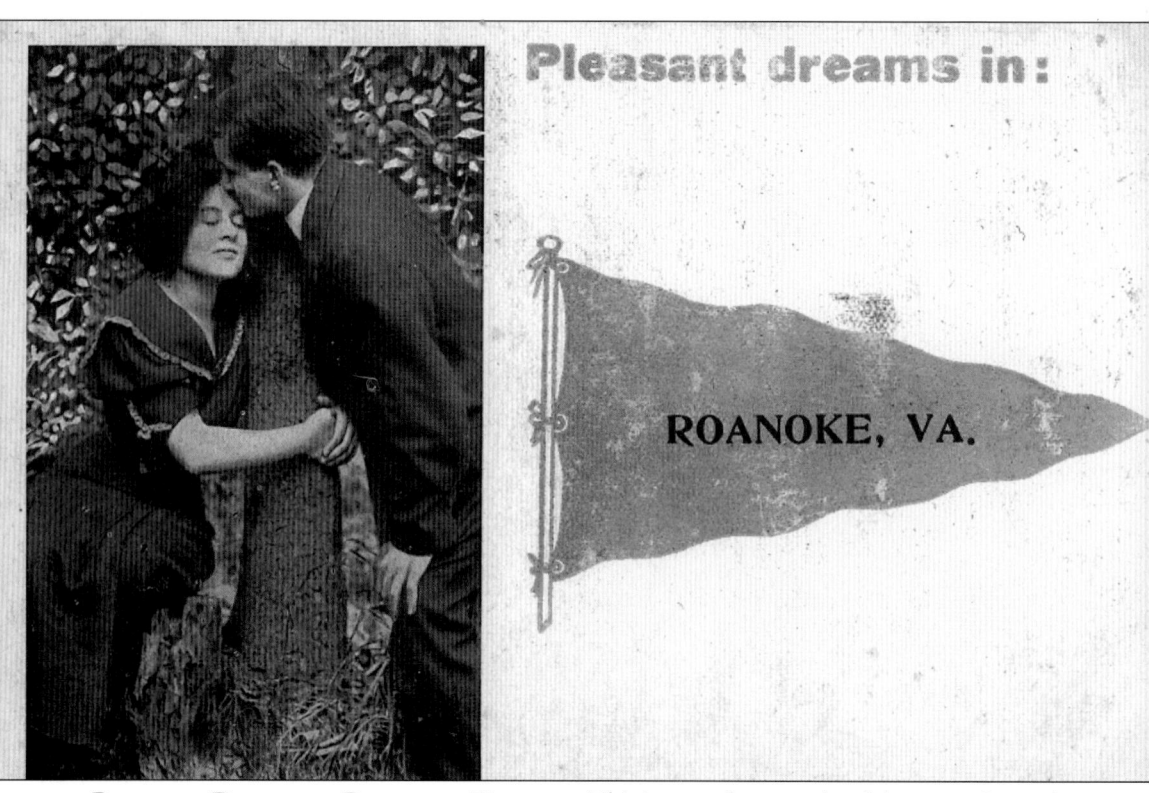

PLEASANT DREAMS IN ROANOKE, VIRGINIA. This is an early example of the many Roanoke postcards that provide humor for the recipient.